Praise for

Stress Free^{TM} Collection

Supply Chain Solutions
Manufacturing Solutions
Work Process Solutions
Changeover Solutions
Daily Management Solutions
Maintenance Solutions

This collection will empower the users
to achieve a rich work environment
that makes coming to work Stress Free..
REM

This collection will empower Leaders to win!
GLM

Stress Free^{TM} Collection
Supply Chain Solutions
Manufacturing Solutions
Work Process Solutions
Changeover Solutions
Daily Management Solutions
Maintenance Solutions

By: Ron Mueller

Around the World Publishing LLC
4914 Cooper Road Suite 144
Cincinnati, Ohio 45242-9998

ISBN 13: 978-1-68223-250-7
ISBN 10: 1-68223-250-6

Distributed by: Ingram
Cover Picture By: Sky Motion, Shuttertock.com
Cover Design By: Ron Mueller

Technical Editor:

Gordon Miller P.E.

Solutions Collection Table of Contents

DEDICATION
*To the organizations and leaders
that develop their people to contribute
to the needed business results.*

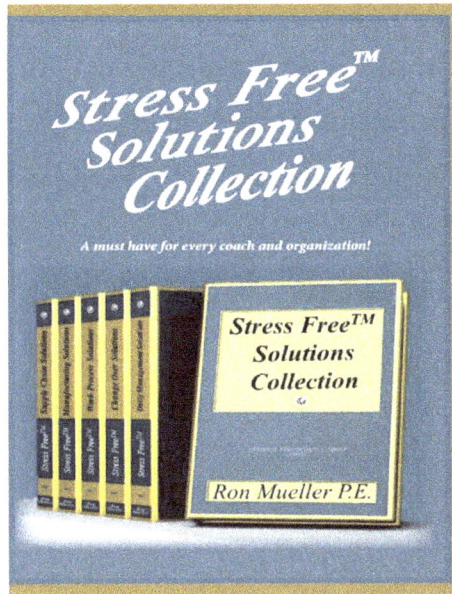

Stress Free^{TM} Solutions Collection Purpose

To present in one book the processes and tools to improve everyone's performance and ability to lead and guide any improvement effort.

- Leaders are change agents and guide the improvement efforts of those they lead.
- Leaders exist at every organizational level.
- Key to leading is to understand, to be able to do and to show success.

This collection will enable leaders at all levels to successfully solve the problems they face.

A Leader's Role is to:

1. Ensure Success and growth of those being coached.
2. To set challenging, measurable goals objectives and strategies.
3. To be the change agent guide and provide the tools necessary to facilitate change.
4. Ensure problem solutions are sustained and improved.
5. Be accountable for the outcome of the organization's efforts and the growth of its people.

1. *Ensure Success and growth*

Leaders ensure the success of improvement efforts by developing the

capabilities of each person that is involved.

Leaders provide skill development by training everyone on,
- Root cause problem-solving
- Work process improvement
- On leadership practices
- Teamwork

2. *Challenging, measurable goals.*

Measurable Goals such as,
- 80% improvement in changeover time.
- 40 % reduction in product inventory.
- 50 % effort reduction

Challenge the improvement teams.

Be the change agent guide

Apply the Five D's,
- Do it first.
- Demonstrate Success.
- Do what you will ask others to do.
- Develop your understanding of the problem.
- Develop your capability

3. Solution sustaining actions

Solutions become part of,
- Daily Management
- Standardized Work for an area.
- Maintenance Management.
- Material handling
- Finished Product handling

4. Accountable for the success

- Gain support of upper management
- Ensure the resource availability
- Supportive hands-on approach

The leader is,
- the guide,
- the coach,
- the quarterback,
- the goalie,
- the top scorer in the game.

The leader learns from small defeats and wins the critical game.

Stress Free^{TM}
Supply Chain
Solutions

Quickly get Products to Market
Free up Trapped Cash
Improve Sales Margins
Satisfy Customers with Superior Service

Money *to the* **Bank** **$**

M**Ron**UELLER P. E.

Stress Free^{TM} Supply Chain Solutions
Flowing production and high productivity

By: *Ron Mueller*

Around the World Publishing LLC
4914 Cooper Road Suite 144
Cincinnati, Ohio 45242-9998

Copyright © 2021 Ron Mueller

ISBN 13:
ISBN 10:

Distributed by Ingram
Cover Picture By: Tassel78|Dreamstime.com
Cover Design By: Ron Mueller and Gordon Miller

SUPPLY CHAIN SOLUTIONS CONTENTS

DEDICATION

To all those who are willing to try some

breakthrough thinking and apply

supply chain flow.

ACKNOWLEDGMENTS

To all the people contributing to

keeping materials and finished products flowing

out to the customer

TECHNICAL EDITOR:

Gordon Miller P. E.

Supply Chain Introduction

The concepts in Stress FreeTM Supply Chain Solutions are a combination of breakthrough, proven concept extrapolation and proven concept efficient and coordinated application.

The role of the leader must change to be that of supply chain orchestration. The Supply Chain leader must envision a supply chain organization that rewards the seamless flow of materials, information, and money to the beat of the purchasing customer.

They must envision the participants to a loss and waste free way to deliver the work required to get the desired product into the hands of the consumer.

These supply chain leaders must develop their capability to be hands on root cause problem-solving coaches. They must be willing to learn each and every required type of work along the supply chain and then they must hold the organization to the standards required to maintain and improve the supply chain.

They must do something different with the supply chain if they expect a breakthrough. They must recognize that a breakthrough in performance is possible, and it is an attractive and desirable business goal.

Stress FreeTM Supply Chain Solutions is the guide to a supply chain organization that achieves a 3-5% margin point improvement, a 40% reduction in inventory and greater than 20% improvement in productivity, an OEE equal to or greater than 85%, increased throughput, a high performance supply chain organization and customer service satisfaction of 99.97%.

A halo effect is the significant reduction in both quality defects, and serious safety incidents.

Statistical Product Replenishment, Material Flow and Production Stability and Supply Chain High-Performance Organizational Design are among the key new and different concepts presented in this book that will yield dramatic supply chain performance improvement.

Statistical Product Replenishment

It is the key concept in freeing up trapped cash.

The Toyota PULL system is not feasible for most supply chains. Statistical Product Replenishment however provides a unique and immediately applicable way for product production to closely meet the customer demand.

The supply chain is the backbone of a business. It must remain fully functional during the transformation. The proposed transformation must yield substantial breakthrough gains. The change benefits must overwhelm the significant effort that change implies.

The concept of Statistical Product Replenishment is a breakthrough concept that has been proven to yield thirty to sixty percent inventory reduction in specific products being managed by leading production planning programs. A production control advisor tool provides guidance that is then utilized to manage production.

The application approach provided in this book provides a risk-free way to test the concept and once the approach is validated the transition to flow can be rapidly achieved.

Flow: The rate that the raw material flows from the supplier to the final customer. All systems have flow. Most flows are stop and go. The approach presented in this book guides the reader to a continuous flow system.

The constant flow quantity, *flow pitch*, the standard daily production schedule and statistically determined response bands reduce the constant change in the production scheduling process.

Flow Pitch: Think of this as the size of the wave that is moving along the supply chain. The limiter to the size of the wave and period of the wave is what is defined as flow pitch.

An increase in operational stability is experienced within weeks of the application of statistically controlled production. The entire supply chain experiences a lessening of variability. Within three months an entirely different stable flowing supply chain begins to emerge.

Trapped cash is reduced enough to pay for all the improvement work along the supply chain. The financials allow for new mutually beneficial organizational relationships to be established among all the supply chain organizations and put into rapid practice.

Material Flow and Production Stability
Material Flow

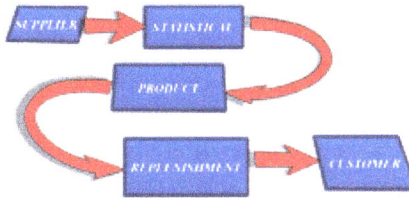

Material flow will follow the behavior of the statistically controlled product replenishment. The timing and quantity of material movement will match the statistically controlled production process.

This coordination will require new relationships with key raw material suppliers. These suppliers will experience a significant reduction in their trapped cash. Renegotiating the contracts with suppliers is normally a very positive experience.

Production Stability

Production stability provides the basis for growing the skills of all the people along the supply chain, creating stable, reliable equipment.

Daily Management, a high-performance teamwork organization and root cause problem-solving capability form the basis for the development of people that bring the production equipment to an OEE (Overall Equipment Effectiveness) that is greater than 85%.

A daily management process focused on fixing problems to root cause provides a bedrock foundation. This is a requirement for longer term continuous improvement. The breakthrough here is the ability to increase the problem-solving skill and capability of the operating team members.

Stress Free^{TM} Manufacturing Solutions and its accompanying excel workbook enables line teams to solve problems at a graduate engineer's level.

Supply Chain High Performance Organization

The Supply Chain High-Performance Organization design builds on the fundamental concepts of the High-Performance Organization Model authored by David Hannah. The natural, organic, extension to supply chain organization design and optimization is key to achieving a breakthrough in supply chain productivity.

Toyota's standardized work concept has been built on and is presented in ***Stress Free^{TM} Work Process Solutions***. This is also applied in improving the work processes along the supply chain.

In summary

The supply chain is as complicated as the Boston Symphony Orchestra. The conductor follows the score, the plan, sets the tempo and ensures the right participation of each section of the orchestra.

The conductor has the vision of how the work being performed is to transpire and works with each section of the orchestra to ensure their participation adds to the total score.

It takes much practice to become great and once greatness has been achieved, the great still must practice. The fundamentals still apply.

This book will focus on showing a few key high leverage changes that provide the breakthroughs that will forever envision and empower the way the supply chain leaders and everyone in the supply chain thinks, acts and performs. It is the score that will lead the organization to greatness.

Chapter 1: Supply Chain

In most cases the supply chain is closer to a pile of wriggling fishing worms than a chain. Designed on paper to be very organized and logical, it is implemented based on the conditions and situations of the moment and the contracts and the money available at the time of execution.

The concepts of PULL extrapolated from the Toyota Production System are a far off and almost impossible dream for most businesses. It requires close coordination of all the organizations involved in transforming the raw material into the final product. Most organizations face contract and sometime legal issues that present very significant and expensive PULL barriers.

Few organizations are able to make the conversion to PULL a profitable choice.

Business leaders face the daunting challenge of improving their business performance. They need to not only out-perform their competitors but must outperform their own previous year's performances.

It would seem they are "between a rock and a hard place". They must envision outside the box and it must be a winning solution. They must do this while they continue to make their current system deliver the results committed for the coming year.

The adaptive, vibrant, dynamic leader looks at his business in a new way. This leader sees a new way to improve it in its entirety with a few short-term changes and a critical longer-term change.

Short-term: Application of Statistically controlled product replenishment.

Longer-Term: Stabilize and Synchronize the production floor and Standardized Work in order to maintain the short-term gains.

The product customer and the consumer at the end of the supply chain define the goals of the supply chain.

This leader looks out to the suppliers of raw materials, the conversion of the raw materials to finished product and the delivery of the finished product to the customer.

This leader can taste the sweet Moscato wine, he can smell apple blossom, and he sees the sparkling mountain stream. A few key changes will dramatically improve the current supply chain performance.

This leader is going to envision his business compatriots to the flowing supply chain.

The supply chain is a complicated network of organizations interacting to move raw materials through to create a finished product. Horizontal organization units interact with vertical support organizations. The flow is horizontal, and the support organizations are vertical.

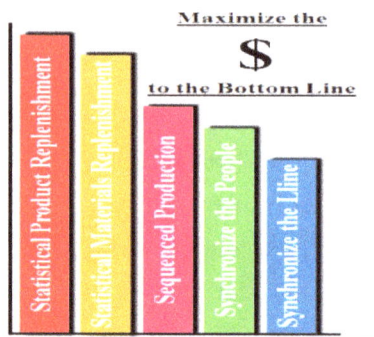

The flow synchronized supply chain system integrates and co-ordinates the transformation work of everyone along the supply chain. The statistical production flow control provides the cadence for the movement of all materials and finished product. The inventory to support flow is thirty to sixty percent lower and productivity twenty percent higher.

Five key flow improvement factors

Addressing the five flow improvement opportunities is key in taking the supply chain organization along the journey to a flowing supply chain.

These five key flow improvement opportunities are,

1. Production at the rate of product shipment – Statistically Controlled Product replacement.
2. Raw Material flow at the rate of production.
3. Mean Time between production runs and sequence order that match customer shipment.
4. Synchronization of the work.
5. Synchronization of the material transformation.

These five opportunities will be addressed in subsequent chapters.

Supply Chain Vision

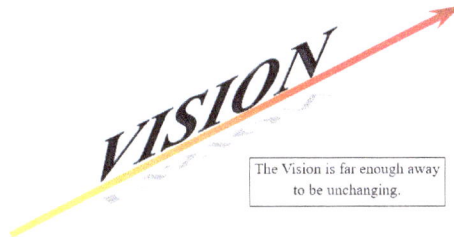

VISION

> The Vision is far enough away
> to be unchanging.

The Supply Chain Vision is a vision that is out three to five years ahead. An example is, "The consumer is always able to buy the product she desires at a price she is willing to pay and every business in the supply chain makes the desired profit margin."

Realizing this vision requires a commitment to a flowing supply chain transformation that starts with a company's top leadership envisioning the benefits of a waste free transformative supply chain, product flow stability improvement, productivity increase.

The leader must declare flow as the supply chain strategy of choice.

This declaration translates into to an organization where everyone will commit themselves to creating statistically controlled flow that will deliver 100% of the winning business results while creating a high-performance workforce that is enabled by an inclusive, team oriented, human focused, learning supply chain culture.

The organization has a long-term vision and all their people support the vision. What actions must be taken to create and operate the supply chain to make progress toward the vision?

Supply Chain Strategy

STRATEGY

The change to something better should not create a business loss. The benefits achieved by making the transition must pay for making the needed changes. It is a business investment decision.

The five key improvement factors provide the basis for deciding on a strategy that generates the money to pay for the improvement.

Strong, hands on, on the floor active leadership is the number one ingredient. *"Give me a strong adaptable leader and I will make a brick productive"* REM.

A requirement is, "A single Supply Chain Leader utilizing statistical replenishment flow control to orchestrate the supply chain across the existing organizational barriers."

Later the supply chain organization will organize as a flow versus a functional organization.

Strategy:

1. Free up cash to pay for the improvement.
2. Understand the main barriers to flow.
3. Enable and empower the people along the supply chain.
4. Create a virtual supply chain organization.

Supply Chain Tactics

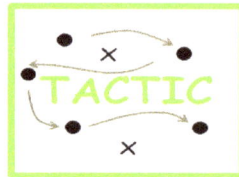

1. Apply Statistical Inventory replenishment control to create a steady material and product flow.
2. Utilize Output tracking to synchronize the work along the supply chain.
3. Sequence the production process
4. Implement Daily Management and root cause problem-solving to guide daily execution and grow the organization capability and improve long term system stability.

The change is holistic. The transition challenge is felt most directly by the leaders. They must,

- Become aware of the opportunity.
- Learn by doing.
- Do the work to show it is important.
- Envision their organization to the value of operating in flow.

Then they must lead their organization by becoming the coach, becoming supportive, becoming adaptive.

Every leader who has embraced this approach has succeeded. The business experienced almost immediate results and five years later the business results were still skyrocketing.

Supply Chain Measures linkage to Continuous improvement

The ability to measure is critical to developing a leader's supply chain understanding. Each measure must be linked to the "production area" and to the capability needed to ensure the measure is maintained or improved.

A supply chain Measures X matrix like the one shown connects the business measures to specific skills and actions needed to maintain and improve the supply chain. This Matrix is available in the accompanying Stress Free™ *Supply Chain Tools*, excel workbook.

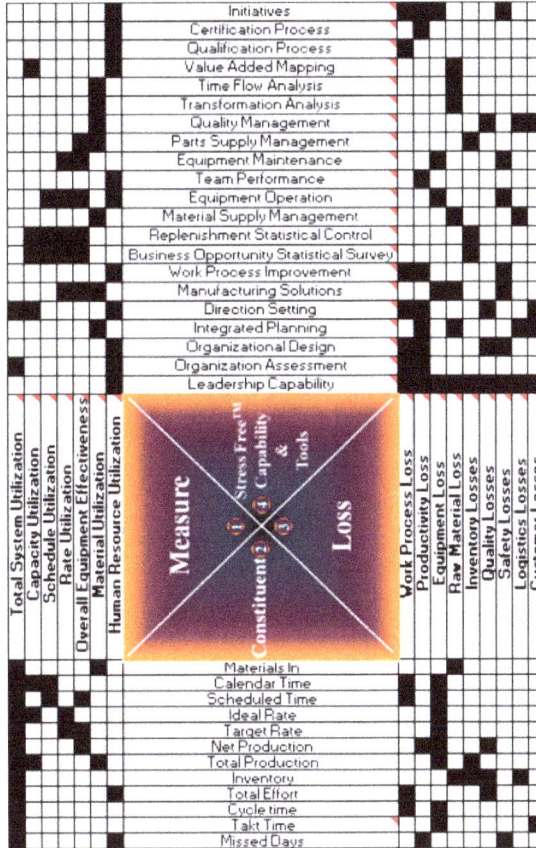

Going counterclockwise the business measures on the left are linked to constituent measures, normally more closely related to the work area. These measures are then related to losses that in turn are linked to specific capability or tools to counter the loss.

This is the stress-free cycle because leaders can find their way to the tools and capabilities that allow them to overcome the waste and losses that hinder them.

Supply Chain Solutions Order

There is an optimum order to all the problems for every supply chain. In most cases the largest barrier to flow is the production planning process.

This can be addressed by,

- Understanding the barriers to flow
- Starting at the dollar income end
- Identifying and prioritizing the barriers to flow.
- Implementing flow countermeasures

It is most interesting that the control signal for production is one of the biggest barriers to flow and flow inventory levels.

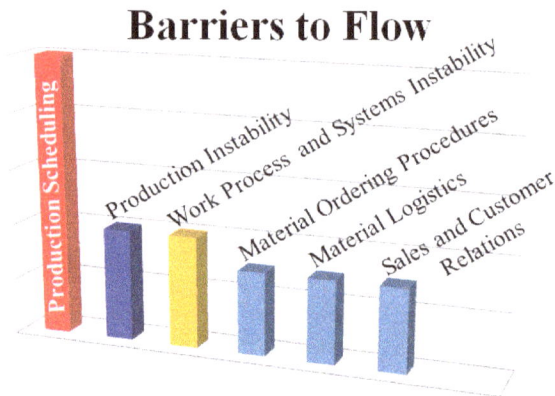

Barriers to Flow

Barrier Countermeasures

- Statistical Replenishment Production
- Root Cause Problem-solving
- Disciplined Daily Management
- Autonomous Maintenance Application
- Planned Maintenance Application
- Supportive Leadership Coaching
- Support functions partnering
- Supplier and Customer Participation

Chapter 1: Tools

Stress Free^{TM} Comprehensive Supply Chain Assessment

Stress Free^{TM} Business Opportunity Statistical Survey

Supply Chain X Measures Matrix

Chapter 1: Learning points

- The comprehensive supply chain assessment creates common supply chain situation understanding and alignment.
- Statistical inventory product replenishment creates more than 60% of the dollar savings opportunity.
- Raw material inventory reduction organically follows the product inventory reduction.
- The quickest and most beneficial improvement order is to begin with the statistical product inventory control.

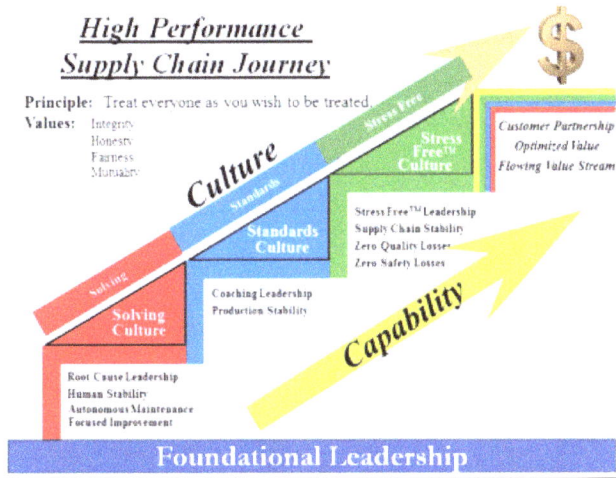

Chapter 1: Summary One Point Lesson

Leadership orchestration is required to lead the people in the supply chain in the continuous improvement journey, to a Stress-Free work environment where people look forward to coming to work.

The culture will change as the capability of the people in the organization grow.

Chapter 2: Supply Chain Leadership

The supply chain leader is the grand orchestra director. More than a mere mortal, this person must have the vision of the flowing supply chain. This person must be able to inspire, to envision, to enable and to empower those compelled by the clarity of the vision that is shared.

In my experience, manufacturing is like the violin section, it delivers the continuous pull for the rest of the orchestra. Each of the organizations directly in the flow of materials and finished product or in support of these organizations are critical in giving the orchestra its depth and resonance.

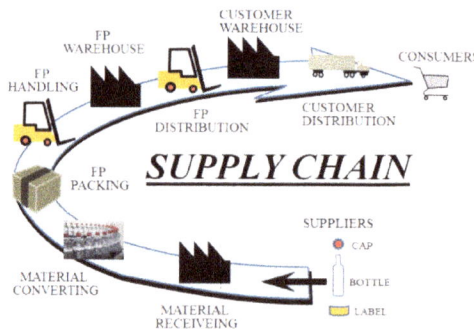

The high standards of the orchestra are maintained by the lead in each instrument section. It is no less so in a production supply chain. Supply Chain leaders hold the standards because they are masters.

The supply chain is long, complex and has many "leaders". Ideally there would be one owner of the entire supply chain to whom all the other leaders reported. They all should be rewarded for actions that support satisfying what the customer wants and the elimination of losses and waste in the transformation of the raw materials to the finished product.

The key ingredient for success is replenishment envisioned leadership. Replenishment based supply chain flow should be thought of as one step short of the Toyota Production System PULL. Every system has its natural, unvarnished, or unpolished flow. It may suffer many significant ills, but it nonetheless has a natural flow. Removing the barriers to this flow will generate substantial, even dramatic, business benefits.

Leadership already knows most of the problems. Every leader can describe what the problem is. In fact, each leader has a slightly different take on the problem, and this often results in disagreement among the leaders.

The ***Stress Free^{TM} Comprehensive Supply Chain Assessment*** is a half day coach guided qualitative assessment that identifies the *gaps in the current system.*

Leaders are guided to discuss and agree on the rating of key questions that expose the performance gaps in the current supply chain.

The rating discussion among the leaders is critical. It exposes the misalignments and provides the forum to gain the required understanding.

A noninvolved, skilled facilitator is often pivotal in ensuring the assessment makes progress and everyone is heard.

The leaders already know the problems and they often know the improvement action necessary. A key step is to determine the priority of the potential problem countermeasures and any interactions contained in the countermeasures. The prioritization capability increases significantly as the concept of a flowing supply chain becomes clearer.

Specific countermeasure actions are identified, and a preliminary action plan is developed. These are evaluated and a weighted priority pareto is developed.

The result often surprises the leaders and additional alignment discussions occur.

This assessment is often extended to facilitate more in-depth planning for implementing immediate action.

This qualitative supply chain understanding can be enlightening and lead to many very significant improvements but… it must be followed by improvement actions that close the identified gaps.

Quantitative Supply Chain Assessment

Stress Free ^{TM} Business Opportunity System Survey (BOSS) is the assessment that has statistical teeth. Product by product it identifies the value of the supply chain improvements that can be made by implementing replenishment control.

Product Replenishment Control System

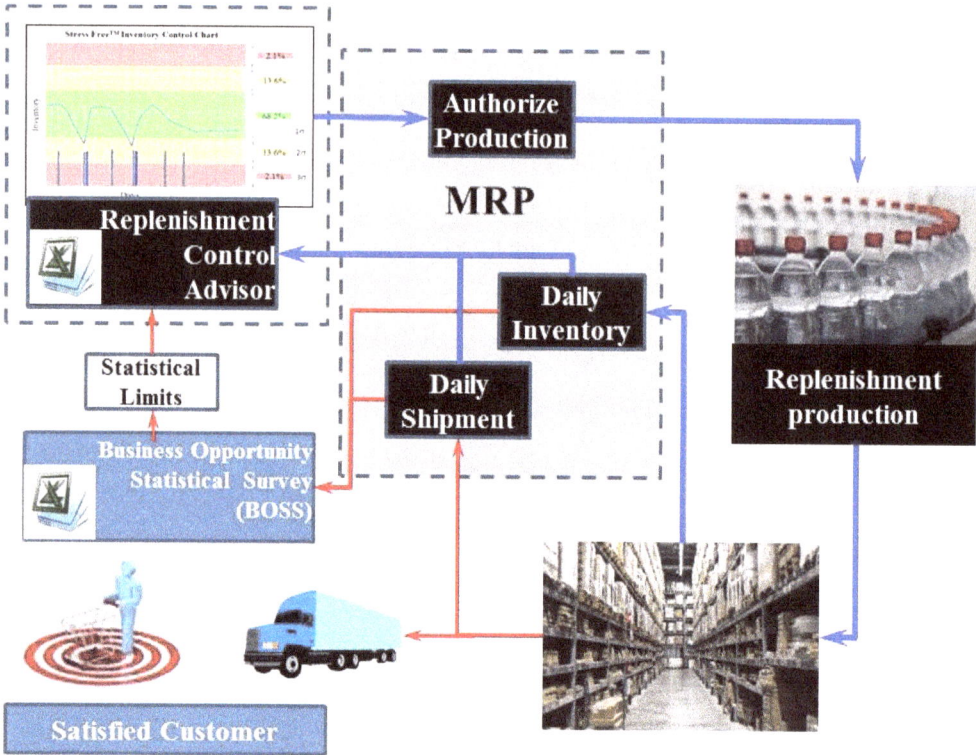

This survey is done using the past year's daily shipment or sales and the past year's daily inventory. This data is analyzed and statistically determined limits provide the guidance for the production. Production planners determine how to keep the inventory in the green band by authorizing or cancelling prescheduled production.

Keeping inventory in the green provides a 99.97% availability rating and an inventory that is normally a dramatic reduction.

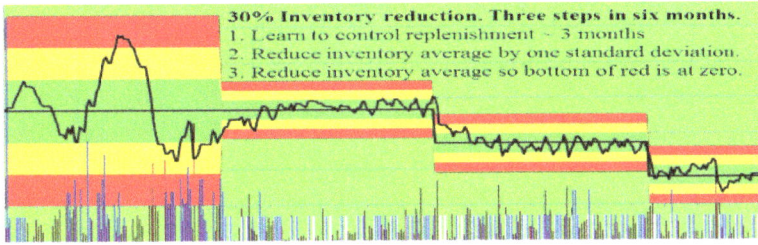

30% Inventory reduction. Three steps in six months.
1. Learn to control replenishment ~ 3 months
2. Reduce inventory average by one standard deviation.
3. Reduce inventory average so bottom of red is at zero.

The transition shown in the chart resulted in a sixty percent reduction in the average inventory. A key element of this approach is to determine a fixed daily and week to week production pattern. This greatly increases the stability of the transformation processes and results in an increased production capacity.

Over and over this analysis identifies the top ten to twenty products that produce 60% of the profits. It identifies the runner, repeater, and stranger products.

Product Classifications

Runner: a high-volume product produced multiple times a week.

Repeater: a moderate volume product produced weekly or biweekly.

Stranger: a product that is produced periodically and sometimes randomly.

Each classification has a different statistical flow control response. Stranger classified products normally fall into the produce to demand or produce to order category.

A Statistical Flow Control Simulator allows the leadership and key personnel a no risk way to practice the statistical flow control. This prepares them to utilize the *Stress Free^{TM} Statistical Flow Control Advisor** to guide them in controlling their MRP (**M**aterial **R**equirements **P**lanning) system.

*OPCG provides initial analysis and prepares the statistical control simulator and final advisor.

Supply Chain Oriented Leadership Perspective.

Think of the supply chain as a multi-lane, super-highway with convenient on and off ramps for all normal traffic and for the support and emergency support vehicles.

The materials flow smoothly and effortlessly along this super-highway and merge to form the desired product. The product consistently reaches its destination, at the desired time, the desired quantity, and the desired quality.

The many drivers along this super-highway do their work smoothly and effortlessly. They enjoy the work that they have helped to optimize. They feel great about helping every one of their constituents. They know and work closely with their immediate customer, and they understand their contribution to the final product and paying customer.

The supply chain leaders, the highway patrollers and maintenance crews, keep the lanes of the highway well maintained and the flow at the required safe speed with everyone in their proper lane. They ensure the support organizations are properly positioned and know when to come on and where to get off.

There are no toll booths, no unexpected reduction in the number of lanes, no unplanned increase in the flow of traffic. The emergency lane is always open but seldom needed.

The designers of this supper highway engaged the patrollers, the maintenance crews, the drivers, the supporters, the material senders and the product receivers in the original supply chain organizational design.

It becomes the supply chain leader's role to:
- Maintain the supply chain in a long-term operational condition,
- Become supply chain oriented versus technically oriented.
- Become an Adaptive, hands on coaches.
- Communicate broadly to everyone along the supply chain.

Chapter 2: Tools:

Qualitative Assessments
Stress Free^{TM} Comprehensive Supply Chain Assessment

Quantitative Assessment
Stress Free^{TM} Business Opportunity Statistical Survey (BOSS)

Statistical Replenishment Simulator

Statistical Replenishment Control Advisor

Chapter 2: Learning Points:

- Leadership defines, creates and maintains the supply chain culture.
- A product by product statistical control replenishment system achieves dramatic business results.
- A master plan to improve the supply chain organization typically has the following elements.

  I.   Supply Chain Organization Design Evaluation
  II.   Information System Improvement
  III. Daily Management Enhancement
  IV.   Work Process Improvement
  V.   Production Equipment and System Improvement
  VI.   Logistics Systems Improvement
  VII. Supplier Engagement
  VIII. Support area engagement
  IX.   Customer engagement

Chapter 2: One Flow One Point Lesson

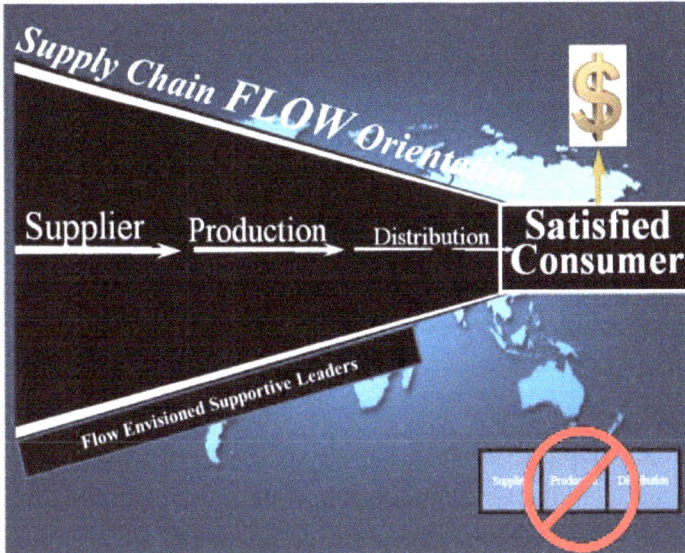

The winning mutually beneficial relationships of a flow-oriented leadership and organization versus a compartmentalized one.

Chapter 3: Supply Chain Statistical Product Replenishment

Toyota has inspired the world with the concept of PULL. The product pulled by the customer is immediately replaced and available for the next customer. Inventories along the supply chain are kept very low. Waste and supply chain cost is targeted for elimination.

The Toyota production system evolved over time and became the fabric of how the Toyota supply chains are established and managed today.

Toyota leadership was requested to provide guidance in the application of PULL to a Consumer Goods Company (CPG).

The Toyota leadership warned that PULL would not be possible for a system running at the high production speeds and the complexities both contractually and physically of the logistical systems associated with one of the simplest products being produced.

The CPG Company leadership insisted we would learn how to do it. At the seventh request for TPS guidance, Toyota relented and assigned a TPS coach to guide the PULL learning effort.

With direct coaching by a Toyota TPS coach, the approach was applied to a consumer goods production system. A very thorough and patient TPS coach[*1] guided us in how to implement the PULL concept.

The project was declared a learning success. We learned the application of Standardized Work[*2] and successfully applied it. We enhanced the root cause problem-solving process. We learned about Kanban[*3] and its application. We learned about Takt[*4] time and how it might be applied to the product flow. The production improvements were many and the project was a success.

Though many of the TPS concepts were deemed very useful and became part of the fabric of the production System, PULL as a system did not happen.

The daily shipment data analysis indicated that by determining production in a similar manner as the concept of Kanban and by leveling the quantity of each production run, inventory could be lowered while at the same time product availability could be maintained or increased.

Learning how to set the statistically determine average ideal daily inventory was a breakthrough.

Subsequent production site trials verified that controlling the flow of production in this new manner supported lower inventory levels while achieving higher customer shipment results.

The statistical analysis and method of determining the ideal inventory level and the width of the control limits were field verified multiple times. In every case, there was improvement. In a few cases the fact that inventory was being held too low was a learning surprise.

Though successfully demonstrated in several other sites, the effort met huge resistance because it was not integrated into the Enterprise Resource Planning (ERP) system, and it does not utilize product forecasting for production control

Current Situation:

The technique is based synchronizing to the daily shipment, daily use, or daily sales history. This history is used to determine the standard deviation of the ideal inventory that when properly replenished will meet all use variation in the future.

Statistical Inventory replenishment works across many businesses, consumer goods production, spare parts optimization, internet sales and distribution, filling operations, and intermediate goods production. All can benefit.

Business Opportunity Statistical Survey (BOSS)

BOSS is a very appropriate acronym. The guiding information it generates has proved to be on target and accurate. Follow the guidance and achieve the desired results.

The key is to provide it with accurate data.

The Data

The Customer

The analysis of the past year's daily product shipment tells the customer behavior story. All product logistical experience is captured and recorded in the daily shipment data.

The Supply Chain

The analysis of the past year's daily product inventory tells the supply chain response behavior and capability. It is the story of the good, the bad and the ugly.

Inventory is the result of the current system to customer demand mismatch and system transformation and transportation constraints and problems.

A perfect match and no transformation problems would result in no inventory need.

The improvement opportunity is to match the production quantity as close as possible to customer demand and to account for the delays of transport.

The Analysis

The daily shipment and daily inventory history provide the basis to identify the ideal inventory. The resulting inventory average and the standard deviation of the ideal inventory, based on the system defined replenishment pitch, are used to set the inventory response boundaries. These boundaries* become the main guides utilized to manage the flow of production.

BOSS Input

Daily shipment for the past year.

Daily inventory for the past year.

Production/throughput/supply chain pitch

BOSS output

The output is by specific product ship unit.

Target product inventory average.

Reaction limit values.

Number of required production runs.

Statistical Replenishment Control Practice

Change requires practice. The work is different. It is more controlled and precise.

The transition to statistical control is facilitated by the use of a Replenishment Control Simulator. This simulator utilizes the same data used for the BOSS analysis. It provides both numerical and visual feedback to the actions authorized by the product replenishment planner.

With the simulator, the product replenishment planner practices maintaining the target average product inventory on last year's shipment data. With this real data, day to day, simulation allows the planner to experience the full range of work processes required to do the work in the highly variable real-world product shipment environment.

The production system issues can be surfaced and discussed. The potential problems can be addressed prior to the transition to actual product replenishment control.

•OPCG provides initial analysis and prepares the statistical control boundaries. Contact Ron Mueller at remwriter95@gmail.com

Statistical Replenishment Control Advisor.

The product shipment and the product inventory value for the previous day is extracted from the existing system Material Requirements Planning (MRP)[*5] being utilized and put into the Statistical Control Advisor.

The Advisor shows the trend of the Inventory and visually enables a decision on whether a production run is needed at the specified pitch. The human replenishment planner evaluates the situation and decides whether to authorize the production as planned. The authorization choice is then put into the MRP system.

The controller is designed to flag the incoming day's data as red, yellow, or green. The replenishment planner is coached to review and address the products in the red band first. Then address those in the yellow band. The products in the green band are within the target limits and do not need immediate attention.

The Statistical Replenishment Control Advisor[*6] provides dramatic improvement by stabilizing the entire supply chain, and product flow to the customer.
The control advisor utilizes,

- Daily Sales or shipment to better understand the Customer.
- Daily Inventory to better understand supply chain situation.
- Utilizes the variability generated by creating the ideal inventory level to establish the red, yellow and green control limits.
- Biases the Ideal Inventory Average up by; + 3 sigma to ensure a 99.97% probability that inventory is available to meet the ordered shipment. This bias can be more conservative than six sigma as may be the case for the medical businesses.

Product Replenishment Control System

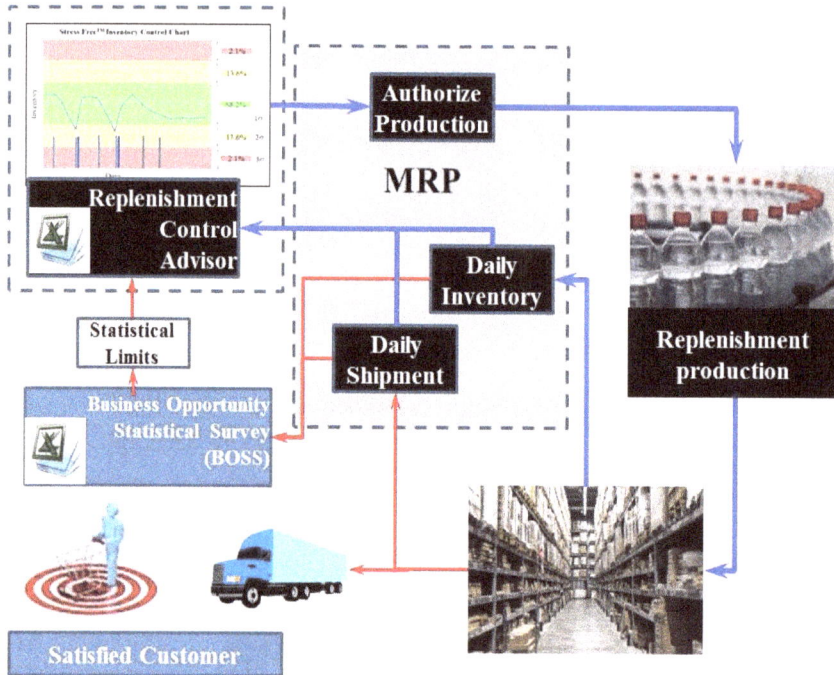

Product Replenishment Control System

This is currently an advisory system that provides the production planner daily shipment and inventory situation. The planner must still look forward to determine the required short-term upcoming production need and compare it to the preplanned scheduled production. This preplanned production is based on meeting the previous year's average shipment.

The planner then follows the simple replenishment authorization rule of only authorizing the production if the inventory level is into the lower yellow control band. If the inventory level is in the green and the forward look does not require additional finished product, the upcoming production is called off.

This approach coupled with sequencing of the production process to an optimum sequence and a repeating fixed daily production pattern creates supply chain wide stability.

Sequencing: Establishing a fixed production order and quantity for each day of the week.

The planner utilizes the power of the MRP system to communicate, to authorize the actual production and to order replacement material.

The Statistical Control Advisor can be linked directly to the MRP system. This allows the planner to quickly, and efficiently, make the required production authorization decisions and have the MRP system operate in its normal way.

The result

The variability of production quantities is greatly reduced by producing to the defined pitch and quantity. In all cases to date, this variability, once reduced allows for the reduction of the average inventory target by as much as sixty percent.

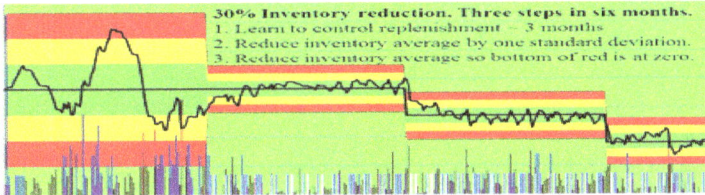

The wide green, yellow, and red bars show on the left side, show the operating variability in a normal production system. The application of the Stress Free^{TM} Statistical Product Replenishment Control results in the greatly reduced red, yellow, and green control bands. This leads to the inventory reduction opportunity.

The first step is to demonstrate this tighter control to maintain the current inventory. This is the first reduction in the green, yellow, and red bars. Then a series of reductions can be taken until the bottom of the lower red band reaches zero.

The replenishment planner, utilizing the control advisor can maintain all product SKU's in the same fashion.

Chapter 3: Tools

Stress Free^{TM} Statistical Product Replenishment Simulator

Stress Free^{TM} Statistical Product Replenishment Advisor

Chapter 3: Learning Points

- Last year's daily product shipment and its standard deviation defines the minimum inventory.
- Control bands based on the standard deviation provide useful guidance for current production decisions.
- A set production pattern with a specific constant production volume target provides flow and work stability.
- Significant inventory reduction is the result of staying in control and in the green.
- Reduction is controlled by the production replenishment planner.

[*1] TPS coach Satoko Watanabe

> Now Head of the:
>> Center of Manufacturing Excellence
>> P.O. Box 1848
>> University, MS 38677

[*2] Standardized Work has three main components:

1. Adheres to takt time.
2. Standard work-in-process (WIP) is specified.
3. Defined sequence of operations for a single person.

[*3] Kanban: A Japanese term meaning "signal". It is used in Just in Time (JIT) manufacturing systems. It authorizes a cycle of replenishment for production and materials.

[*4] Takt is the German word for the baton that an orchestra conductor uses to regulate the tempo of the music. It is a measurable "beat time," "rate time" or "heartbeat." Takt time is the rate at which a finished product needs to be completed in order to meet customer demand.

[*5] Material requirements planning (MRP); a production planning, scheduling, and inventory control system used to manage manufacturing processes.

[*6] Statistical Replenishment Control Advisor is a product supplied by Optimum Performance Consulting Group (OPCG). OPCG also has the Replenishment Control Simulator.

Chapter 3: One Point Lesson

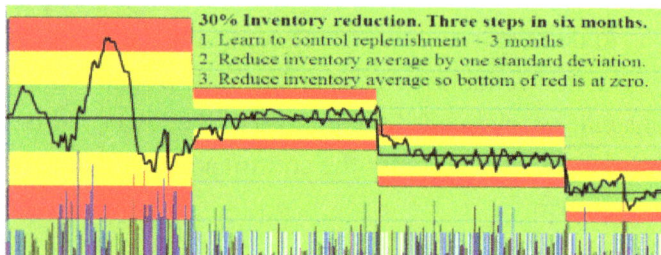

30% Inventory reduction. Three steps in six months.
1. Learn to control replenishment ~ 3 months
2. Reduce inventory average by one standard deviation.
3. Reduce inventory average so bottom of red is at zero.

Key aspects: Production Quantity prescheduled, fixed frequency control bands with reaction guidance.

SUPPLY CHAIN SYNCRONIZATION

Chapter 4: Supply Chain Synchronization

Supply Chain Optimization focuses on the improvement of existing product delivery systems. The best approach would be to design and implement cost efficient supply chains. For many reasons, from taxes to previously existing systems, most supply chains get designed and implemented in a less than optimum configuration.

Good supply chains slowly get buried under layers of change and incident triggered practices. These practices at one time were improvements or defensive in nature. Later they became imbedded in the normal practices of the delivery stream.

Just reviewing the flow of materials, information and observing the transformation and transportation taking place along the supply chain will yield improvement opportunities. Applying a series of simple tools and practices in a strategic way will yield fast and lasting continuous improvement.

The cultural change in the organization is critical to superior results over time.

Supply chain synchronization means that time, material quantity and flow get coordinated along the entire supply chain. This includes the support from engineering, quality, maintenance, logistical, sales, finance personnel and many other groups.

Leadership must cross the organizational lines. The organization needs to change to a supply chain focus versus a functional focus. Synchronization requires each functional organization to change its work process to match the timing required by the product flow drumbeat.

All supply chain participants must be "dancing" together to whatever music the supply chain plays.

Statistically controlled product replenishment requires that the **entire supply chain follows the metronome established by the** practice of producing in the green with fixed volume sequenced production authorization. The constant rhythm of flow moves up the supply chain to the supplier and his supplier. It moves out to the supporting organizations and must be reflected in the monitoring and control systems. The material flow to the final product is the backbone of the supply chain. The information and communication systems are very critical in synchronizing the supply chain.

Material Flow

Material flow will follow the behavior of the statistically controlled product replenishment. The timing and quantity of material movement will match the statistically controlled production process.

Follow the raw materials from the product production line to the material supplier. Note every time the material gets touched by another person. Each touch by another person represents a flow boundary. The more touches, the more boundaries and the more losses.

Touch: Any time the product or packaging material gets handled. This occurs during material receiving, materials staging, and materials delivery to the line, line feeding and when the finished product is moved to the warehouse and finally loaded into a truck.

Boundary: Raw Material Truck loading, Transport, Raw Material unloading, Delivery of Raw material to production line, finished product removal, finished product storage, finished product loading into truck, delivery to customer.

The material flow boundaries must be seamless, and they must be synchronized in time and quantity to the authorized statistically controlled production replenishment.

Boundaries are most often the points where rework and waste are generated. Resolving the problems at each boundary results in the reduction of supply chain operating cost.

Stabilizing incoming material flow implies replenishment control of raw materials from the raw material suppliers. The coordination to ensure material flow stability will require new relationships with key raw material suppliers. Key raw material suppliers become part of the improvement team. These suppliers will experience a significant reduction in their trapped cash. Their hands-on personnel interact with your material receiving hands-on personnel.

Output tracking is implemented on the supplier end and material receiving tracking is implemented on the receiving end.

If the logistics between the supplier and the customer includes a transport company, the transport leadership and schedulers are brought into the supply chain stability work.

Stabilizing line delivery requires the flow from the material delivery truck to the line to be studied. The focus is on the materials associated with key high-volume SKU's. Understanding and reducing the number of touches will yield significant productivity improvements. The quantity and the frequency of delivery to the line is now determined and authorized by the replenishment planner. The variability of this delivery is monitored by the use of delivery tracking

Information and communication system

These systems are critical in the longer term in establishing the supply chain synchronization. In the short term, they actually are part of the problem! They are replete with problems that must be fixed. These problems self-identify with the use of output tracking.

Information Systems

Data may not be kept in the granularity that supports longer term improvement. Daily shipment and daily data may not be linked or even measured at the same time. The data is often stored and then forgotten.

Communication systems

These systems are used most often as the means to call for help versus a means to prevent a problem. Communication must utilize the visual, the audible, the computer, and internet avenues to be fully effective. Wireless communication now enables equipment to communicate directly to people, no matter where they may be located.

This area is rapidly changing, and new opportunities are constantly surfacing.

Boundary hourly throughput tracking is the primary way to identify the material and product flow issues. Clarity on how to measure the flow across the boundary and then the flow through the system to the next boundary is critical to establishing and maintaining flow.

Output Tracking

The tracking sheet is the same at every boundary. It may be titled differently but the tracking is normally done in the same manner.

Output tracking, Input Tracking, Throughput Tracking are all basically the same. "A rose is a rose by any other name," and so it is with Output tracking.

- **Supplier Shipment Output tracking**,

  The supplier leadership is trained by on replenishment control.

  Output tracking is implemented on the supplier end and material receiving tracking is implemented on the receiving end. If the logistics between the supplier and the material receiving includes a transport company, the transport leadership and schedulers are brought into the supply chain stability work.

- **Material receiving Input tracking**,

  Stabilizing incoming material flow implies replenishment control of raw materials from the raw material suppliers. Key raw material suppliers become part of the improvement team. Their hands-on personnel interact with the material receiving hands on personnel.

- **Line delivery Output Tracking**

  Stabilizing Line Delivery, defined as movement of raw material from storage area to the production line, requires the flow from the material delivery truck be studied. The focus is on the materials associated with key high-volume SKU's. Understanding and reducing the number of touches will yield significant productivity improvements. The quantity and the frequency of delivery to the line is now determined and authorized by the replenishment planner. The variability of this delivery is monitored by the use of delivery tracking.

- **Production Output Tracking,**

  Stabilizing finished product replenishment is the focus for the production area. Work on the reliability of the equipment yields increased production area stability. The average and 3 sigma determine the inventory that must be held due to transformation instability.

- **Finished Product Loading Tracking,**

  Stabilizing finished product loading focuses on how effectively the loading process is managed.

  "Any loader, any SKU, any truck" is an approach that will reduce the miles traveled by the forklift truck. Truck loading variability, as measured by tracking each truck load time, highlights the variability of loading. Reduction of the variability normally results in reduced loading time.

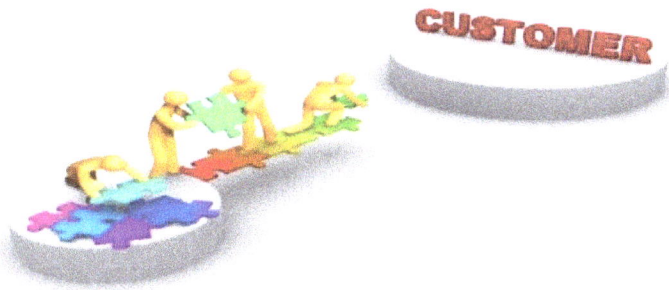

- **Customer Receiving Tracking**

  Stabilizing finished product delivery to key customers is a first step in engaging our paying customer. This should be done in mutual learning mode. It requires the engagement of top customer leadership. This is a big deal and only customers known to be willing learners should be approached. They need to become partners in the flow improvement team.

  True customer need understanding must be the driving factor for every boundary in the organization. This need should be visually recognizable and a miss in need delivery should immediately raise a red flag.

  Once the customer is engaged, they can utilize receiving tracking and communicate any issues back to their supplier

  Customer receiving tracking will become the ultimate in determining the customer service achieved by the Supply Chain.

Summary

Variations based on time span or quantity may make the input or output tracking appear slightly different, but they all serve to measure the performance variability in a specific area. Every boundary is measured, and the variability problems are addressed as the continuous improvement focus for the area.

The critical element is that it:

- is managed by the working shift,
- has a specific flow target for each shift,
- follows the production pitch drumbeat,
- it is visually graphed,
- it is deployed on every boundary.

Chapter 4: Tools

Output tracking

Stress Free^{TM} Manufacturing Solutions

Chapter 4: Learning Points

1. Shipment frequency and volume is the supply chain synchronization signal.
2. Synchronization is managed with output tracking.
3. Output tracking identifies the boundary issues or irregularities impeding flow.
4. Issue countermeasures are usually rapidly implemented.
5. Today's communication technology can be leveraged to accelerate synchronization.

Chapter 4: One Point Lesson

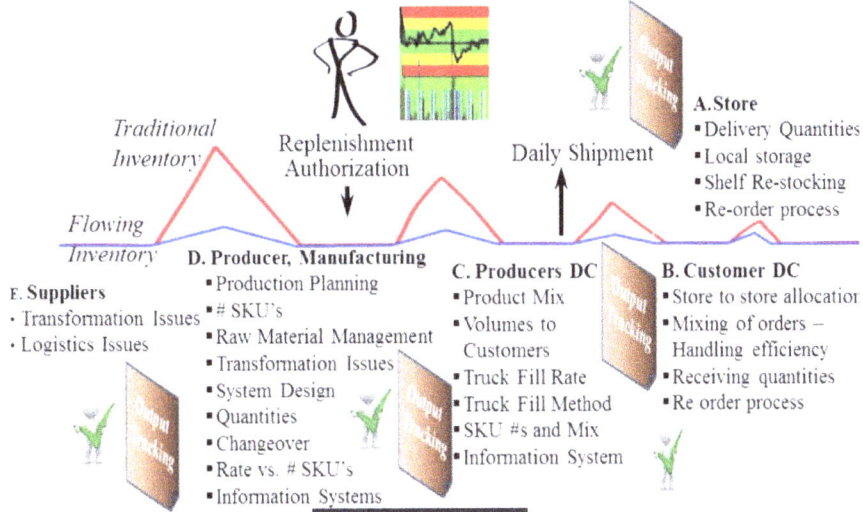

Output Tracking
Supply Chain Synchronization

- Implementation along the entire supply chain is key.
- The replenishment planner authorizes replenishment.
- The replenishment value is tracked on the output tracking sheet.
- The output tracking sheet is a daily management tool.

Chapter 5: Supply Chain Organization

Flowing Supply Chain Organization

The chief operation officer must envision the top thought leaders to the benefits of moving from organization driven to a capability building Supply Chain focused approach. They can then invest their time and energy in developing an organizational design and structure to deliver the transformation and enable and energize the organization to build capability to move the supply chain organization forward.

Supply Chain improvement deployments leverage the scale and power across the entire business.

The supply chain organization can expect 3-5% margin point improvement, a 40% reduction in inventory and a > 20% improvement in productivity, significant reductions in both quality defects, and serious safety incidents, increased throughput, and customer service improvement.

The resulting high-performance culture will ensure the retention of the champions in the organization

Achieving a waste / loss free, long term sustainable supply chain from raw materials to a consumer preferred product will provide a breakthrough. The waste / loss free approach is more profitable, agile, and flexible. This winning way can only be achieved when all resources work harmoniously together against common goals and a clear vision.

With hands on experience, the leading champions have the means of bringing the flowing supply chain vision to life. They are able to convey how they see it improve the lives of everyone and improve the long-term results of the business.

The vision becomes more than a slogan. It becomes the rallying point for all the people. It encompasses the entire organization. It becomes the Supply Chain Vision.

Every champion goes through the emotional high when they experience firsthand the power of the Stress Free™ Approach.

To create value, the customer need must be immediately addressed, waste must be reduced, throughput must match the need, and new initiatives must be brought efficiently on-line.

Each supply chain organization needs an improvement coach. This improvement coach provides an external perspective. The coach has a broad level of hands on capability. He/she sees many businesses. These coaches normally coach four to five sites.

An external coach provides the supply chain a different set of eyes. This external perspective allows the losses that have become a part of the supply chain to be identified and eliminated.

A series of workshops provide the hands-on experience to the key supply chain improvement leaders. These leaders along with the supply chain coach develop a comprehensive, pay as you go deployment plan.

The vision is to start from any situation and to take the journey to waste / loss free with all the people involved.

This never-ending drive to eliminate waste and loss will deliver breakthrough business results.

Supply Chain Organizational Assessment

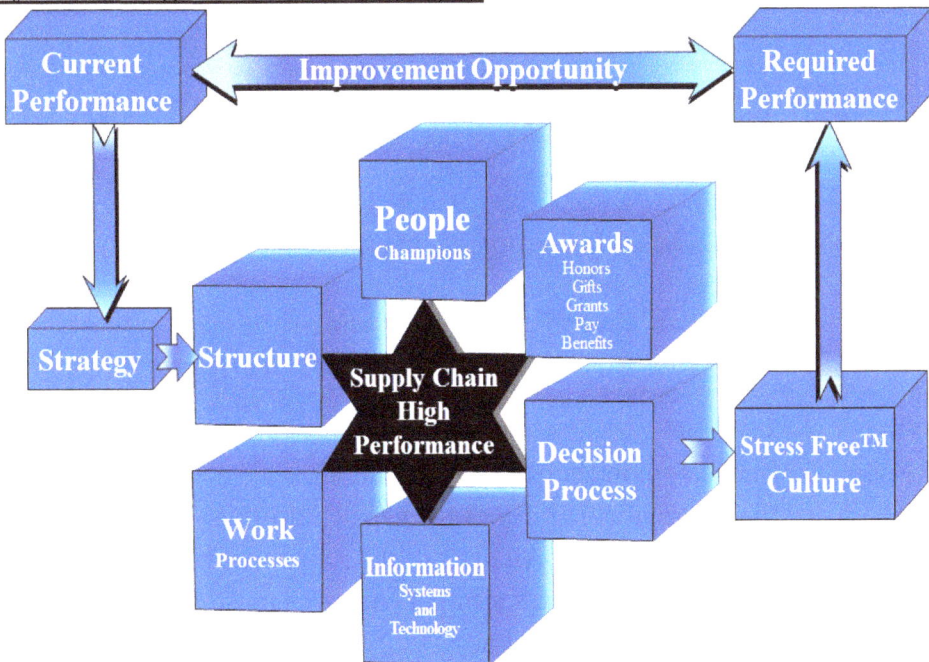

Leaders need a clear understanding of the entire supply chain situation. They need alignment to the most critical maintenance and improvement actions to take.

A comprehensive supply chain assessment on at least a yearly basis provides the leaders an aligned understanding of the supply chain situation. The assessment effort need only be in as much depth as required to get leadership consensus on the continuing supply chain improvement effort.

The high priority improvement efforts should surface during the alignment to the assessment question answers.

The assessment questions need to evaluate the condition of the supply chain in:

- leadership and the business situation reward
- organization
- information and material flow processes
- material transformation production processes
- finished product handling and distribution processes
- product to the shelf processes
- support and new initiative processes
- rewards and people

The assessment provides the supply chain leaders a clear understanding of the gaps and guides them to make the improvement selection.

Visual output of a Supply Chain Assessment

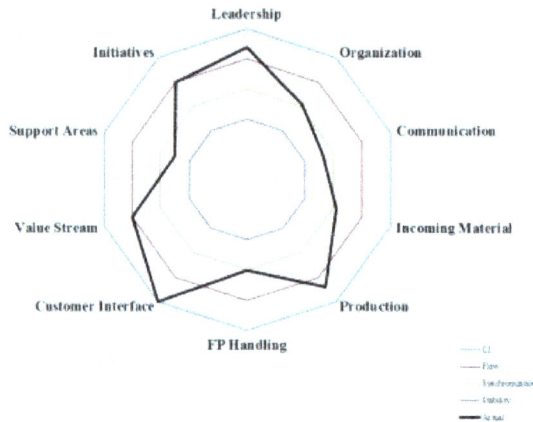

The supply chain champion leaders gain and embrace the concept of a flowing supply chain and the assessment highlights the gaps. Enrolling the supply chain organizations as a whole is critical. All parts of the supply chain need to move forward together. Not all at the same speed but each area must identify their role and part in the continuous improvement journey.

"When the mind functions, the muscles respond automatically, the heart pumps at the rate dictated by the muscle and the muscle responds based on the load."

The supply chain functions in a similar manner. The relationships between its various parts have been established on the basis of need. These relationships and the established organizational boundaries require examination. The boundaries are normally where waste is created.

Today communication technology allows every business result champion to know immediately when a sold unit goes out the door.

There is no primary, no support, and no secondary functions. There are only supply chain result Champions.

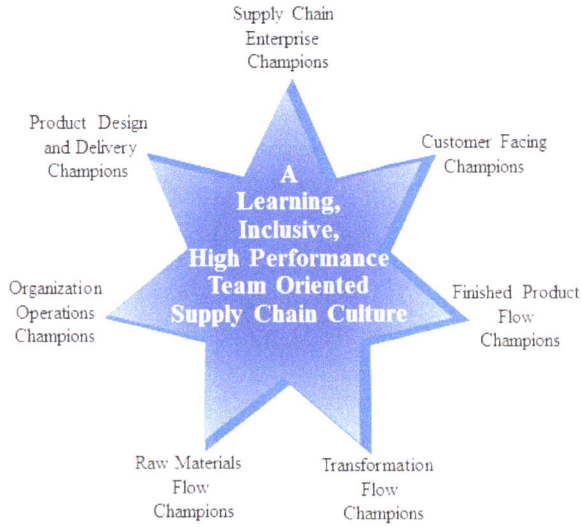

Supply Chain Result Champions

Supply Chain Enterprise Champions

- Supply Chain Leader; site, region, country, international.
- They are the orchestra conductors that keep all the members synchronized.

Customer Facing Champions

- The Site Manager
- The Sales Managers
- The Financial Contract Managers
- The Logistics Managers

These are the champions that must envision the customer to the impact that a steady statistically controlled flow closely meeting his consumer demand is an opportunity to free the cash trapped in the back room and on the shelf.

Product Design and Delivery Champions
- Product Development
- Process Development
- Engineering and Initiative Delivery

These folks deliver the new or improved product that seamlessly comes into the stably flowing supply chain.

Supply Chain Organization Operations Champions
- Site Manager
- HR manager
- Safety Manager
- Quality Manager
- Engineering Manager
- Support office managers

These are the people that ensure the supply chain organization has the quantity and quality of people and functions as intended. They monitor and ensure standards are followed and continuously improved.

They support and coach the organization in maintaining high safety standards and behaviors.

Raw Material Flow Champions
- Material receivers
- Line material deliverers

Material touches are minimized, and the quantities taken to the line exactly match that authorized to maintain flow. The precision of material delivery quantity reaches the point that line clearance is less than a kitchen trash bag.

Transformation Champions
- Line operators
- Maintenance personnel
- E&I and Electrical personnel
- Team Leaders
- Line Leaders
- Department Managers
- Operations Managers
- Site Manager

These are the people that ensure the material is safely transformed to the desired product at the specified quality and authorized quantity. They keep the equipment at target performance and operating speeds.

These folks become expert root cause problem solvers and continuous improvement champions.

They make work easy to do, mistake proof and are always improving its efficiency.

Those directly handling the materials and interfacing with the equipment know their leaders are capable and ready to support them as needed.

Problem-solving resources are visually signaled when needed and resolve problems immediately.

Finished Product Flow Champions

- Finished product to Warehouse handler
- Warehouse Forklift driver or other order loaders
- Truck Scheduler
- Customer order verifier

The product flows to replenish the inventory that has been loaded onto the out bound delivery trucks or into containers for rail or ship transport.

The customer orders are accurately filled and the finished product flows to the customer on time, on quantity and quality.

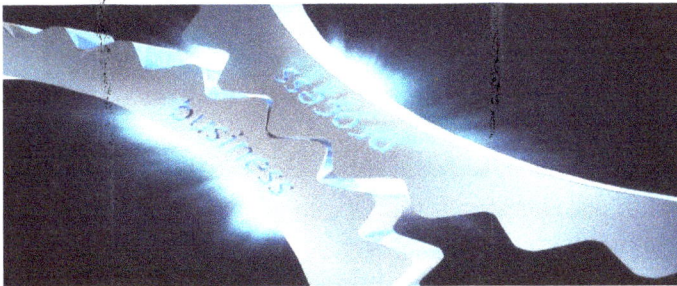

Supply Chain Optimum Organization Design

The Comprehensive Supply Chain Assessment questions and the evaluation of answers are a reflection of the Supply Chain Organization Design and the current social and work culture. The high-performance supply chain design is not monolithic nor structurally rigid. It needs to be organic and adaptive. It must keep up with technology and rapidly changing social culture.

Understanding the situation is critical. The supply chain crosses multiple organizations and though they may be in constant contact, leaders seldom take the time to gain a common alignment on the issues before them.

A comprehensive supply chain assessment utilizing key questions that expose the performance gaps in the current supply chain form the basis for a common alignment. Specific countermeasure actions are identified, and a preliminary action plan is developed. This assessment is often extended to facilitate more in-depth planning for implementing immediate action.

The opportunity may be immediately known, and a specific action taken.

Organizational Design (1977) by Jay R. Galbraith led to the codification of P&G's High-Performance Work System HPWS organizational model. This was further developed by David P. Hanna at P&G and later published by him externally as *Designing Organizations for High Performance* (1988).

Neither Galbraith nor Hanna was thinking in supply chain organization terms. Neither of them had the information technology of today. The basics they described have not changed but organization design implementation then, is now similar to baking a cake in a wood burning versus a microwave convection oven.

Now in 2020 thirty years later it is time to think in terms of the High-Performance Flowing Supply Chain Organization.

The organization must empower all people and make them champions. This is accomplished by implementing the High-Performance Supply Chain Work System Design.

The foundation of this design is the foundational principle of treating everyone as you wish to be treated.

How the supply chain works, how it grows, how results are measured and delivered and the strategy that holds it all together leads to an organization of champions.

Each element must be designed to produce the desired output at each supply chain boundary. Previous chapters highlighted the strategy of flow and flow implies an organization with as few boundaries as possible.

High Performance Supply Chain Work System

Supply Chain Structure

The flow-based supply chain structure implies the material transformation process management is the primary element that defines how to organize to win.

Supply Chain Tasks

The supply chain tasks are designed to operate the transformation processes and maintain the steady flow that matches the statistically controlled replenishment authorization.

The supply chain daily management system can be tuned to support replenishment.

Supply Chain Information System

The information system continuous to be one of the most rapidly evolving opportunities. Given the right application of technology, every individual can be synchronized to the replenishment authorization signal. Every task can be adjusted and tuned to this signal. Non-value-added work can be minimized or eliminated. Required work can be scheduled appropriately.

Supply Chain Rewards

The Supply Chain Champions deliver the business objectives and goal. The reward system must recognize this with social recognition as well as monetary rewards.

Supply Chain Decision Making

The supply Chain decision making must be designed to occur at the lowest level possible and the capability to make good decisions trained to each individual.

Supply Chain Champions

Continuously developing and renewing people's skills creates an organization of winners. Organization winners challenge and reinforce each other as they deliver superior results.

Supply Chain Optimum Organization Performance

The creation of winners occurs in a learning organization supported by strong adaptive capable leaders. Leadership creates the culture and the people he or she supports create the superior business results that allow the business to win in the marketplace.

Tools for Chapter 5:
1. Comprehensive Supply Chain Assessment
2. Leadership Capability Assessment
3. Organization Assessment
4. Vision Creation Guide
5. Master Plan Creation
6. Measures to Capability Matrix

Chapter 5: Learning Points
- The Principle of Inclusion is the supply chain foundation.
- Team-work concepts make it happen.
- A learning supply chain environment fuels improvement.
- Delivering results is critical.
- Supply Chain Flow maximizes results

Chapter 5: One Point Lesson - Supply Chain Operation

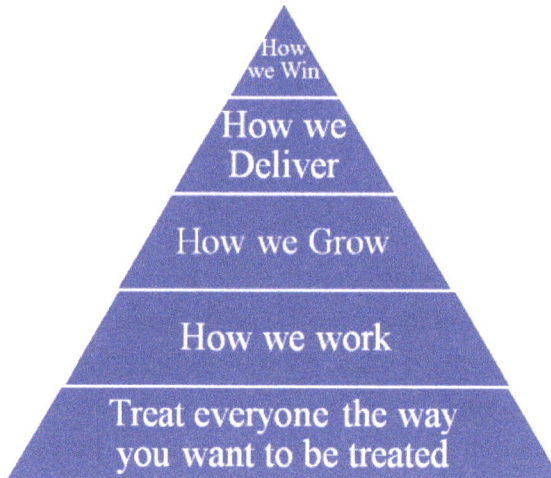

- Leadership behavior establishes the culture.
- Supply chain organizational design, maintains and continuously keeps it current.

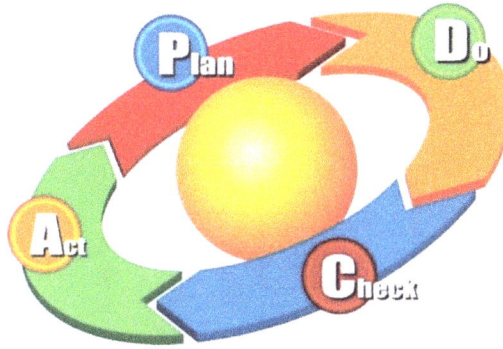

Chapter 6: Supply Chain Daily Management

Supply Chain Daily Management (SCDM) provides the supply chain leader the ability to understand, manage and synchronize the flow of information, and materials to ensure resources are functioning optimally. It is a systemic means of ensuring high supply chain performance.

The elements of daily management all come together to ensure the future twenty-four hours will perform flawlessly. The previous day supply chain performance is examined, countermeasures correcting any shortcomings are assured, the next twenty-four hours are anticipated, and any continuous improvement actions are reviewed.

The supply chain daily management is the last level of the daily management chain that begins at the production line level and rapidly progresses to the supply chain level. The daily management at the line level is based on the operating shift line team and may occur seven days a week. At the supply chain level and for the support functions it occurs once a day, and in most cases only five days a week.

The primary purpose of every level of the daily management system is to organize and apply the existing resources to ensure an, as planned, loss free performance, for the next twenty-four hours and beyond.

Daily supply chain daily management does deploy the company's strategy and goals. It does share the appropriate KPI's at each level of application. It is based on teamwork.

The daily management activity is not about deploying from the top but requesting resources as needed from the production line operating level all the way to the supply chain level.

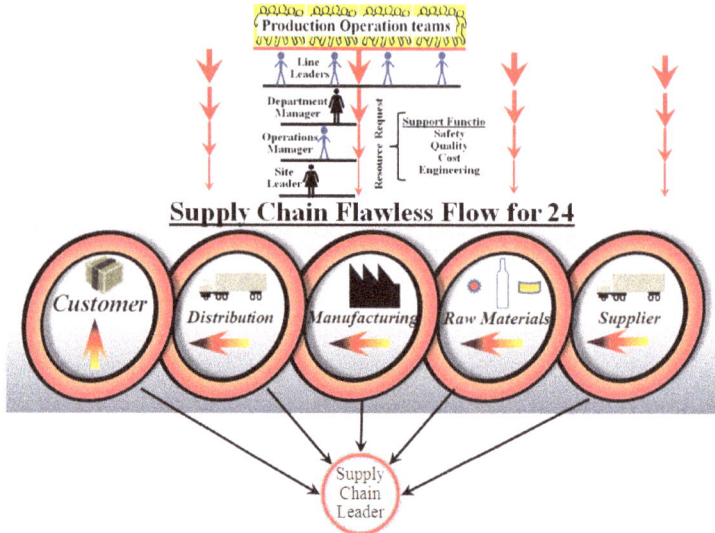

The diagram, Supply Chain Flawless Flow for 24, depicts the operating teams at the top. Daily Management is designed to ensure the operating teams have the skills and resources to keep the production lines running at the required statistically controlled product replenishment pace.

Output tracking provides the details of any issues and is brought to the daily direction setting meeting when an issue resolution requires resources outside of the line operating team.

Daily Management of course is also an excellent organizational structure to deploy the business goals as well as to capture operational performance. This is visually displayed on the daily meeting board but needs little discussion unless a performance gap exists. On a yearly or major event basis the business strategy and Key Performance Indicators (KPI's) are deployed via the daily management interaction.

Coordinating the Supply Chain Daily Management system requires one to understand the vertical resource management occurring on the vertical axis from the production line to the supply chain and horizontally along the supply chain back from the customer to the raw material supplier.

The supply chain organization has many interacting, interdependent elements. The focus in this book will intentionally be kept to the vertical flow from the production line to the supply chain organization level and from the customer to the supplier. This approach will show the materials handling, manufacturing and product distribution practice of the daily management. The supporting organizations play partnership roles in ensuring the materials get transformed into the desired product.

Daily Management is a foundation system for all organizations. It must flow from the transformation work point to those at each level that control resources. In each case, resource allocation decisions need to occur at the lowest level possible.

Resource allocation is a key issue for all organizations. A robust daily management system reaching across the entire organization that strategically optimizes resource utilization, accelerates the business results and at the same time creates the on the floor culture critical for continuous improvement.

There are some basic requirements that need up front definition and clarification.

1. **On the floor:** the location where material or data transformation takes place in the journey to becoming a product.

2. **Line Operating Teams:** A team of people that work on the same line and set of equipment on a regular basis.

3. **Operating team leader:** One team leader for each line operating team. The operating team leader maintains the line output tracking chart. Any hourly, off target production is a defect to be evaluated. This implies immediate problem-solving capability.

    The operating team leader determines if the operating team has the appropriate problem-solving skills. If so, the team solves the problem immediately. If not, the team leader makes a call for support to the line team leader.

4. **Line leader:** has 24-hour line performance accountability. This person manages the teams assigned to one line. This person may manage multiple lines. A key responsibility is to monitor the hour by hour line output tracking.

A miss on quantity, time or quality is a defect to which corrective resource effort must be allocated.

The line team leader may have the supportive problem-solving coaching skills and helps resolve the problem. If not, the line leader will take this resource need request to the department daily morning meeting.

By addressing the defects as they arise, the production transformation process is continually improved.

At the beginning of the journey to supply chain flow, the department and operations managers must step in to lead this problem resolution. At each intervention they must strive to develop their people into becoming master problem solvers.

Daily Management – from the line to the supply chain
Production Area Daily Management

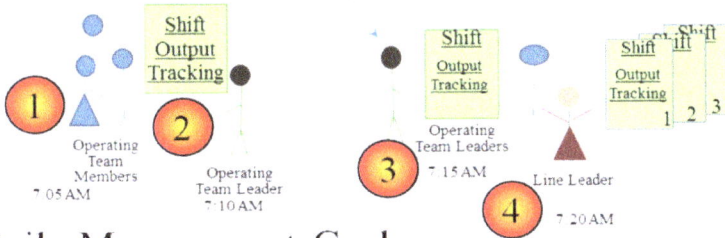

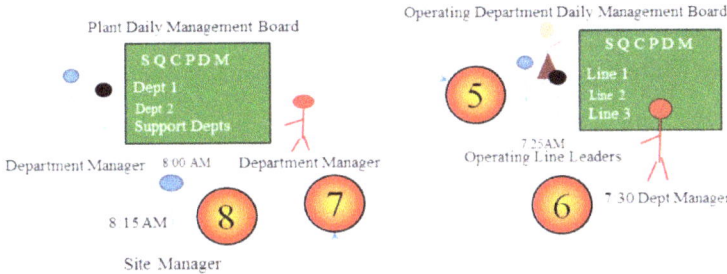

Let's look first at how the daily management flows from the floor to the site leadership and then let's look at how Leadership interacts with this flow.

The night shift operating team, at the end of their shift meets briefly at their operation line team board to review their output performance. The operating team leader joins them to better understand the overall shift performance.

Then the operating line team leader meets with his on-coming counterpart and shares the off going shift's output tracking chart. The line leader joins them and reviews the last three shift output tracking sheets. Together they look ahead to the actions necessary to make the next twenty-four hours loss free.

The line leader takes this information and any resource needs to the department meeting where she meets with the other line leaders and department manager. Resource needs are identified and allocated if available.

The department manager takes his needs and the needs of his line leaders to the site managers meeting. There he and the other managers share their situation. The resources still needed get evaluated and help allocated on a priority basis.

Site Manager and Leadership Team Tour

The site manager follows a set, weekly and monthly operations interaction, routine. Each day of the week, the site manager will tour a specific path through the site.

Day one: Outbound truck loading to finished product storage.
On tour: Site manager, Department Manager, Quality Manager

Day two: Finished product storage to production line one,
On tour: Site Manager, Receiving Manager, Safety manager

Day three: Finished product storage to production line four,
On tour: Site Manager, Quality Manager, Engineering Manager

Day four: Line delivery to the line back to raw material receiving.
On tour: Site Manager, Department Manager, Finance Manager

Day Five: Support areas, Maintenance areas, Environment,
Safety, Health, Quality, Engineering, Finance, Office area.
On tour: Site Manager, Department Manager, Logistics manager.

Each day's tour begins immediately after the Daily Morning DMS meetings. The weekly tour cycle is repeated every week. A leadership designate is appointed to make the tour even when the site manager is absent. The tour focus is on the adherence to standards, safety and cleanliness, everything in its place and in recognizing and giving feedback to the good work that is being done.

Supply Chain Daily Management

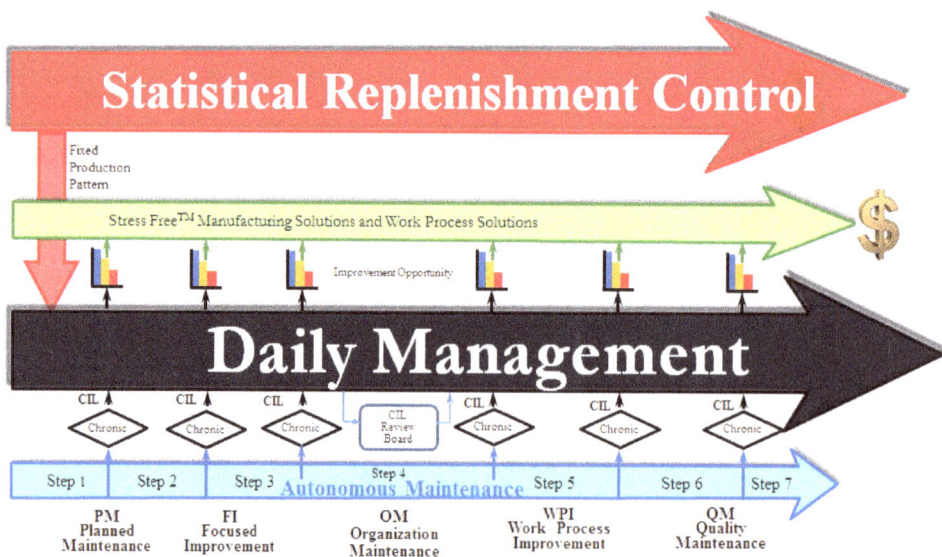

The Supply Chain Daily Management meeting occurs at the same time every day. Each of the supply chain organizations hold similar meetings to what has been described above and then these supply chain organization leaders attend the final daily supply chain management meeting.

This meeting is held at high noon every day. It is a short meeting unless there is a high-level issue that one of the organizations has not been able to resolve.

Boundary flow Issues for the next twenty-four hours are resolved. Longer term continuous improvements are reviewed.

In Summary

The daily management system and the daily leadership tour form the center or power rail of continuous improvement.

Money to the bank, manufacturing and work process solutions workshops along the improvement journey create a pay as you go improvement process.

The application of continuous skill improvement, root cause problem-solving and technical skills development all combine to increase the capability of the supply chain personnel.

A statistical inventory replenishment system using a fixed production pattern to replenish the shipped product provides production stability.

Tools for Chapter 6:

1. Standardized Daily Management
2. Check, Act (PDCA) cycle
3. TPM – Total Productive Maintenance (TPM) organized in pillars,
   AM – Autonomous Maintenance
   PM – Planned Maintenance
   FI – Focused Improvement
   QM -- Quality Maintenance

Leadership and Daily Management Tips:

Short Term:
- Do a Stress FreeTM Leadership Capability Assessment
- Do a Stress FreeTM Organization Capability Assessment
- Implement a Stress FreeTM Daily Management Workshop.

Longer Term:
- Engage the Stress FreeTM Leadership Workshop Series
  (See chapter 7)

Chapter 6: Learning Points

- A structured, standardized daily management system is fundamental.
- The PDCA cycle is used to manage the daily management process
- Synchronized Daily Management along the entire supply chain is a fundamental element

Chapter 6: One Point Lesson - Daily Management

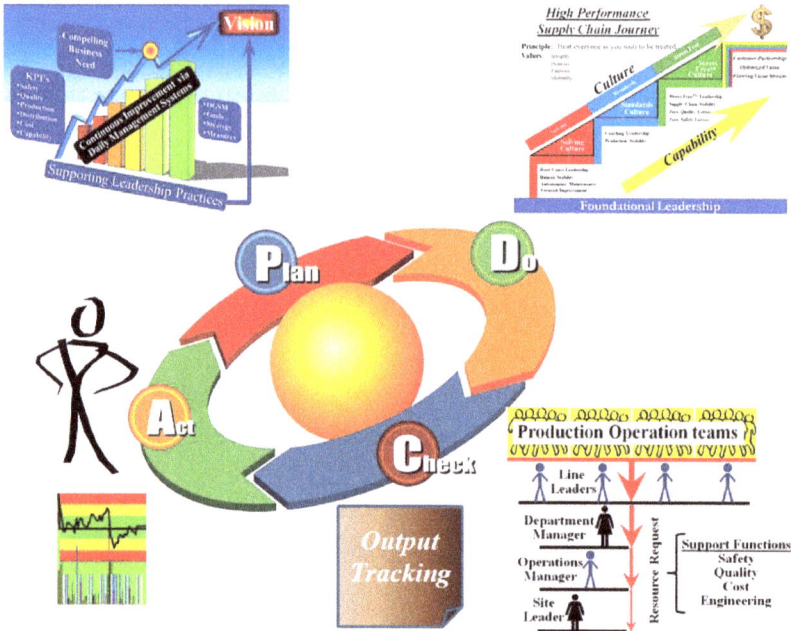

- Output Tracking begins the cycle
- Immediate response by the team to issues
- Longer term resource needs get planned
- The teams deliver to plan

Output Tracking OEE DMS

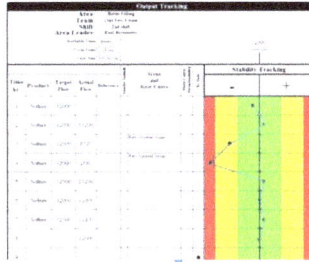

Target ~ 80%

Target 800
Produced 770
OEE=770/800= 96.25 %

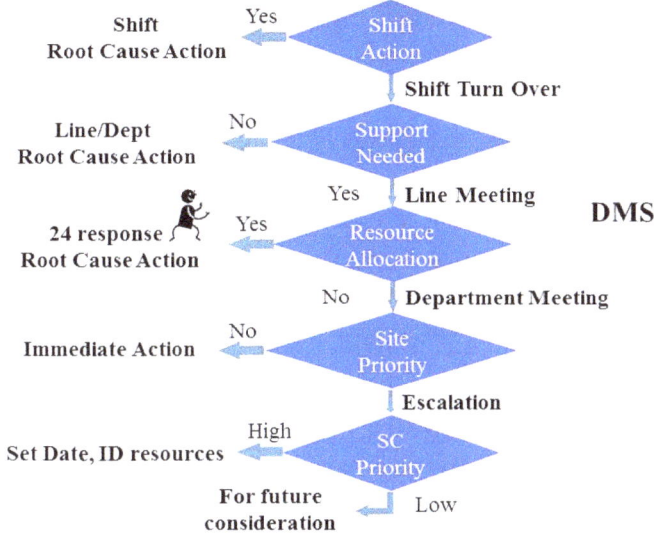

Shift
Root Cause Action ← Yes — Shift Action

Shift Turn Over

Line/Dept
Root Cause Action ← No — Support Needed

Yes — Line Meeting — DMS

24 response
Root Cause Action ← Yes — Resource Allocation

No — Department Meeting

Immediate Action ← No — Site Priority

Escalation

Set Date, ID resources ← High — SC Priority

For future consideration ← Low

Chapter 6: One Point Lesson – Output Tracking and Daily Management

- Line output tracking begins a problem resolution resource allocation process that goes all the way up to the supply chain level if necessary.
- It stops at which ever level has the resource to solve the problem needing the resource. The Daily Management meetings are the points where the problem gets discussed and the solution resource gets allocated.
- The least that is done is to ensure the next twenty-four-hour window is address.

Chapter 7: Supply Chain Putting it all together

The supply chain gets established to meet the business situation existing at a specific time. It may have been perfectly designed but more than likely it was based on the best compromises available at the time. With time the supply chain was changed based on new supplier contracts, changing customer demands and the transformation process was changed to reduce cost and improve profit.

The Supply Chain leader is faced with the challenge of staying competitive, flexible, and continuously improving. The leader looks along the supply chain and lists the following tools available for use:

- Leadership hands on development
- Qualitative Assessments
- Quantitative Assessments
- Root Cause Problem-solving
- Work Process Improvement
- Rapid Change Over

Leadership hands on development

The supply chain leadership development is narrowly focused to the behaviors required to support the organization and the people being led. There are four specific leadership practices,

1. Supply Chain Organization Assessment and Enhancement

Every Leader needs to be out on the "floor". They must see, hear, smell, and feel the environment. They must engage the people and understand the environment. They must ensure safe, healthy work processes and a supportive environment is present.

The on the floor assessment experience and personally practiced enhancement approach, in partnership with the on the floor champions assures the success of the resulting improvement.

2. Stabilization Behavior

The workday actions at each level of each organization is clarified and the "on the floor time" organized and standardized. This allows the supply chain organization leaders to work together. The Organization behavior and requirements for a "successful twenty-four hour" becomes the evaluation criteria.

A shared continuous improvement application plan provides the basis for continuous improvement.

3. Synchronization of Leaders

Synchronization of the key supply chain work, communication and material flow is the next step toward the continuous improvement organization.

Leaders at all levels and along the supply chain make sure that everyone is operating to standards.

Reapplication along the entire supply chain is the practice.

Leaders reassess and adjust their organization to reflect increased organization capability.

4. Pull Activities and Behavior

Pull may not be achievable by the supply chain but high-quality products flowing close to the customer desired rate is possible.

The leadership behaviors supporting this environment focus on waste elimination, supply chain synchronization, organizational partnering and the empowerment and enablement of all persons in the supply chain.

Qualitative Assessments

There are many types of assessments. The ones described here are simple, facilitate a close to the action assessment, and are effective and usually only takes a half day when facilitated by an expert resource.

Comprehensive Supply Chain Assessment

Understanding the situation is critical. The supply chain crosses multiple organizations and though they may be in constant contact, leaders seldom take the time to gain a common alignment on the issues before them.

A comprehensive supply chain assessment utilizing key questions that expose the performance gaps in the current supply chain forms the basis for a common alignment. Specific countermeasure actions are identified, and a preliminary action plan is developed. This assessment is often extended to facilitate more in-depth planning for implementing immediate action.

The opportunity may be immediately known, and a specific action taken.

Additional rapid assessments may shed more light on specific opportunities. These assessments are:

Leadership Capability Assessment

Leadership behavior sets the culture. This assessment identifies the gaps in the key behaviors, leaders' desire. If an organization does not have the culture leaders say they want, it most often is the result of rewarding the wrong behavior. This assessment identifies this situation.

Supply Chain Organization Assessment

The supply chain organization achieves exactly what it is designed to deliver. If it falls short, it is often due to the supply chain organization design. Leaders must design their supply chain organization to deliver the business results and the culture required to have a prosperous company.

The supply chain organization assessment identifies the gaps as compared to the winning world class design and guides the organization in developing countermeasure activities.

Quality Assessment

The customer buys the product because they inherently see the product quality value. The Quality Assessment provides insight to the gaps in the key elements that maintain the desired product quality level. The Assessment points to specific actions aimed at the elements that maintain the quality the customer desires and pays for.

Equipment Assessment

Equipment is the primary material to product transformation work agent. Keeping it performing and improving on the design is a fundamental activity of the production system.

This assessment highlights specific daily and long-term maintenance system gaps and links countermeasure actions to them.

Work System Assessment

People do work. They maintain and keep equipment and systems working and performing as desired. People grow, people contribute improvements, people represent a malleable resource that need to be supported, developed, encouraged and empowered.

The Work system assessment looks at the specific work of the organization or work system being studied. The identified gaps can often be addressed immediately following an assessment.

Dramatic productivity results have consistently been achieved.

Safety Assessment

Safety is the number one consideration for every organization. This assessment examines safety behaviors, practices, and safety systems. The safety gaps are identified, and the leaders of the organization are guided in their safety improvement countermeasure plan.

BOSS

Quantitative Assessment
Business Opportunity Statistical Survey (BOSS) (see Chapter 3)

Inventory is the result of the current system capability. The analysis of the past year's daily product shipment tells the customer behavior story. The analysis of the past year's daily inventory position tells the supply chain behavior story. Knowing how to combine the two to determine the optimum way to synchronize product flow to customer demand in any system defines the improvement opportunity.

This analysis applied to key distribution points along the supply chain provides critical insight to the studied situation.

Two repeatedly used capabilities.

Assessments provide knowledge the root cause problem-solving and work process improvement are fundamental skills that support all other actions.

Root Cause Problem-solving

There are many root cause problem-solving tools. The goal is to have one root cause problem-solving process that can be applied by those champions dealing directly with the material to product transformation and also be used by the top leader in the company.

A single process for the supply chain that meets the line to the board room criteria creates a powerful communication bond and understanding for each in between organizational layer.

Work Process Improvement

Work is synchronized to the customer need and to that work that directly produces the desired product. It is the current best and easiest way to do work. It is defined and improved by the people doing the work.

Improvement is driven by the desire to make it easier to do, the desire to eliminate the waste of time, effort, or materials. The goal becomes a mistake proof, easy to, low effort work environment.

Rapid Changeover

In today's world, the supply chain manufacturing organization must utilize their production lines to make multiple products and variations of these products. Many times, this means frequently changing their lines over to a different configuration. The time it takes to change over is time not available for production. Reducing the changeover time to that required to ensure the statistical product replenishment rate ensures the most revenue from the capital utilized.

Stress Free^TM Continuous Improvement

The following steps closely follow the content of this book. These steps define the implementation of the concepts covered in this book in a step by step process. The timing to get to step 9 is a three to five-year period.

Steps 1-3 takes about twelve months.

Step 4 is takes 18 to 24 months.

Step 5 takes about 12 months.

Step 6 -7 takes about 12 months.

Step 8 is the continuous improvement state that goes on forever.

Step 9 happens incrementally after Step 6, first with key customers and continues along with Step 8.

Stress Free^TM Continuous Improvement

Step 1: Comprehensive Supply Chain Assessment

Read Chapter 1

Step 2: Define the Opportunity

Improvement should be defined, planned and tracked.

Read Chapter 1

Step 3: Envision and Empower Supply Chain Champions

Make people want to come to work. Let them experience the power of making things better. Make them champions.

Read Chapter 1 and 2

Step 4: Deploy Supply Chain Stability Actions

Create a supply chain Continuous improvement master plan as an integral part of the business plan. Operate the supply chain within a single business master plan.

Step 5: Develop the Organization

Make continuous improvement a strong pattern in the fabric of the organizations culture. It has to be more than a thread.

Read Chapter 5

Step 6: Synchronize the Work

The calendar, the clock and the control chart make synchronization possible. Technology provides the volume control and facilitates low cost solutions.

> Read Chapter 4

Step 7: Create System Flow

Flow allows all supply chains to leverage their current capabilities and work toward the longer-term vision of achieving PULL.

> Read Chapter 6, 7

Step 8: Create Adaptive Organization

The business world is in constant change turmoil. A flexible responsive organization will be able to adapt and ride the wave.

> Read Chapter 6, 7

Step 9: Partner with Customers

The customer is the focus. An adaptive organization is capable of flawlessly dealing with the needs of the customer.

Once the customers realize that partnering is to their advantage business will continually improve.

Tools for Chapter 7:

1. The four leadership practices
2. Statistical Replenishment control
3. Root Cause Problem-solving
4. Work Process Improvement
5. Rapid Change Over
6. Stress FreeTM Continuous Improvement
7. Quality Assessment
8. Equipment Assessment
9. Work System Assessment
10. Safety Assessment

Chapter 7: Learning Points

- Daily leadership action is required
- Daily improvement reviews
- Daily Management System action.

Chapter 7: One Point Lesson - Putting it All Together

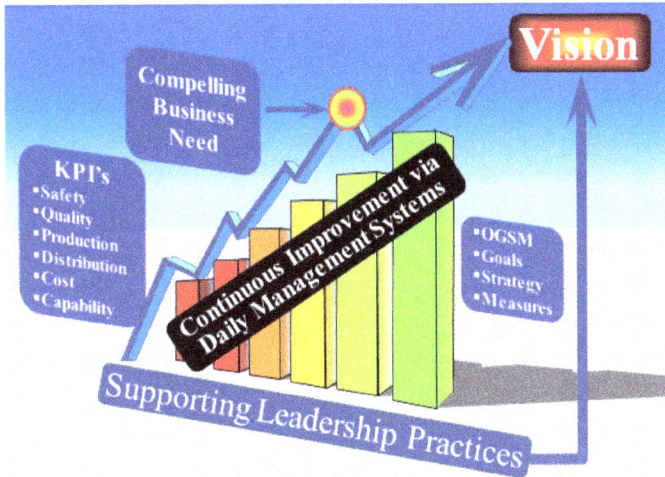

A vision out beyond the shorter-term compelling business need

- Leadership supply chain orientation is a critical factor
- Supply Chain oriented goals with Key Performance Indicators
- A strategic, measurable action plan.
- Continuous improvement via supply chain daily management.

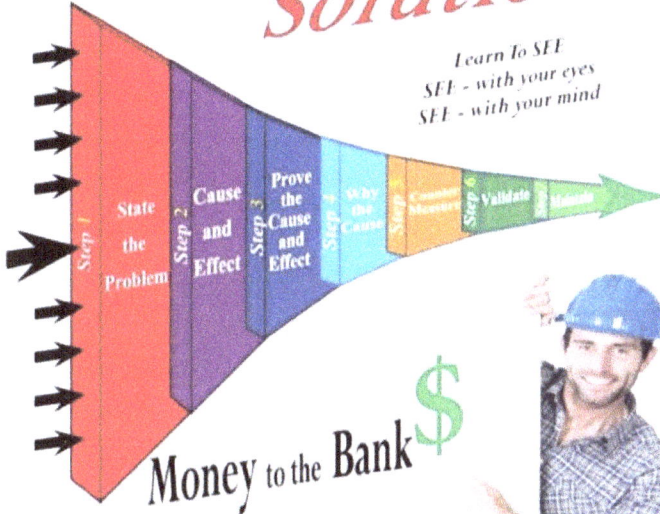

Stress Free^TM Manufacturing Solutions

**Root Cause Solutions
for
Manufacturing and Production Systems**

By: *Ron Mueller*

Around the World Publishing LLC
4914 Cooper Road Suite 144
Cincinnati, Ohio 45242-9998

Copyright © 2021 by Ron Mueller

ISBN 13:
ISBN 10:

Distributed by Ingram
Cover Picture By: Andrey Popov, Dreamstime.com
Cover Design By: Ron Mueller

DEDICATION

To *Hien Nguyen Mueller*,
the *family problem solver*
and the person
who has enriched my life.

Technical Editor:

Gordon Miller P. E.

Manufacturing Solutions Table of Content

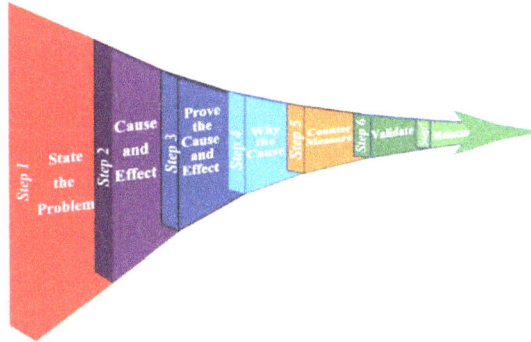

Manufacturing Solutions Introduction

You want the problem solved. A world class leader is a world class problem solver who has a series of thoroughly documented solved problems as case studies used to coach others in solving problems.

Do you have your problem-solving coaching guide?

There are leaders at every level of the organization. Operating team leaders, Maintenance team leaders, Line Leaders, Area Leaders, Department Leaders, Operations Leaders, Site Leaders, Business Leaders, Lab Leaders; I could go on with the list, but you get the point.

All people are in problem-solving roles and they need to be **great** problem solvers.

The production line stops. The call for help is made. Demanding customers get less than they ordered. The Vice presidents valiantly give assurances of a quick fix.

Numerous problem-solving actions are implemented but the problem reoccurs or in many cases continues un-abetted.

Good intentions but not the required solution.

Then promise of Stress Free^{TM} Manufacturing Solutions, Learning To See with the Mind and the Eye and the promise of "Money to the Bank" is recalled.

"Give me a week and five key production area people. We will give you the root cause solution," replies the **problem solver** as he brandishes his Stress Free^{TM} Manufacturing Solutions book.

"I can't free up that many people for that amount of time. They are too busy keeping the line running. Let's get some engineers or those process improvement folks," is a common reply.

"That's fine call me when you all have the people and the time," is the **problem solver's** reply.

The people and the time are grudgingly agreed to and production line cooperation is assured.

The team of five convene. The operator closest to the problem knows it is hopeless. The maintenance technician knows his area will be blamed. The young degreed process engineer figures her career is over. The data hunter resource is willing but confused. And the person responsible for the final resolution has said their prayers and sent out the resumes.

The group is ready to become a team.

The problem persists. The team is asked to define the problem.

The team is asked what is the Phenomenon that must be solved?

"What is a phenomenon," asks one of the team members who gets immediate support from all the rest.

This is team building at its best.

They learn phenomenon and all the rest. The theories are written for each cause and effect. The testing is rigorously done. True causes go into the Why-Why Analysis and countermeasures get identified.

In only five days, the team solves the problem and a few more. Like all heroes they get recognized as the best.

The line keeps running, the product is shipped.

The Stress is over, and people feel free.

Stress Free

Stress Free!   **Really?**

What makes this problem-solving approach stress free?

Solved problems reduce stress.

The approach in this book has been used to solve hundreds of problems all to root cause, reinforcing my statement to you:

"Give me the right five people and any problem can be solved."

Stress Free^{TM} Manufacturing Solutions

- is a closely guided process that documents each step.
- follows the scientific thought process.
- leverages team knowledge.
- has more than twenty years of a 100% success rate.

"Any problem you can see you can solve."

Stress Free^{TM} Manufacturing Solutions teaches you to **SEE!**

> ***SEE:*** *with your eyes*
>
> ***SEE:*** *with your mind*

The accompanying:

Stress Free^{TM} Manufacturing Solutions Workbook

Is an excel workbook that guides the user and creates a documented solution for each problem.

Stress Free^{TM} Manufacturing Solutions Examples,

Provide solution examples of common manufacturing problems.

The main focus of this book is to teach the user how to focus, how to clarify, how to fully understand a problem and finally how to permanently eliminate a problem.

Problem-solving is based on the scientific method.

> **Stop!** Don't run. ***Stress Free^{TM} Manufacturing Solutions***
>
> *"Keeps it simple"*

The scientific method simply implies the laws of physics, of chemistry and of gravity are fundamental.

Any other team will be able to validate the result utilizing the solution test plan. The test will be measurable, thorough, meticulous, precise, and accurate.

Value of the Loss

A key focus for problems solving is the loss recovery expressed in dollars per year. Problem-solving may be fun but problems cost businesses significant dollar losses. A key and first step in understanding the problem is to understand the value of the solution. This value should always be front and center for those working on solving the problem.

Defining the value of the loss is critical. The value of the solution needs to be important enough to warrant the effort and cost expenditure of the problem-solving team.

Conservatively a problem-solving team costs ten thousand dollars per week. The goal is to solve all problems to root cause in one week and to have solutions in place in a month.

The most appropriate way to state the value of a loss is in **dollars lost per year**. Most business cycles and budgets are yearly. The decision to support a problem-solving effort must compete with other choices the resources could be working on.

Business Linkage

The dollar loss per year, due to the problem, **must be defined**. It is critically important to create this linkage. What specifically will be gained and how will this gain be measured when the problem is solved.

General improvement goals are certainly important - inventory reduction, speed to market, net outside sales (NOS) gain. However, these are longer term and harder to realize.

Measurable:

- 15 min package change over down to 5 min.
- Work in Process (WIP inventory) reduction from fifteen times the customer "pull rate" (Takt) to two times the customer pull rate.
- Manipulation line staffing reduction from six to two

System Layout

Immediately walking and doing a hand drawing of the system is an important activity that grounds the individual in the understanding of the physical system that they are trying to improve.

It is also important to understand the organizational structure that maintains the current situation. If the improvement change is to be maintained, the organization's leadership must understand how to do so.

The system lay out provides an understanding of,

- People placement and activities
- material placement and handling issues
- current behaviors and practices by individuals
- synchronization issues i.e. - long conveyance, bottlenecks, surge points

It is important for the improvement team to discuss what they have seen and understood from the on the floor walk to make the system layout.

No matter what the problem may be, the leaders of the area and the problem-solving team should step back and understand,

- The Customer,
- The Material Flow
- The Equipment
- The Human Connection - how the Work gets done.

Customer Connection

It is critical to get away from the thinking of only meeting the demand of the equipment.

Takt Time is the measure that provides the direct customer pull signal to the production system.

It is worth the struggle to determine how Takt Time is connected to every improvement that is made to the production system. To bypass this struggle makes the improvement temporary.

Takt time should be kept as pure as possible and have no safety/buffer factors associated with it.

Available time:

Calendar or clock time minus planned activities that have blocks of time specifically calling for the production system to be down.

This measure should be kept pure and used to help find the barriers to a pull-based production system. Every proposal to change it to accommodate a current measurement approach only serves to hide the improvements required to establish and maintain a flow enabled pull-based system.

C/O time relates to inventory reduction. Inventory should only be held to maintain top level customer service. Inventory Reduction is only possible when the system provides reliable flow. Reliable flow is required to support a pull-based production system.

Material Connection

The supply of the raw materials and the synchronized handling of the finished product are both critical in ensuring the flow of the production system.

Raw material quantity and placement is critical in optimizing the flow of the production system.

The logistics of bringing the materials to the line and returning material remnants for later use is a critical element the must be analyzed. Flow and time analysis are important analysis to utilize.

Equipment Connection

Physical layout and material supply layout to the equipment are often related to specific problems or are due to previously experienced problems.

The problem may be the number of stops, or break downs or the amount of effort it takes to keep an area up and running.

There are many opportunities to better utilize the equipment at hand.

- Create flow by the synchronization of filler, capper, labeler case packer by shortening the distances between the equipment to the optimum so the line can start and stop in a synchronous fashion and generate no scrap during a changeover.

- Minimize the raw material inventory in the production area; bottles, caps, KDF's by delivering at Takt or at a pitch.

The equipment layout needs to be drawn to scale. The time that a single product spends having value added and the time it spends traveling needs to be analyzed. The travel time then needs to be eliminated or shortened.

The Human Connection

Once the initial production system drawing is completed then the actions of the people involved in the production of the product should be studied and understood.

Standardized Work

This is *only the work done directly on the product to produce it to the customer need*. All other work though being done to standard is not considered standardized work. ***Standardized means synchronized to the customer.***

Many organizations produce to a production schedule. This schedule is the equivalent of the "customer". In many cases it is designed to cover the many problems experienced by the logistics associated with moving materials and finished product.

Within this concept people will work to the required standards as defined by safety and product quality requirements and the that required by law.

For continuous improvement to be possible, the critical and repeatable work must be done to standard. The time for this work is normally synchronized with the cycle of the equipment that is being supported. It may also be a service that is synchronized with an accounting or other process cycle.

Stress Free*^{TM} *Work Solutions is the companion guide in solving problems of manual and office work.

- People and equipment do work,
- Both need to be maintained.
- Both break down.
- Both periodically need fixing.
- People maintain, people fix, people think and solve problems.

Stress Free*^{TM} *Manufacturing Solutions focuses on the production system, equipment and material flow.

Realize that given five knowledgeable people you too can solve any problem in the world.

Following the ***Stress Free*^{TM} *Manufacturing Solutions*** Process will give you the root cause solution in three to five workdays.

You will always solve your problem.

If not contact **Ron Mueller**

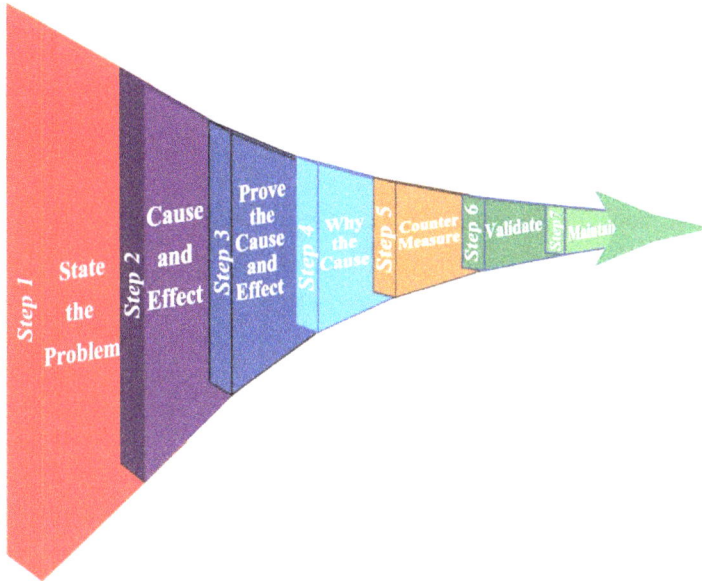

Chapter 1: Problem Understanding, Focus and Solution Value

Before going into problem-solving let's talk about; *Measurement*, the *Type of problems*, *True Value* problem selection and how leaders must *Focus* the problem before organizing a problem-solving team.

Measurement

It is important to understand the business cost of the problem before launching into the problem-solving process.

A fundamental requirement before beginning any problem-solving is the requirement of a *flawless measurement process* or system. In problem-solving the ability to exactly measure and have confidence in the measurement is a must. The first problem-solving example is one where this fundamental had been overlooked.

Measurement

A team was called together to solve the problem of missing actives in a product. They worked for almost six months with no progress.

I was asked whether I would add this problem to a problem-solving workshop.

"If you give me the right five people," I replied.

I described to them the five people that would be acceptable. There were around ten people involved, including people in China, Japan and the US.

"The five people must be physically present and only five people," was my reply when the bargaining began.

On the second day of the workshop, I reviewed the cause and effect diagram.

There on one branch was Measurement.

"Measurement can never be a cause," was the point I made.

If you suspect you have a measurement problem, it must be the head of the fishbone or the "effect".

After putting this at the head of the fishbone, the team solved the problem in **two hours**.

Types of problems

Knowing the type of problem allows the leaders of an area know how to select the right people to be on the problems solving team and to determine what tools they would expect a problem-solving team to utilize.

There may be other types or more types than are listed but these have served to categorize and organize all the problems I have ever worked on. There are variations and differences in specifics or how a problem may be described but in general they all will end up in one of the six.

1. **Equipment Problems**

   These are problems occurring in the equipment. The equipment function is either reduced or stopped. Action must be taken to re-establish the transformation work the equipment is expected to provide. Often the equipment just needs to be restored to base conditions.

2. **Material Problems**

   These are problems occurring in the material being transformed. The material performance either is inadequate or it prevents the transformation from occurring. The material needs to be evaluated and action taken to ensure the material is within the specification required for easy and consistent transformation.

3. **Processing Problems**

    Processing problems are similar to equipment problems but often they are chemical reaction or flow and mixing oriented. Since visibility is often the problem the analysis tools for these problems aid the investigator by providing visibility of the problem via secondary measures.

4. **System Problems**

    System problems are problems experienced in the management, maintenance, and assurance of the fundamental value stream flow. There are quality requirements, safety requirements, government, and financial requirements. Adherence to these requirements is a fundamental expectation.

5. **Human Problems**

    The problems in this area are problems in how people work together. These problems lend themselves to very different problem-solving tools. These types of problems are covered in Around the World Standardized Work

6. **Information Problems**

    Information flow, timeliness, accuracy, and understandability are critical in holding complex transformation processes together. It is often the single most significant problem in complex transformation processes.

    There are many ways information can flow,

    - Visually – red light to stop cars, signs, symbols, a smile or frown
    - Electronically – internet, e-mail, phone, computer.
    - Paper – reports, certificates, orders, receipts, lists
    - Audibly – voice, horns, music

    Usually, information flows in a mix of the media described. Problems often arise due to incomplete or misinterpreted information.

    Problem-solving relies heavily on the clarity of information

    All of these problem types have been experienced and solved in every part of the world. They are universal in nature.

True Value Problem Selection

Problem solutions must result in a budget reduction. This is what "Money to the bank" means. The expense of the solution should be quickly recovered.

The problem focusing process breaks what some might think of a single problem worth five million into ten projects worth five hundred thousand each. Key is the understanding that whatever the size of the prize, the team will take the prize to the bank.

It is leadership's responsibility to ensure the problem-solving team is solving the most business needed problem (s).

Problem Focus

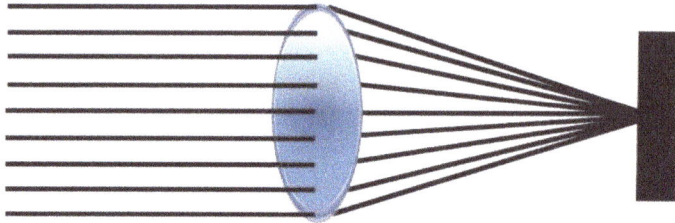

It is the leader's responsibility to focus a problem or aim the effort before asking a problem-solving team to solve a problem. The leader must be a problem-solving coach. The leader must have the skill to aim a problem-solving team and the ability to ask the questions that help the team define the phenomenon.

The pareto chart is the world's best focusing tool.

The ***Pareto Interview Process*** (PIP) is simple, fast, requires no data collection, utilizes the knowledge of the "right people", creates organizational alignment and is about 85% accurate.

It is a key tool that helps make problem-solving stress free!

Most often I have coupled the *Pareto Interview Process* with the *Material Transformation Analysis* process (MTA).See the chapter: Tools for understanding

When and how to merge the two depends whether the organization has a specific problem on hand or whether they have multiple problems in a production process and are trying to set action priorities.

The *Pareto Interview Process* (PIP) for a specific problem is an interview technique that relies on the knowledge of the people in the room.

The facilitator has the simple task of asking three questions.

What is the worst problem you experience?

What is the next worst one?

How does it compare to the worst one that ranks higher?

This initiates the aiming process.

Aiming Process (example)

Step 1: On a chart pad draw the first bar of a pareto

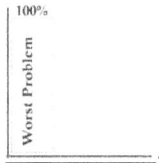

By definition this problem is the worst and gets a 100% value.

Step 2: Ask: What is the second worst problem?

Ask: Relative to the first how bad is the second problem?

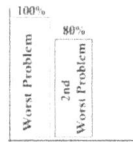

Draw this out on the chart pad.

Step 3: Ask: What is next worst problem?

Often the third problem is a significantly lower issue.

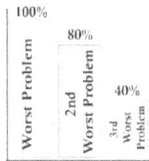

There may be problems beyond the fourth or the fifth bar but normally they are of significantly lower value.

Step 4: Repeat the process for each of the three pareto bars in step three. Go down another two levels if possible.

Step 5: Select the problem at the lowest level that the people in the room choose. At this point the team often chooses to split up and attack more than one of the pareto bars.

The problem-solving team is now *FOCUSED*!

They will walk out knowing two things,

1. Their leader is a capable problem-solving coach
2. They have a problem-solving process, examples and guidebook that will ensure they solve the defined focused problem.

The number of Pareto that are defined may be relatively high.

One problem I helped focus had thirty-two Pareto for one stated problem. After the **Aiming Process** I gave the operators the choice of which ONE pareto bar to solve.

The leaders in the area began to argue that all thirty-two bars needed solving.

"Solve the one and then come back and talk to me," was my reply as I shut down the discussion.

The reality was that in the process of fixing the one, many of the other bars were eliminated.

At the end of the following half year that area became known for their flawless operation.

Note: The **Pareto Interview Process** (PIP) is often coupled with the *Stress Free*^{TM} *Material Transformation Process* to identify the worst ingredient, then the worst transformation, then the worst work point in a production process.

This is a way to use the hands-on knowledge of those at the point of cause to clarify and aim improvement efforts.

See Chapter 4: Problem-solving tools.

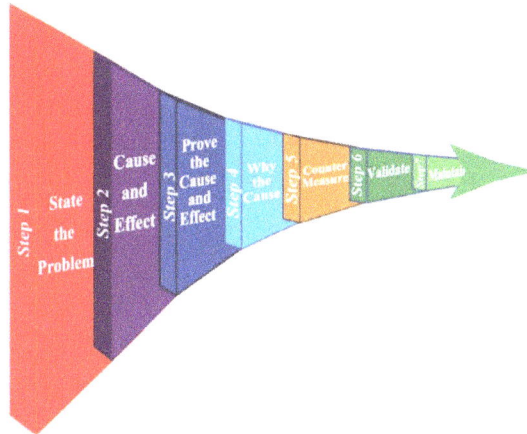

Chapter 2: The Manufacturing Problem-Solving Process

Most problem-solving processes are similar. They vary in the number of steps and what the steps are called but in the end they seek to identify a root cause for a specific problem.

Stress Free Problem-solving reduces all the approaches to a single, simple and very successful one.

Pieces, parts, and practices from all processes are acceptable. I never argue with someone wanting to use a tool they know how to use. In the end all have put those tools away and have utilized the simple approach presented.

The "Stress Free" Problem-solving Process

Step 1: State the Problem.

Step 2: Cause and Effect

Step 3: Prove the Cause and Effect

Step 4: Why the Cause

Step 5: Countermeasure

Step 6: Validate

Step 7: Maintain

Stress Free Problem-solving

This process is available in an Excel workbook.

The workbook provides a way to organize the problem-solving effort.

It is an aid to standardize the approach and provides a way to maintain discipline essential in problem-solving .

See the example in the back of this book.

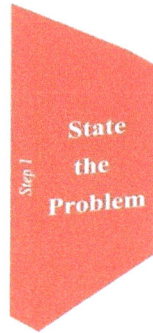

Step 1: State the Problem

To understand the situation the problem statement must be precise. The problem statement must focus on only one ***phenomenon***. This is a big word with a simple meaning.

Phenomenon: **What you see: Singular**

This simple concept seems to be the hardest for problem solvers to accept. The problem examples in this book were solved when problem solvers were able to focus on a single phenomenon.

So, the problem is worded to ***what is seen***.

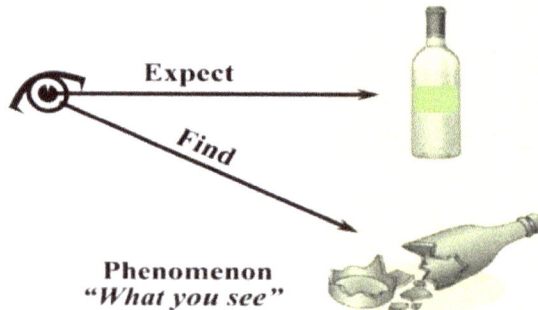

The person was expecting to see a whole bottle but instead saw a broken bottle. In a chemical process what is seen may be a measurement that is outside an expected range, in web process it may be the jam etc.

The statement of the problem often gets mixed with other important but distracting information. The observer of the problem must state only what is seen. To say anything else projects solution thinking into the understanding of what the problem's root cause might be.

Knowledge and understanding about, what is seen must be developed. The situation must be investigated

There are a several important knowledge development tools,

1.   **Material Transformation Analysis.** (MTA)[1]

This tool examines the transformation of each material that is in the product. The transformation point where the problem exists can then be further examined using work point analysis.

2.   **Work Point Analysis** (WPA)[2]

Work Point Analysis examines the elements that are associated with each work point.

3.   **Direct Observation Sheet and Stopwatch** (OSS)[3]

This is used to understand the human to equipment and material interaction.

4.   **Travel Chart**[4]

This is used to understand the human movement around the work area.

These tools must be practiced out on the floor. They are useful only to the problem solver if they get used "on the floor" during the problem-solving effort.

The saying is,

"If you haven't seen it. You are not allowed to talk about it."[5]

When the phenomenon statement can be stated with simple, *what you see* clarity, the problem will be solved to root cause.

These tools are in the Stress-Free Problem-solving workbook and shown later in the examples in this book.

[1] This is an industrial engineering tool modified to material transformation system evaluation

[2] WPA from TPM and is invaluable in determining the 100% quality condition for each component in a production system.

[3] OSS is used to observe the individual

[4] Follow someone, draw a line for each from here-to-there movement. See what you get.

[5] From Toyota stories by Satoko-san.

Step 1: Tips on Stating the Problem

1. Keep asking those involved in the problem,
2. What do you SEE?
3. If the problem is inside where one can't see the problem then ask, "What is your theory or problem model?
4. If there are competing theories, accept them and have each person postulating the theory write down their thinking.
5. Make sure the learning tools get thoroughly exploited and that they get use "out on the floor".
6. Utilize use photographs and video to better see the problem.

Step 1: Tools for Aim and Understanding

1. Material Transformation Analysis
2. Pareto Analysis

Step 2: Cause and Effect (C&E)

This is the next most critical step.

- The Effect, the problem or phenomenon defined in step 1 is the focus.
- Each cause MUST have a **direct** relationship to the Effect.

Effect: The bottle is broken.

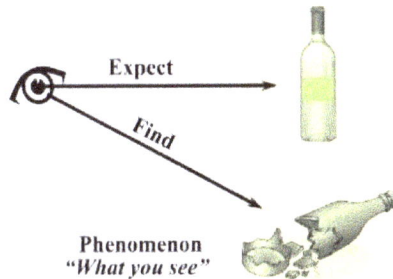

Cause:

- the bottle was dropped
- a rock hit the bottle
- the bullet from the gun hit the bottle

It is critical each cause has a **direct** relationship with the Effect. The practice of having this direct relationship creates the situation that a relationship proven to be true leads to a root cause.

The cause and effect relationship are always written as if true.

Cause and Effect Workbook-Cause input lists.

These lists automatically fill in the cause and effect worksheets associated with each list item.

Most input into the worksheets will only need to be done once. It will then be copied into all forms that use the same information.

Steps 2.1 through 2.5 are the input areas below.

This is about identifying the CAUSE. The cause must have a direct impact in creating the EFFECT or PROBLEM.

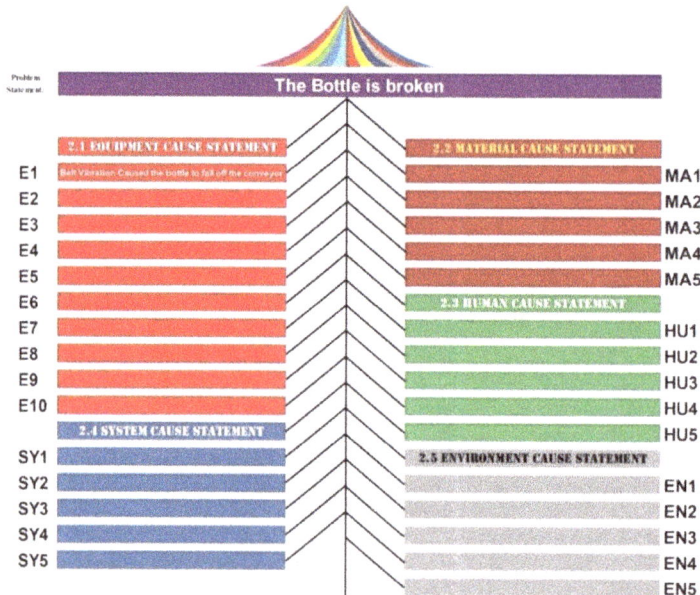

These lists automatically fill in the cause and effect worksheets associated with Cause listed.

Step 2.6 Create Cause and Effect proof of Cause worksheets.

This is the central PRINT SELECTION AREA

This Step provides a link to each cause and effect worksheet that must be filled out.

Cause and Effect Worksheet

Cause statement	This comes from each input area (Equipment, Material, Human, System and Environment
Effect Description	This is what you see – the broken bottle.
Standards	Exist Name ... If standards exist, then a check of adherence to standards is the first step. If no standard exists, then at the end of the problem solving a standard is often set for that solution ... Applied
Cause Thesis / Theory	The Cause Thesis or theory is written in the positive sense. If proven true then this cause has a contribution to the effect. If the theory proves to be false this particular cause is put aside.
Thesis Diagram	A visual diagram often aids in explaining the thesis
Proof / Test Plan	This is step by step test plan. The intent is that it can be validated by anyone following the steps. This allows for follow up if there is any disagreement
Data	Fresh, Optained from the source / From Computer System / From the Expert Action Immediate corrective actions the best practice. This allows for quick verification of the solution

Example Cause and Effect Worksheet
This form is used over and over for each type of Cause. It documents the work done and should be kept as the record or the case study documentation for each problem

Step 2: Tips on Stating the Cause and Effect

1. Test each cause and effect relationship.
   "Because of this – the problem happened.

2. Write each cause and effect relationship. Then ask the problem-solving team members to analyze the statements for clarity.

3. If there are competing or opposite theories, accept them and have each person postulating the theory write down their thinking.
   Do NOT debate the opposing theories. Accept both and allow the individuals the opportunity to learn.

4. Whenever possible draw the cause and effect relationship.

5. Use engineering documents or pictures to describe the problem.

Step 2: Tools for Cause and Effect

1. Field observation
2. Travel Chart
3. Scientific thought process

Step 3: Prove the Cause and Effect

The cause is written in a manner implying it is true.

"Because of this cause, the observed effect happens."

The theory of how the cause creates the effect is written down in the work sheet shown. This is the thesis or theory that describes the relationship between cause and effect.

Often two people have opposing theories. This process facilitates each writing their theory and then designing a test to prove it to be true.

A thesis diagram provides a visual, showing the relationship between cause and effect. This visual often is all that is needed to align the problem solvers on the problem.

The proof or test plan is the way defined to verify the truth of the thesis.

The importance of being rigorous in this proof cannot be overstated.

- Each test plan must be measurable, verifiable, and repeatable.
- Done well this step greatly focuses the problem down to a few or only one cause.
- Every Cause and Effect work sheet must be rigorously field tested.

Step 3: Tips on Proving the Cause and Effect

1. Field verify the test plan by a simulated walk through.
2. Adjust the test plan based on field learning and operational discussions.
3. Make arrangements with the on the floor operation for their participation.
4. Ensure all necessary data will be gathered and preserved. If product or material samples are to be analyzed make sure a sampling plan exists and includes marking each sample.
5. Do a thorough results evaluation. Whenever possible make the evaluation a "statistically valid" one.

Step 3: Tools for Proving Cause and Effect

1. Test Plan
2. Field Observation
3. Control Charting
4. Statistical Analysis

Step 4: Why the Cause

Theories proven to be **true** in the Cause-and-Effect process are brought into the Why–Why analysis process.

- The Cause is the item in the left-hand column of the Why-Why worksheet.
The question then is why does this cause occur?
  - There may be several first level whys. Each first level why must be field checked and verified **before** the second level whys are asked.
  - The Why-Why is executed in a vertical direction

The process of asking the next level of why continues if the next level can be clearly stated.

  - In most cases when the Cause and Effect has been rigorously executed, it is very difficult to go beyond the third level Why.
  - Each first Why Level must be field checked before defining the second level whys. The same approach is then followed for each subsequent why level.

Getting out to the fifth why is often a sign of a not properly stated effect or phenomenon.

WHY-WHY ANALYSIS

True Cause	Why 1	Field Check	Why 2	Field Check	Why 3	Field Check
Corona power goes low	Not running at Centerline					
	Low Corona Power	True	Power System low power	True		
			Power System interuption	True		

The last two columns identify who is responsible for executing the root cause correction and by when it will be done.

If you get beyond three why's with any of the true cause and effect worksheets that were true, it is a sign that you did not do as thorough and rigorous cause and effect analysis as you should have. The benefit of the why-why at this point is that it makes your mind look at the cause in an almost opposite direction. This causes one to see some additional reasons of why the problem existed.

Additionally, it captures all the counter measures in one location and creates a countermeasure action plan with dates and people responsible for the countermeasure.

The right-hand side of this chart is the root cause.

Tips on Why-Why and Root Cause

1. Make sure each true Cause and Effect is taken through Why-Why. Do this even if "Root Cause" has been found during the use of Cause and Effect.
2. Why-Why is the mirror image of Cause and Effect. It causes one's mind to think about the problem differently.
3. Each Root cause when implemented should eliminate the final why in the why-why analysis.
4. Training all personnel is always a required action. It is not a root-cause. Remember "Direct Cause and Effect Relationship,"
5. The form shown has steps 5 and 6 included. Often this is all the "plan" that is needed.

Step 4: Tools for Why-Why

1. Field Observation
2. Control Charting
3. Statistical Analysis

Step 5: Countermeasure

It is critical to execute the countermeasure and then validate the elimination of the problem.

Many times, the Why-Why form is sufficient as a countermeasure plan.

On larger or longer solution execution time frames a counter measure plan with measurable milestones is critical.

Safety should be verified before counter measure implementation.

Countermeasure Plan Example format

	Counter Measure Plan											Plan Owner:
				Mile Stone (MS)								
Cause	Counter Measure	Owner	Measure of Success	MS 1	MS 2	MS 3	MS 4	MS 5	MS 6	MS 7		Completion Date

At this point you should check for:

- the specific fix to physical objects or chemical reactions.
- that standards will be written
- that the storeroom will be updated based on the countermeasure
- maintenance and operating procedures will be appropriately adjusted.
- training of everyone associated with the counter measure will occur.
- validation and follow up will occur

Step 5: Tips on Counter Measure Implementation

1. Make an immediate improvement.
2. Act immediately, standardize or meet system requirements over time.
3. Make sure all shifts know about the countermeasure.
4. Train all personnel on the countermeasure.
5. Follow up on the countermeasure implementation.

Step 5: Tools for Counter Measure Implementation

1. Project Plan
2. Maintenance Calendar and Planning System
3. Daily Log

Step 6: Validate

The "goodness and ease of maintaining" a root cause solution directly affects the probability that the root cause loss free condition will be maintained.

	Questions	No	Not Sure	OK	Mostly	Good	Best in Class
	Equipment						
1	Equipment operating condition is easy to see.						a
2	Equipment operational and physical settings are easy to set.						a
3	Equipment settings are fixed for each specific product.						a
4	Production variations are easy to prevent.						a
5	Operational centerlines are automatically maintained.						a
	Material						
6	Material Quality Characteristics have units and tolerances defined.						a
7	The supplier is certified and the material Cpk>1.33						a
8	Only logistical damage inspection is required of incoming materials.						a
9	Damaged incoming materials are not unloaded.						a
10	In process material issues are rare and easy to recover from.						a
	Human						
11	Expert problem prevention skills are the norm.						a
12	Advanced condition management skills are the norm.						a
13	Adherence to Standards and following Standard Operating Procedures is the norm.						a
14	Mistake proofing has eliminated mistakes.						a
15	Our people are highly motivated, continuous improvement leaders						a
	Systems						
16	Systems exist and are well documented						a
17	Systems ensure Cpk>1.33 and no defects						a
18	Systems ensure required production rate is maintained.						a
19	Systems are explained and trained using the lastest techniques						a
20	Systems are easy to learn requiring less than five days to get qualified.						a
	Environment						
21	Support Organizations accept our solutions and integrate it into their design.						a
22	Purchasing adjusts its buying based on the problem solution.						a
23	Material specifications are adjusted based on specific problem solutions.						a
24	Operational conditions are changed as required to maintain improvements						a
25	Logitics are adjusted to support specific problem resolution.						a
	Leadership						
26	Leaders review the root cause of all key problems.						a
27	Key problem resolution always get public recognition.						a
28	Leaders schedule root cause validation time.						a
29	Leadership goes to the root cause to see and get understanding.						a
30	Leaders participate in stress free problem evaluation.						a

It is critical to prove the correction in a statistically defined fashion. The scientific method stipulates anyone can follow the solution path and be able to duplicate the approach.

Statistical performance or correction validation is one of the best ways to ensure the solution is the root cause.

If a solution has requirements that are difficult to maintain, the problem will return in the future. Stress Free Evaluation provides a way to evaluate the solution. If the evaluation is 80% or higher the probability of maintaining the conditions that keep the solution in place is very high.

I have had what I believed were phenomenal solutions that had low evaluations. They required the constant attention of the operators. They do not appreciate the solution for very long if they must attend to it on a daily basis.

Visual Stress Free Evaluation

Stress Free Solution Score Minimum Goal is 80 %

80.0%

These types of Solutions are acceptable but should then be put on checklist for future improvement.

Step 6: Validation Tips

1. Enroll affected personnel in the evaluation.
2. Listen to what the conversation during the evaluation.
3. Take notes of suggested improvements.
4. Use Cause and Effect to capture suggested improvements.
5. Have the people involved try out the improvements.
6. Set a fixed time to call an end, celebrate the success and focus on the next critical problem.

Step 6: Tools for Validation

1. Statistical Analysis
2. Control Chart
3. Time

Step 7: Maintain

All documents and drawings affected by the countermeasure must be updated. All operating procedures must be modified to reflect the counter measure.

Each solution should have a standard that maintains the solution.

When everything is in order everyone associated with the problem and its solution must be trained and if necessary qualified in the new procedure.

Maintain Items

- Scheduled training and qualification
- Periodic Re-retraining and re-qualification
- Maintenance Calendar
- Maintenance Contract updates
- Operational Calendar
- Periodic Inspection
- Engineering records update
- Purchasing/Spare parts records update
- Visualization

Step 7: Tips on Maintain

1. Use the hand edited field paperwork immediately. The formal paperwork may take longer to get through the system. Assign an owner to update all documents.
2. Make sure the spare parts area gets the information on any parts that have changed and if anything was made obsolete.
3. Make sure all training documents get changed appropriately.
4. Make sure all maintenance procedures and documents are addressed.
5. Schedule the requalification of all people as required.
6. Train, train, train

Step 7: Tools for Maintaining

1. Maintenance Calendar
2. Training
3. Periodic requalification of people and equipment

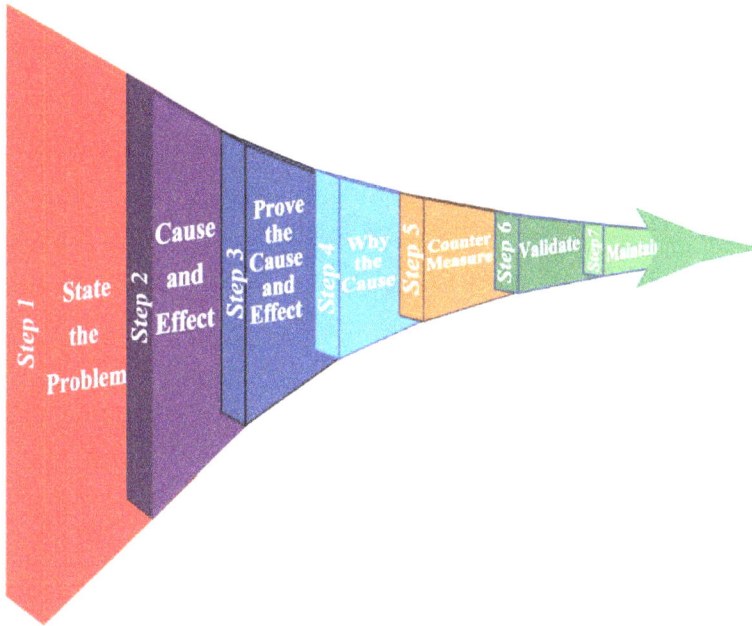

Chapter 3: Excel Workbook Solved Example

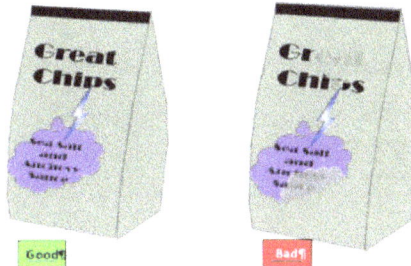

The makers of Great Chips experienced a quality problem with their packaging. Consumers complained that the artwork was smudging off. This was a problem that needed immediate attention.

A problem-solving team was put together to solve the problem. The team coach was an expert problem solver. He guided the team to the use of Stress Free^{TM} Manufacturing Solutions book, and its accompanying Excel Workbook. Guide.

The first step was to clarify what the problem or phenomenon that needed to be solved. The team studied the defects that had been obtained. They then went on to evaluate the process of making the package and the printing of the artwork on the package.

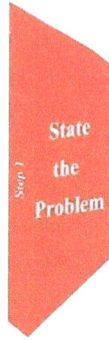

Step 1: State the Problem

The team flow charted the packaging material. The three major steps were Extrusion Blowing, Printing and Finishing. Each of these major steps had sub processes that might contribute to the phenomenon.

The team followed the PPS guide and spent some time clarifying the Phenomenon.

Step 1: State the Problem

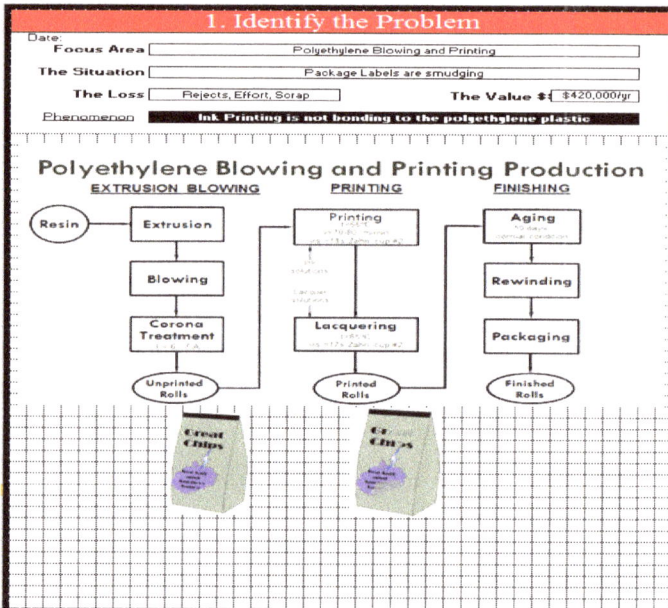

The initial problem statement had been that the ink was rubbing off of the package.

A better description was the ink was not bonding to the polyethylene plastic.

The next step was to postulate the potential causes of the phenomenon (problem).

Step 2: Cause and Effect

The team was guided to identify the potentially direct causes of the ink not bonding properly to the polyethylene plastic.

Their problem-solving coach made several key points about the cause and effect exercise.

1. The relationship between cause and effect had to be **DIRECT**.
2. Since the problem was physical neither **Method** nor **huMan** could be a direct cause.
3. The environment might be a contributing factor but again it was not a direct cause.

The direct relationship requirement greatly simplifies the identification of causes. This is not brainstorming for new ideas. The intent is to clearly identify all potential causes that can directly cause the problem.

There may be contributing factors that create the situation that result in the cause, but these will be addressed later as part of the solution as counter measures to prevent the recurrence of the problem.

It is a scientific cause and effect. These worksheets each test the cause and effect hypothesis using scientific principles.

E1	equipMent Cause Proof Worksheet
Cause statement	Corona power goes low
Effect Description	Ink Printing is not bonding to the polyethylene plastic
Cause Thesis / Theory	Corona treating increases the surface energy of plastic film, to improve wettability and adhesion of inks. A dip in the corona power will lead to spots of untreated poly where ink will not properly bond
Thesis Diagram	
Proof / Test Plan	1 Check history of the Corona System 2 Induce the situation most suspect 3 Evaluate results

	Exist	Name	Applied
Standards	Yes	Corona System Centerline CBA	Yes

Data

Fresh. Optained from the source
From Computer System
From the Expert

Action

Corona Low Power caused the film treatment to be negatively affected.

Enter True Or False > TRUE

The expectation is that the hypothesis can be verified by any other person or team.

- The cause and effect worksheet provides a focused document that brings all the information together on one sheet.
- The Cause and Effect sheet becomes the record for later review and for ensuring the right work is being done to prevent recurrence of the same problem.

Step 3: Prove the Cause and Effect

There were seven equipment, three material and two environmental cause thesis postulated. Each was clarified using a cause and effect worksheet. The worksheet begins with the cause statement. It is additionally clarified with the effect statement.

The next block is where the scientific thought process is put into action. The person proposing the cause must write up his or her thesis or theory of how the cause can create the effect.

Often there are competing theories. This is OK. Have each person write up their theory. They will then test their theory. They will either prove the theory true or they will prove it false.

The act of drawing out the thesis diagram and the accompanying theory test plan often resolves competing ideas. If not, the subsequent scientific test will do the trick.

Before going too far into the problem-solving , check whether standards that affect the problem exist and that the standards are being followed. If they do exist and are not being followed, the first step is to re-establish the standards and check to see if the problem is solved.

In this case the history of the corona system power was checked. The loss of power and some periods of low power were documented in the historic production system data. This seemed to support the theory.

The coach suggested that low voltage should be induced on the corona system. This low voltage test created the situation where the printing ink did not properly bond to the polyethylene surface. The theory had been proven to be true.

False theories die immediately.

True theories go on into why-why analysis.

Step 4: Why the Cause

The problem-solving coach pointed out the reverse relationship of cause and effect and why-why. This reverse relationship often causes the problem solver to see the situation in a different light.

The true cause is tested as to why it happens. In each case the test is a fresh in the field test. These tests should be managed to minimize the loss, but it is critical to learn if the problem can be turned on and off.

When this ability to turn the problem on and off is achieved, the countermeasures are very precise and effective.

Step 4. WHY-WHY ANALYSIS							
True Cause & Effect	**Why 1**		**Why 2**		**Why 3**	**Root Cause**	**Counter Measure**
Equipment							
Corona power goes low	Low Corona Power	True	Power System low power	True		Power System low power	Corona System Power Back up- Investigate cost
			Power System Interuption	True		Power System Interuption	Reject product when power system dips
			Loose power connection				Reject product when power system Interuption occu

Action	
Who	When
Jose	Immediate
Maria	Immediate
Maria	

Step 4: Why the Cause

The counter measure addresses the last why and only the last true why.

The action may be as in this case one that does not resolve the root cause but makes practical sense for the business. This does sound a bit off the root cause mantra but let's be clear. This is a business oriented problem-solving process and not about the purity of the process.

Having no power dips requires the investment in an un-interruptible power supply. In this situation the power company was not dependable and having no power dips requires the investment in an un-interruptible power supply. This requires investigation into the cost benefit of the power supply.

A red light and an automatic poly position logging system was implemented to indicate a low power condition and to reject the poly made during that period.

This solution greatly improved the ability to deliver high quality poly and not make the immediate high cost expenditure the company could not afford.

This is the End of this Example. Step 5,6,7 are not included.

Chapter 4: Manufacturing Problem-solving Tools

This chapter presents an ***array of tools*** that are used to develop focus understanding and help guide the problem solver to root cause.

Not all the tools have been used in the examples in this book but have been employed in solving the many problems addressed by the process and the reader should be aware of them and pull them in as necessary when needed.

Tool for Focusing

Pareto Analysis:

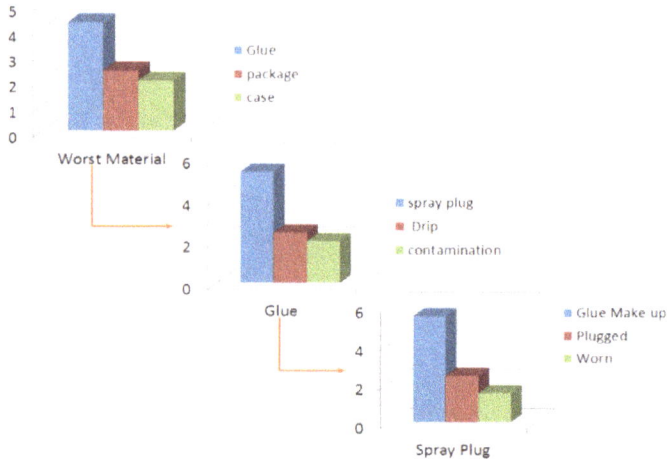

Three levels of Pareto analysis are an excellent way to guide an improvement effort to an actionable level. It later allows the logical selection of the next improvement area.

The Key step in clarifying the problem is to quickly establish a cascading Pareto.

In this example ask, "What is the worst material?"

The agreed to answer becomes the first Pareto bar.

Then continue to ask about the second, third materials. Always proportion the next worst to the one before it.

Repeat this process to identify the worst problem within the worst material.

Do this to create the three sets of Pareto.

Notice how it aims the process.

Tools For understanding
Material Transformation Analysis:

Material Transformation analysis is one of the most powerful ways to quickly learn how a product is produced. Each ingredient in the product is identified and placed down the left side of the paper. Then the transformation of each ingredient is shown. How each ingredient is combined to make the product is represented by conveyance lines and arrows, transformation points, inspection points, delay points etc.

The entire diagram provides a means of seeing very complex processes in a very simple way.

The output of this analysis provides a means of prioritizing the improvement efforts in the production process.

Only the green elements add value.

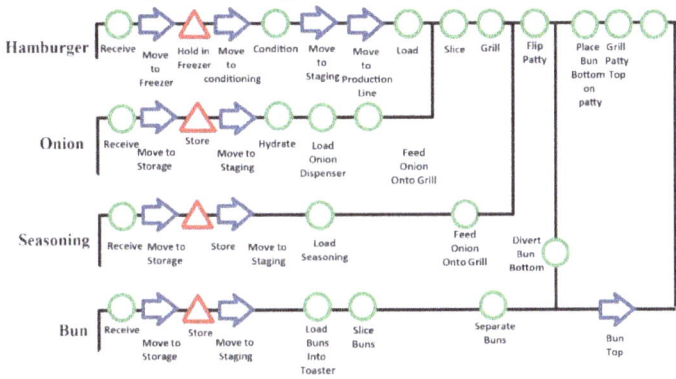

Stress Free Material Transformation
Burger Making and Packing Process

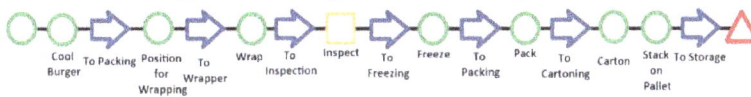

Stress Free Material Transformation
Burger Making and Packing Process

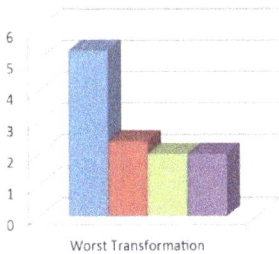

Value Stream Mapping:

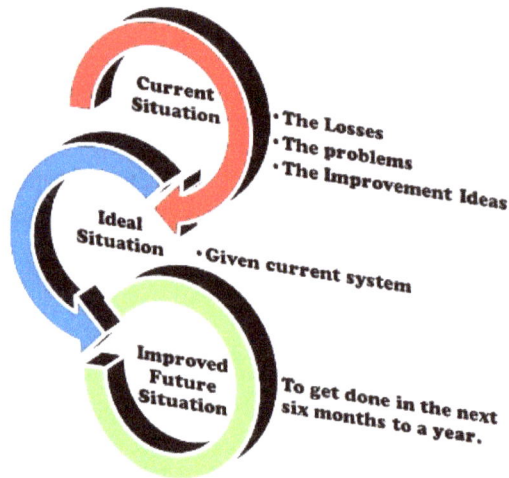

This tool provides essential information of the status of the value stream. Key elements on a value stream map are:

Material flow, quantity, and time.

Information flow and to whom.

Transformation points

Number of people in the process and where

Learning to See by Mike Rother and John Shook is an excellent resource to understand Value Stream Mapping.

Time Flow Analysis:

The focus and the visual associated with this analysis are material movement and transformation time in seconds or minutes. The amount of time material spends in the system at each point along its travel indicates where delays and inefficiencies exist.

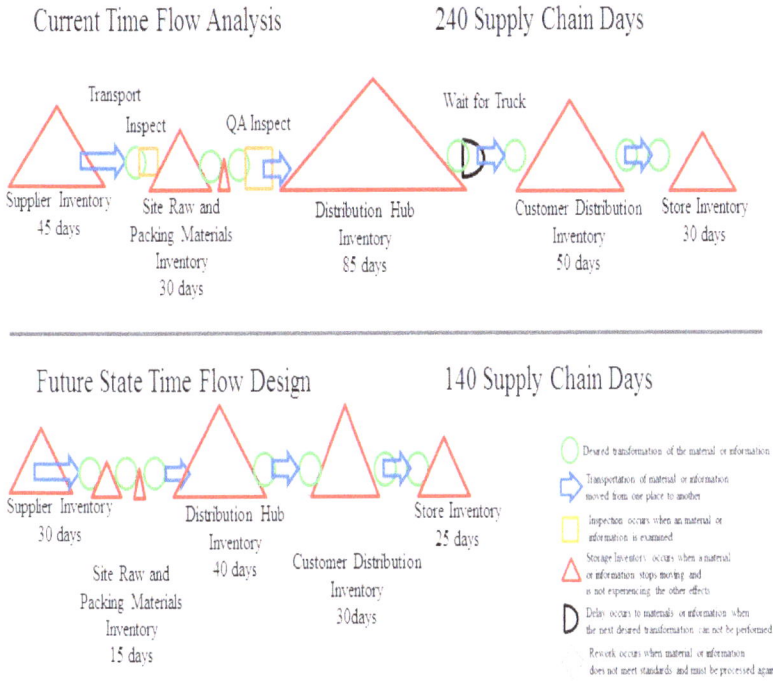

The visual elements are sized according to the amount of time the material being transformed spends at a specific transformation point. The triangles above are inventory or stop points in the transformation process. The current state diagram and the future state diagram are shown. The future state is the target that the improvements and solved problems aim to achieve.

Work Point Analysis:

Work point analysis is the process of examining a work point to determine the defect free condition of all components associated with the work point.

This analysis produces a zero-loss component inspection check list. This check list covers all systems and components associated with the material transformation into the product desired.

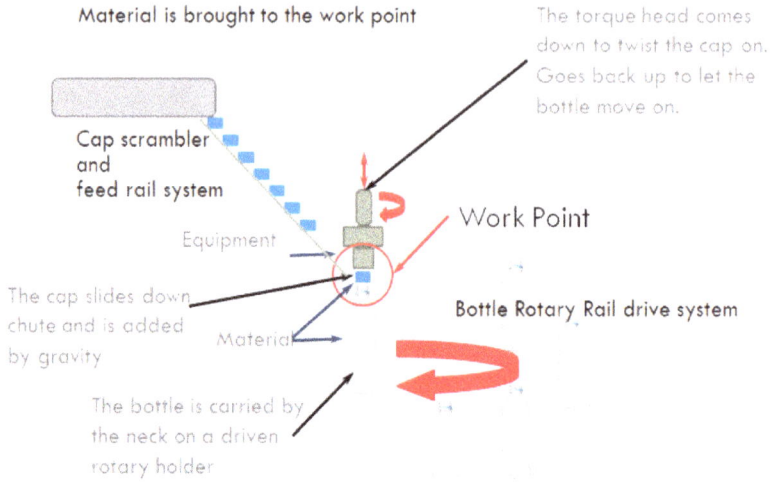

Keeping all components within tolerance will result in zero downtime or quality problems.

This form guides its user to create a new deeper understanding for the transformation work point.

Work Point Summary Form

1. Work Point: *Where the equipment and materials make contact to transform "Work"*

2. Operating Principle: *What happens as the product and equipment make contact at this point. How does it work?*

3. Standards: *List known standards for this point: CIL, centerline checks, etc.*

4. Loss Impact: *Loss that occurs at this work point*

5. Define Work Point: *Where the product & equipment make contact – show main structure and components*

6. Sketch the Work Point *Draw or show point of contact diagram*
   Equipment Components

   Product/Material Components

   Process Conditions / Variables
   Temperature, pressure, Flow, Speed, etc.

   Processing Aides
   Air-blow, anti-friction spray, catalysts, etc.

Step 7: Determining Work Point POSITION		Step 8: Determining Work Point CONTINUITY	
Fasteners		Fasteners	
Piping		Piping	
Rotating		Rotating	
Lubrication		Lubrication	
Pneumatics Hydraulics		Pneumatics Hydraulics	
Electrical & Instruments		Electrical & Instruments	
Static Elements		Static Elements	

Tools For Root Cause Identification
Cause and Effect Analysis:

Cause and Effect Analysis provides a simple means for identifying multiple contributors to a specific phenomenon. It is one of the primary tools utilized in the examples shown in this book.

It is especially useful on complex problems since it allows the elements of the problem to be examined one at a time. This provides the people on the floor a simple means of addressing very complex problems.

By using the problem-solving approach presented in this book, multivariable problems requiring complex design of experiments is reduced to minimum.

Tools for Root Cause Identification
Why-Why Analysis

Why-Why analysis was developed in the 1940's in the US. Procter and Gamble has a 1947 copyright with this process described.

It came back to the US in the late 1980's and 1990's from Japan and the Quality Circle focus.

It can be used by itself. However, my experience with Why-Why analysis causes me to recommend the use of Cause and Effect first followed by Why-Why analysis. This approach ensures a focused Why-Why. It reduces Why-Why analysis often shown on a C size drawing to a normal 8.5 by 11-inch paper size.

This is an example from the *Stress Free[TM] Problem-Solving Workbook.*

Phenomenon Mechanism (PM) Analysis

Phenomenon Mechanism Analysis engages simple statistics and chemistry to analyze a problem at a more detailed level. It is similar to moving a microscope slide from a 10- x magnification to a 10- x magnification. The problem or phenomenon definition does not change. However, the description of the problem must now be described in the terms of physics, force diagrams and equations.

PM analysis is required in less than 2% of the problems if the "Stress Free" Problem-solving process is rigorously followed.

Example:

Goal: serve a full cup of tea with no spillage.

Phenomena: 7% of time some tea is spilled outside the cup

Phenomenon 1   Phenomenon 2

Phenomenon Mechanism (PM) Analysis (Continued)

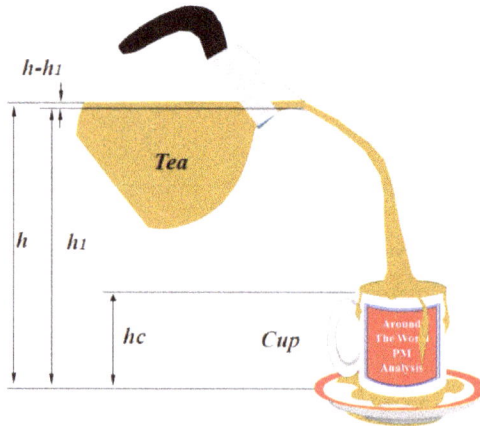

There are two phenomena that result in tea outside of the cup. The analysis of these phenomena using the basic laws of physics allows for the exact definition of all the contributing factors leading to tea outside of the cup.

Chapter 5: Stress Free^{TM} Manufacturing Problem-solving Workbook

The companion ***Excel Stress Free Manufacturing Problem-solving Workbook*** provides a guided way to successfully analyze, solve and thoroughly document a problem.

Around the World Publishing Website; www.ATWP.US

There the excel workbook can be purchased via PayPal and immediately downloaded.

A series of Solved problem workbooks are also available. These solved problems are ones that may be similar to a problem you are currently facing. The intent is to provide a solution that may accelerate the problem solver in attaining their solution.

Entry page for the Excel Spread Sheet

Each step is linked to the work area for that step. This is a fully linked workbook that allows the user to navigate to the different work areas and then back to the beginning.

The result of using this spread sheet is a fully documented process for a solved problem.

Excel Workbook Sample:

Step 1 Example: Problem understanding, and focus must be documented. If it is not written down and clarified the problem-solving team may be resolving some problems but they will likely not get to root cause.

The thought process to clarify the problem or phenomenon is to compare the problem situation to the situation when there is no problem. The difference is the phenomenon. It is the problem that must be solved.

Once the problem has been clarified and focused it is time to go on to **Step 2**

Step 2 Example:

In step 2 there are five cause and effect categories to examine and define. In the production area equipment, material and sometimes the environment are the primary focus.

In workplaces and offices areas human, systems and sometimes materials are the primary focus.

In laboratories it would depend on the problem focus. If the problem is mechanical then it will mirror the production area, if the problem is work process oriented it would mirror the office area.

The Cause and Effect Worksheet is the document that will be used the most. It will be a summary of the relationship between one cause and the theory of how it creates the unwanted effect. This CE worksheet also has the test plan to prove the cause and effect relationship.

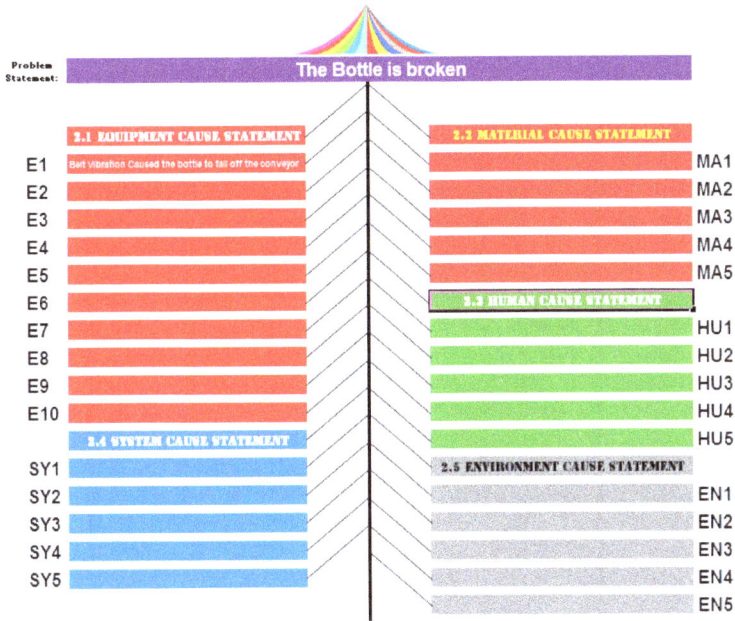

Problem Statement:	The Bottle is broken

2.1 EQUIPMENT CAUSE STATEMENT		2.2 MATERIAL CAUSE STATEMENT	
E1	Belt Vibration Caused the bottle to fall off the conveyor		MA1
E2			MA2
E3			MA3
E4			MA4
E5			MA5
E6		2.3 HUMAN CAUSE STATEMENT	
E7			HU1
E8			HU2
E9			HU3
E10			HU4
	2.4 SYSTEM CAUSE STATEMENT		HU5
SY1		2.5 ENVIRONMENT CAUSE STATEMENT	
SY2			EN1
SY3			EN2
SY4			EN3
SY5			EN4
			EN5

Excel Workbook Sample:
Step 2 Example:

Steps 2.1 through 2.5 provide a one stop location to put in the Cause Statements associated with equipment, material, human, system, and environment.

Step 2.6 Create Cause and Effect proof of Cause worksheets.

Equip 1	Material 1	System 1
Equip 2	Material 2	System 2
Equip 3	Material 3	System 3
Equip 4	Material 4	System 4
Equip 5	Material 5	System 5
Equip 6	Human 1	Environment 1
Equip 7	Human 2	Environment 2
Equip 8	Human 3	Environment 3
Equip 9	Human 4	Environment 4
Equip 10	Human 5	Environment 5

This is the PRINT SELECTION AREA

Step 2.6 Provides one location linked to each of the *Proof of Cause* worksheets.

If the relationship is proven to be true the owner of this worksheet will state whether the relationship was true or false. **All** true Cause & Effect relationships go on to the Why-Why analysis.

Example of proof of cause material worksheet five.

Step 2 Example:

All false Cause and Effect relationships are marked if the test shows not meaningful or statistical relationship between cause and effect.

The EquipMent, Material, huMan, SysteM, and EnvironMent links go to all the worksheets.

The cause for each equipment-oriented relationship is entered in the equipment cause statement area. There are ten equipment cause statements. If the problem-solving team comes up with more than ten equipment causes they should consider,

1. Doing a work point analysis of the problem work point area to get better problem understanding.
2. Revisit the problem statement and clarify the phenomenon.
3. Use the unused human and method worksheets to add their equipment problems.

The Cause and Effect Worksheet is the main problem-solving focus. Once this worksheet is filled in, the owner of this worksheet will follow the step by step test plan as written in the proof test plan block.

This worksheet is the backbone of the problem-solving process. It facilitates the breakdown of complex, multivariable problems into a set of simple checks to identify the key problem contributors.

This is the time for rigor and discipline. Get it right here and the problem will be solved.

There is a similar worksheet for every cause and effect category.

Step 3 Example:

Each defined cause and effect will need to be field verified to determine if it is true or false. Many problem theories require that certain events or conditions occur. When the condition required to cause the problem can be manually generated, the problem solver should set up the failure condition.

However, this must be done safely.

- **Personal and Equipment safety must be the first concern.**
- **Never create an unsafe or dangerous situation.**
- **Never simulate a problem that risks high financial loss.**

The ability to turn the problem on and off is a signal that the largest contributor to the root cause has been found. Sometimes the cause only creates a portion of the problem. This indicates that it is a multivariable problem with contributing factors that are of similar importance to each other. This is why all true cause and effects are taken into a Why-Why analysis.

Each filled in cause and effect worksheet should be printed out and given to the problem solver that generated the cause and effect theory. The problem solver will then go to the field or area of the problems and follow the test plan. The workbook has each worksheet ready for printing. This is currently one worksheet at a time.

This is normally the point where other personnel must participate to execute the test plan. This participation should have been planned early on and communicated throughout the organization. It is important for all the people affected by the problem to understand what is being done and how they may be asked to contribute to the effort.

Often data must be collected across multiple shifts. Such efforts require some planning, definition of how to collect the data, data collection sheets and some basic training across three to four shifts of personnel.

Do not surprise already hardworking people with the request of extra work! Early engagement will often ensure better problem definition and problem information.

Step 4 Example:

Every true cause becomes the focus for the why-why.

The Why-Why analysis forces the problem solver to think in the reverse order to the Cause & Effect analysis process. This often uncovers additional contributing factors.

Remember: All Why 1's must be field tested before stating a why 2 for each true why 1. This approach maintains a clear logic from true cause to root cause.

Each root cause then must have at least one direct countermeasure. This direct countermeasure must fix the problem. Additional countermeasures may be needed to ensure there is no sliding back into the problem. If the problem has the potential for returning then a periodic check needs to be put into place. This check should be put into the daily inspection standard or the longer-term maintenance standard.

Here is where many of the items that did not make the cause and effect list show up. They were countermeasures.

Step 5 Example:

The Counter Measures Listed on the Root Cause sheet may need an Execution Plan.

The key is to act to implement the countermeasure in a timely manner.

Do not try to develop a complex execution plan. Sometimes it is just "go do".

If multiple problems are being worked on at the same time, the owner of the effort allocation should have an execution plan.

The Counter Measures Listed on the Root Cause sheet may need an Execution Plan. The key is to act to implement the countermeasure in a timely manner.

Counter Measure	Owner	Measure of Success	Mile Stone (MS)							Completion Date
			MS 1	MS 2	MS 3	MS 4	MS 5	MS 6	MS 7	
Corona System Power Back up- Investigate cost	Maria	Report back in two weeks								

Simple example plan format.

Step 6 Example: Stress Free Evaluation

Questions	Evaluation
Equipment	No. / Bad / Base / OK / Mostly / Good / Best Class
1 Equipment operating condition is easy to see.	
2 Equipment operational and physical settings are easy to set.	
3 Equipment settings are fixed for each specific product.	
4 Production variations are easy to prevent.	
5 Operational centerlines are automatically maintained.	
Material	
6 Material Quality Characteristics have units and tolerances defined.	
7 The supplier is certified and the material Cpk>1.33	
8 Only logistical damage inspection is required of incoming materials.	
9 Damaged incoming materials are not unloaded.	
10 In process material issues are rare and easy to recover from.	
Human	
11 Expert problem prevention skills are the norm.	
12 Advanced condition management skills are the norm.	
13 Adherence to Standards and following Standard Operating Procedures is	
14 Mistake proofing has eliminated mistakes.	
15 Our people are highly motivated, continuous improvement leaders.	
Systems	
16 Systems exist and are well documented.	
17 Systems ensure Cpk>1.33 and no defects.	
18 Systems ensure required production rate is maintained.	
19 Systems are explained and trained using the lastest techniques.	
20 Systems are easy to learn requiring less than five days to get qualified.	
Environment	
21 Support Organizations accept our solutions and integrate it into their	
22 Purchasing adjusts its buying based on the problem solution.	
23 Material specifications are adjusted based on specific problem solutions.	
24 Operational conditions are changed as required to maintain improvements.	
25 Logistics are adjusted to support specific problem resolution.	
Leadership	
26 Leaders review the root cause of all key problems.	
27 Key problem resolution always gets public recognition.	
28 Leaders schedule root cause validation time.	
29 Leadership goes to the root cause to see and get understanding.	
30 Leaders participate in stress free problem evaluation.	
Savings	
31 Solving the problem is more important than immediately trying to restart the line.	
32 Problem Elimination savings are a key concideration.	
33 Problem cost elimination is evaluated during the budget and elimination goals setting	
34 Problem cost elimination savings is prioritized and a key improvement concideration	
35 Problem Elimination Savings are a key conciceration	

So, the root cause has been found. A counter measure has been executed. This countermeasure and how long it is kept in place, is directly related to how much more work the persons that have daily contact with the problem solution area are required to do.

If the fix made the situation better and the work is less the solution will stay in place for a long time.

If maintaining the conditions for zero loss is difficult and hard to do. The root cause will return in the near future.

Step 6 Example: Stress Free Evaluation

Visual Stress Free Evaluation

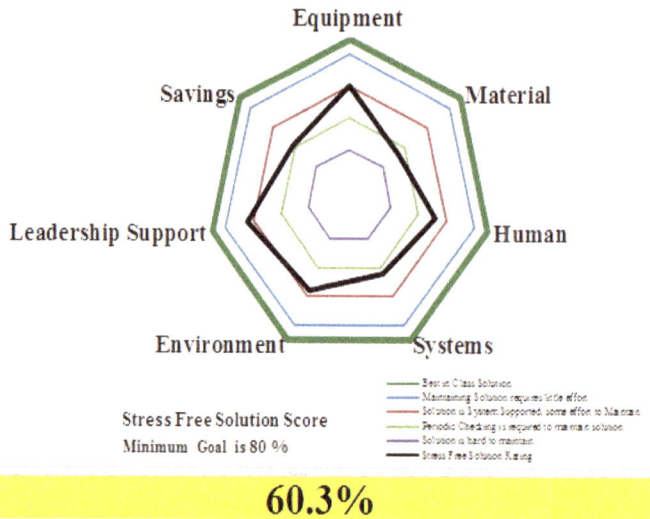

Equipment

Savings   Material

Leadership Support   Human

Environment   Systems

Stress Free Solution Score
Minimum Goal is 80 %

Best in Class Solution
Maintaining Solution requires little effort
Solution is System Supported, some effort to Maintain
Periodic Checking is required to maintain solution
Solution is hard to maintain
Stress Free Solution Rating

60.3%

Answer the evaluation questions and see the easy to maintain score.

The target should be a minimum of **80** %.

Some of the most difficult root cause problems that I have solved and felt so good about ended up with very low easy to maintain scores. The low scores are an indication that additional improvement is needed, and that the problem area will need to be monitored.

Step 7 Example: Document, Standardize, Train

If this step is not done well, the ability to maintain the root cause solution is put at risk. Training is most often addressed but the upgrade of standards and the system documentation is often overlooked. Missing any of these areas puts the solution in jeopardy.

1. Update all Documentation:

    All business, control documents, drawings etc. must be upgraded to reflect the solution. Not doing so jeopardizes the final outcome.

    Examples:
    - Engineering Equipment Drawings
    - Maintenance Procedures
    - Operating Procedures
    - Clean, Inspect, Lubrication procedures
    - Safety guidelines and procedures
    - Set up and Start up procedures
    - Spare parts purchasing specifications and amounts

2. Establish and Maintain the use of Standards:

    Document the new or improved standard(s) to ensures the problem will never occur again.

    Examples:
    - Quality Standard
    - Safety Standard

3. Establish a Qualification and Periodic Requalification System

4. Train all those who must maintain the countermeasure.
    - All Operational Teams
    - All Maintenance Teams
    - All Engineering resources
    - All Leadership

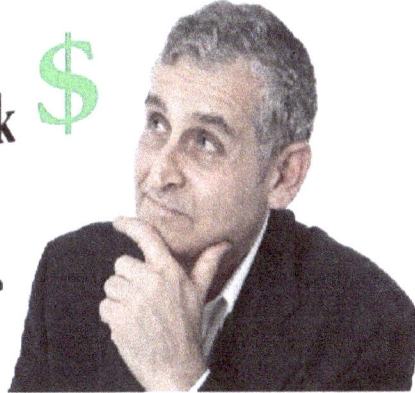

Praise for Stress Free^{TM} Work Process Solutions

"The human matters! The human produces the product. The human fixes the problems in the Supply Chain. The human can be developed and grown.
Equipment and systems decay and must be maintained by the human.
The human matters!"
REM

"Capable, well trained people working in a well-designed work process will win!"
GLM

Stress Free^{TM} Work Process Solutions

For All Work Processes

By: *Ron Mueller*

Around the World Publishing LLC
4914 Cooper Road Suite 144
Cincinnati, Ohio 45242-9998

Copyright © 2021 by Ron Mueller

ISBN 13:
ISBN 10:

Distributed by Ingram
Cover Picture By: Suria Photo, Shutterstock, Inc.
Cover Design By: Ron Mueller

Technical Editor:
Gordon Miller P. E.

DEDICATION
To: All the hard-working people,
in all the countries of the world.

Work Process Solutions Table of Contents

Work Process Solutions Introduction

This book is a guide to make work easier, less stressful, more effective, and more efficient. The primary and most important person is the one doing the Value-Required (VR) and Value-Added (VA) work. Implementing this seven-step approach will improve the work process experience and improve the resulting output. Waste will be reduced.

How to do the work, documented by those doing the work, is the way to stabilize and improve it. The documented, standardized work process becomes the basis for continuous improvement. It allows technology to be leveraged to create an even better environment.

Work accomplished easily will be done to the defined standard. When this easy-to-do way is visually displayed and documented, it is consistently followed. New people can quickly learn the standard way to execute the task at hand.

Clarifying and defining the specific actions that add value to the product and then eliminating the non-value-add (NVA) effort is a critical improvement activity.

The people directly involved in the transformation of raw materials or data into products and information are the key in improving the work process. Any approach that does not put them in the center and in leading the improvement will lack the deep understanding of the current situation and forfeit the subsequent ownership for the improvement.

External resources provide a very important role in asking the why questions and in providing new perspectives.

Leaders must recognize their work process improvement support role and provide encouragement, resources, and improvement time.

The approach shared in this book has been successfully applied to work processes in every kind of work and applied in many countries around the world.

Stress Free^{TM} Work Process Solutions and the companion Excel workbook provide a solid basis for successful and maintained work process solutions.

This approach is a bottom up approach. It guides the leader to get out on the floor and work with those doing the work. This on the floor leader is then in position to understand the work situation and participate in improving it. By definition the "floor" is where the work is being done. The "floor" is the place where raw materials are transformed into a product. It is the place maintenance work or manual assembly is performed. And it is in the office area where data is turned into information.

This critical relationship between the person who will experience the workday after day and the business area leader responsible for the delivery of production is crucial. It is the ingredient that creates ownership by those doing the work and a willingness to work to a documented, fixed process that is positioned to be continuously improved.

Ownership of the standardized work process should be by the person or team responsible for doing the work. The person that validates adherence to the standardized work process is the first level budgetary leader in that particular organization.

Well documented, visualized, standardized work enhances knowledge renewal and requalification. It is a very good tool in training new people and accelerates their ability to contribute to the rest of the team. The visualized step-by-step documentation provides a visual guide to the external part of the work. The work of the mind, a crucial part of the work, must be captured and made part of the documentation.

The culture is set and maintained by leaders. The best way to shape the culture is by doing. What is practiced and what is rewarded is what shapes the culture. Adherence to standardized work must be recognized and rewarded.

When standardized work is not the way people are doing the work, the leader must call for an improvement review. People always gravitate to doing work in the easiest way possible. Standardized work must continually strive to be the easiest way work gets done.

When hard work is required to meet regulation, quality or safety, all other ways of doing the work must be made harder or the required work easier.

The environment of an organization actively engaged in adhering to standardized work is invigorating. Leaders are on the floor supporting workers focused on making improvements. All of them are connected to the business and understand the work needs to be done only as fast as required by the customer.

This is a mutually supportive environment where everyone is treated like an owner.

"Stress Free"

Stress Free!   **Really?**

What makes this approach stress free?

1. Work processes become effective and efficient.
2. *Stress Free^{TM} Work Process Solutions* closely guides the user in the creation and improvement of the work.
3. *Stress Free^{TM} Work Process Solutions teaches* and leverages teamwork**!**

           Team Balance

           Team Value Add

The accompanying *Stress Free^{TM} Work Process Solutions Workbook* is an excel workbook that provides tools, guides the user, and creates a documented standardized work process.

The main focus of this book is to teach how to focus, how to clarify, how to fully understand work processes and how to set up a sustainable, friendly work area.

Stress Free^{TM} Work Process Solutions – The Process

           Step 1: Business Need

           Step 2: Define the Improvement.

           Step 3: Improve

           Step 4: Evaluate

           Step 5: Repeat (Steps 2-4)

           Step 6: Integrate

           Step 7: Utilize

This process is available in an Excel workbook. The workbook guides the user through one of three types of work process improvement. The workbook provides a way to organize the work process improvement effort. It is an aid to standardize the approach and provides a way to maintain the improvement.

The examples in this book are given in detail in the supporting Excel workbook.

Value of the Improvement

A key focus for improving work processes is the improvement value expressed in dollars per year. Work process improvement may be fun, but the solution must save money, it must provide a financial benefit. A key and first step is to understand the value of the improvement. This value should always be front and center for those working the improvement.

Defining improvement value is critical. The value of the improvement needs to be enough to warrant the improvement effort and cost expenditure.

The most appropriate way to state the value of an improvement is in **dollars per year**. Most business cycles and budgets are yearly. The decision to support a work process improvement effort must compete with other choices the resources could be working on.

Business Linkage

The dollar value per year, due to the work process improvement, **must be defined**. It is critically important to create this linkage. What specifically will be gained and how will this gain be measured when the work process is implemented.

General, high level improvement goals are important; - inventory reduction, speed to market, and net outside sales (NOS) gain. However, these are longer term and harder to realize.

Example of specific, clear, measures:
- 15 min package changeover down to 5 min.
- Work in Process (WIP) inventory reduction from fifteen times the customer "pull rate" to two times the customer pull rate.
- Manipulation line staffing reduction from 6 to 2

These are directly linked to the work process improvement.

System Layout

Immediately walking and doing a hand drawing of the system or documenting or obtaining the flowchart of the work being done, is an important activity that grounds the individual in the understanding of the physical system that they are trying to improve.

It is also important to understand the organizational structure that maintains the current situation. If the improvement change is to be maintained, the organization's leadership must understand how it will be sustained.

The system / work process lay out provides an understanding of,

- People placement and activities
- material placement and handling issues
- current behaviors and practices by individuals
- synchronization issues i.e. - long conveyance, bottlenecks, surge points
- Quality and Safety issues,
- Work balance issues

It is important for the improvement team to discuss what they have seen and understood from the, on-the-floor, walk or direct work observation and interviews.

The leaders of the area and the work process improvement team should step back and understand,

- The Customer,
- The Material Flow
- The Equipment
- The Human Connection - how the Work gets done.
- The Environment

Customer Connection

It is critical to get away from the thinking of only meeting the demand of the equipment.

Students of Japanese TPM theory will recall Takt. The Customer Cycle Time (Takt Time) is the measure that provides the direct customer need signal to the production system.

It is important to connect every production system improvement to the need of the customer. This connection defines the value of the improvement.

Generally, organizations tend to work faster and produce more than they need. This speed desire often leads to work process issues.

The customer cycle time should have no safety/buffer factors associated with it.

Available time:

Available Time is equal to Calendar or clock time **minus** planned activities that have blocks of time specifically calling for the production system to be down.

Available time should be used to help find the barriers to a customer focused production system.

Material Connection

The supply of the raw materials and the synchronized handling of the finished product are both critical in ensuring the flow of the production system.

Raw material quantity and placement is critical in optimizing the flow of the production system.

The logistics of bringing the materials to the line and returning material remnants for later use is a critical element the must be analyzed. Flow and time analysis is an important analysis to utilize.

Equipment Connection

Physical layout and material supply layout to the equipment are often related to specific problems or are due to previously experienced problems.

The problem may be the number of stops, or breakdowns or the amount of effort it takes to keep an area up and running.

There are many opportunities to better utilize the equipment at hand.

For example:

- Create flow by the synchronization of filler, capper, and labeler and case packer by shortening the distances between the equipment to the optimum so the line can start and stop in a synchronous fashion and generate no scrap during a changeover.
- Minimize the raw material inventory in the production area; bottles, caps, KDF's by delivering at Takt or at a pitch.

The equipment layout needs to be drawn to scale. The time that a single product spends having value added and the time it spends traveling needs to be analyzed. The travel time then needs to be eliminated or shortened.

Change Over (C/O) time:

C/O relates to inventory reduction. Time spent changing from one SKU to another is non-value added. No sellable product is produced during the changeover. Inventory should only be held to maintain top level customer service. Inventory reduction is only possible when the system provides reliable flow. Reliable flow is required to support a customer focused production system.

The Human Connection

Once the initial production system drawing or work process flow chart is completed then the actions of the people involved in the production of the product should be studied and understood.

It must be noted that if the work process is being done by the human, the system drawing will be a flow chart showing the work of, writing, or analyzing, or evaluating etc. The "production system" is this flow chart that must be documented and verified.

Standardized Work

Standardized Work is *the work done directly on the raw material, to produce a product to meet the customer need.* All other work being done is not considered standardized work. **Standardized means synchronized to the customer.** It forms the basis for making continuous improvement.

Many organizations produce to a production schedule. This schedule is the equivalent of the "customer". In many cases it is designed to cover the many problems experienced by the logistics associated with moving materials and finished product.

Within this concept people will work to the required standards as defined by safety and product quality requirements and that required by law.

For continuous improvement to be possible, the critical and repeatable work must be done to standard. The time for doing this work is normally synchronized with the cycle of the equipment that is being supported. It may also be a service that is synchronized with an accounting or other process cycle.

Stress Free^{TM} Work Process Solutions is the guide in solving problems of manual and office work. This applies to office work where computer software is a key contributor to getting work done. Computer software doesn't necessarily break, but it must be adjusted to be in synch with any changes to the work processes being used.

People and equipment do work,
- Both need to be maintained.
- Both break down.
- Both periodically need fixing.

People maintain, people fix, and people think and make improvements. People are the key.

Stress Free^{TM} Work Process Solutions **focuses** on the people working in the production system, on the equipment and maintaining material flow. It focuses on the work people do whether on the production floor, assembly area or in the office environment.

Following the *Stress Free^{TM} Work Process Solutions* guidance will lead to improvements in three to five workdays.

You will always deliver a superior, easier way of doing the work.

If not contact Ron Mueller

Work Processes and the Working World.

Every working person follows or implements a work process. Most of these work processes are documented in a very general way. Many do not have clear measurable accomplishment metrics. Many are done routinely and have no current documentation.

Work can be broken into two major kinds:

- Knowledge Work
  - o Frequently intangible result
  - o Mental process not visible
- Physical Work
  - o Tangible and measurable results
  - o Visible and public work behaviors

In both cases work is a process, and it has a specific result.

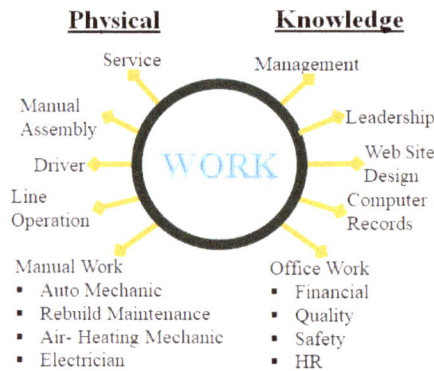

This is a simple example of the physical and the knowledge-based work processes.

There are often overlaps or a mix between the physical and knowledge work.

These processes exist around the globe.

The country, the culture, the color of the people may vary but work processes exist everywhere. They are all quite similar.

Work Improvement

Work improvement implies that there are problems. Here are the six problem categories:

1. System Problems

System problems are problems experienced in the management, maintenance and assurance of the fundamental material to product transformation process. There are quality requirements, safety requirements, government and financial requirements. Adherence to these requirements is a fundamental expectation. *Stress Free^{TM} Work Process Solutions will address many of these problems.*

2. Human Problems

The work-related problems in this area are problems in how people work together. These problems lend themselves to very different problem-solving tools. We will cover a few problems in this book.

The human problem associated with the design of the organization is covered in; *Stress Free*^{*TM*} *Organization Design Solutions*.

3. Material Problems

These are problems occurring in the material being transformed. The material performance either is inadequate or it prevents the transformation from occurring. The material needs to be evaluated and action taken to ensure the material is within the specification required for easy and consistent transformation.

To do this please refer to: *Stress Free*^{*TM*} *Quality System Solutions*.

4. Equipment Problems

These are problems occurring in the equipment. The equipment function is either reduced or stopped. Action must be taken to re-establish the transformation work the equipment is expected to provide.

To do this please refer to: *Stress Free*^{*TM*} *Manufacturing Solutions*.

5. Processing Problems

Processing problems are similar to equipment problems but often they are chemical reaction or flow and mixing oriented. Since visibility is often the problem, the analysis tools for these problems aid the investigator by providing visibility of the problem via secondary measures, mathematical models or physical models.

To do this please refer to: *Stress Free*^{*TM*} *Manufacturing Solutions*.

6. Information Problems

Information flow, timeliness, accuracy, and understandability are critical in holding complex transformation processes together. It is often the single most significant problem in complex transformation processes. There are many ways information can flow,

- Visually – red light to stop cars, signs, symbols, a smile, or frown
- Electronically – internet, e-mail, phone.
- Paper – reports, certificates, orders, receipts, lists
- Audibly – voice, horns, music

Usually, information flow is a mix of the media described. Problems often arise due to incomplete or misinterpreted information. Problem solving relies heavily on the clarity of information. All the books highlighted rely on the clarity and correctness of information.

Every one of these problem types have been experienced and solved in every part of the world. They are universal in nature.

The state of work processes
Varieties

- Undocumented
- Documented but not followed
- Work process with no defined metrics
- Inter-related, dependent, uncoordinated

Documenting and defining the evaluation measure for each work process is critical. They work for pride first, but people will do what they believe is necessary to satisfy their bosses and the "system".

Effectiveness

One VP at a global company developed The Million Dollar Loss report to be generated weekly. The Million Dollar is an example of a very powerful but ineffective, poorly aimed tool. Great name but when examined, it made no sense. It was however, expected to be on the VP's desk every Monday morning. He used it to brow beat various production plant managers about their poor performance.

Because of their dollar expenditure, large plants, even when they were performing well remained on the loss report list. Small plants though they might perform poorly seldom made it into the Million Dollar report.

I stopped compiling the report to see what would happen. Three months later, the VP called wondering about the Million Dollar report.

Once he understood the situation and got over the fact that I had unilaterally stopped compiling the report, he began using better metrics to evaluate the various sites. These more focused measures put the right production plant managers in front of his desk for additional guidance.

Documentation

Are your work processes documented?
Is the documented work process the actual one that is followed?
Are the performance measures for the work process clear?
Are the inter-relationships with other work process clear?
These questions will guide the improvement process.

Work Process Solutions-A Global Look

Let's take a global trip and examine work processes with the mindset that this improvement work is applicable globally. It has been done in more than sixty countries.

But let's have some fun and learn a bit about each country.

Thailand

Serious Facts

Capital: Bangkok
Population: 66,000,000
Ranked: 50th in size of population
Population Growth – 3 million in 6 years

Fun Facts

When traffic is bad in Bangkok, the sky train quickly fills with riders eager to by-pass the hours of delay in taxis, cars or buses.

Best Beer: Singha

Thai Work Process Problems (3)

1. **Work on automated line** – More value- add work

The request was for more productivity from an existing production line. Often productivity means cutting people. This is counter to my thinking. I will seldom work on cutting people unless the competitive viability of the business is on the line. This to me means we will go out of business if more productivity is not achieved. Getting more profit margins at the expense of the worker is counter to my thinking. Fire about six vice presidents and you will get a terrific productivity boost throughout the organization.

A small team observed the line and provided solutions yielding significant improvement in throughput with the same staffing.

How was it solved?

The Pareto Interview Process (PIP) in Step 1 of the Seven Steps of *Stress Free^{TM} Work Process Solutions* provided new insight to the work process problems.

2. **Standard Work on Sashay line** – 9 people to 2 people solution

Nine operators were stationed to operate nine sashay shampoo filling units. The nine units were packed out as a single line. On the floor observation and detailed documentation of the value-add work indicated that less than three people could accomplish the tasks.

A small improvement team was assigned to evaluate and to devise a more efficient way to operate this line. In four days, the team devised and implemented a way to operate the line with less than two people.

In step 3 Improve, the site manager and the area manager demonstrated that two people could indeed keep the line running in a "stress free" way. This demonstration by the leaders made a significant impression on those operators normally doing the work.

How was it solved?

By using the Seven Steps of ***Stress Free^{TM} Work Process Solutions***.

3. **Standard Work in Customization** - 47 to 16 solution

Customization of production is on a dramatic increase in the consumer products business. Consumers desire a more convenient mix and presentation of products. This desire causes the packaging of the product to take on many variations. Each variation may require special manipulation. This manipulation often requires manual intervention of already automatically packaged material.

The site was preparing to spend several million dollars to expand the customization area and double the staffing. The request for the improvement work session was to evaluate how many people and how much space would be required for this expansion of customization.

The improvement team evaluated the current customization process. In Step 2 the team identified the value-added work. They modified the work process. In four days, it demonstrated a reduction from forty-seven people down to sixteen people to accomplish the same production throughput.

The expansion and additional hiring were cancelled. The reduced staffing requirement meant the projected increase in customization could be handled with current staffing.

Two additional savings were identified,

1. a reduction from sixteen to twelve people by improved raw material presentation, packaging and
2. Transport loss elimination by moving customization to the end of the production line.

How was it solved?

By using Seven Steps of *Stress Free^{TM} Work Process Solutions.*

Romania
Serious Facts
Capital: Bucharest

Population 22,200,000

Ranked 80 in land size

Population Growth – (-100 thousand) in 6 years

Fun Facts
Bucharest is a great city to walk in. It has great restaurants and good food.

Best Beer: Timisoreana

Romanian Work Process Problem (1)

1. **Bottle Blowing Extruder Centering** – Immediate action

This problem was causing the site to generate a large amount of scrap at the start of the bottle blowing process or when bottle sizes were changed. The plastic extrusion called the "sock" had to have an even wall thickness all the way around.

The set up consisted of centering the central guide to ensure an even thickness of melt would get extruded from the nozzle. Multiple adjustments were needed to get the thickness even all around the bottle sock.

"It is an art to get the sock to come out right the first time," was the comment of the line leader as we watched the setup procedure.

The improvement team watched three setups. The best set up took a minimum of three adjustments. One took eight adjustments. Every adjustment resulted in at least three lost bottles. Every adjustment and evaluation took at least fifteen minutes.

There was plenty room for improvement.

The team applied mistake proofing discussed in Step 3: Improve and developed a special tool. Then, working with a key operator, the improvement team demonstrated a one step, one adjustment, and mistake proof procedure in the afternoon of the following day.

The result was zero lost bottles.

How was it solved?

By using the Seven Steps of *Stress Free^{TM} Work Process Solutions.*

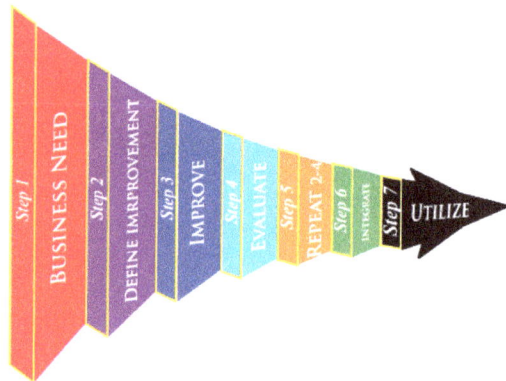

Mexico
Serious Facts

Capital: Mexico

Population: 110,000,000

Ranked: 14 in land size

Population Growth: 6 million in 6 years

Fun Facts

The country of the honorable cab driver thief. He charged three times the rate but provided three receipts!

Best Beer: Corona with a lime

Mexico Work Process Problems (2)

1. Blocked Payments

The purchasing office was experiencing blocked payment issues with several top material suppliers that threatened to impact the ability to produce the final product in a timely manner at the quantities desired.

The process seemed to be the problem of the entire organization and all suppliers. An improvement team, utilizing the tools of *Stress Free™ Work Process Solutions* focused the effort and resolved the issue in a matter of a few days.

The problem was consistently occurring with three suppliers and with one person in the purchasing office. The fact that the documented procedure was outdated and not followed was also a key factor.

The team, along with the one person experiencing the most problems, flow charted and tested an effective payment process. The flow chart was refined over the next week and final documentation entered in the organizations standards file.

The following quarter there were no blocked payments.

How was it solved?

By using the Seven Steps of *Stress Free™ Work Process Solutions*.

2. <u>Core Waste elimination</u> – Take it to the core

This was an embarrassingly simple, immediate $500,000 per year to the bottom line on the same day as observation. It is included here to demonstrate that work process and equipment problem solving relies on understanding the situation.

The improvement team went to the floor to observe the operation of the tissue combining stand. This transformation combined two sheets of tissue to create a double layer. Imagine a roll of toilet paper that proportionally is ten feet wide.

The team observed the large paper roll being unwound. As the paper came closer to the core the operator watched it get to the metal retaining ring holding the large roll on the machine. Then just before the unwinding paper got to the retaining ring the operator initiated the start of the new roll.

There was almost a foot of paper still on the core. When asked about this, the operator's response was sensible. The interaction of the paper with the retainer ring often caused the web to tear. When this happened, the broken web went through the entire unwind stand. Then the web needed to be totally rethreaded. This rethreading often took up to thirty minutes. By stopping it early and making a controlled cut, the end of the new roll and the tail of the old web could be tied together. The system then would rethread automatically in less than a minute.

This was why the site continued to allow almost a foot of paper to be left on the core and "recycled" back to papermaking.

"Why is the retaining ring so large?" I asked the improvement team.

"So, the core can be held solidly by the machine," was the reply.

"What if the retaining ring was the exact size of the core outer diameter?" was my question.

A spare set of retaining rings were immediately taken to the machine shop and modified. On the next paper roll change the new ring was put in place. The operator was asked to take the paper down to the edge of the metal retaining ring. No change in the work process.

There was no problem and the core and less than a half inch of paper was removed from the machine. The new retaining rings were tested for the rest of the day. By the next morning the retaining rings on all combining machines had been modified to the new design.

In this case there was no need to retrain any of the operators.

How was it solved?

By using the Seven Steps of *Stress Free*^{TM} *Work Process Solutions*.

United States

Serious Facts

Capital: Washington, DC

Population: 326,474,013

Ranked: 3 in land size

Population Growth: 23 million in 6 years

Fun Facts

The "why should we do it" country. This has been the hardest country for me to get folks to do it better.

Yet by far the best country in the world to live.

It fulfills the saying "It is hard to get the good to be better."

Best Beer: Bud Light.

US Problems (2)

1. Late payments by Finance

The production site was experiencing problems with consistently being on time with the payment for production materials. Each morning the finance manager would allocate the invoice closing work to the purchasing folks. She was trying to ensure a balanced workload across her employees.

Yet quite often the required work did not get done in the appropriate amount of time. It seemed the problem was random and was not due to any specific individual.

A request for an additional employee was turned down.

Her next step was to hold a work process improvement workshop. She had experienced a *Stress Free^TM Manufacturing Solutions* workshop and wondered if there was something similar for the office area.

She sponsored a *Stress Free*^{TM} *Work Process Solutions* workshop. Her three improvement teams investigated the Materials Payment process, closing the books each month and closing the books at the end of the year.

By the end of the week-long workshop all three processes were improved. The time to close the books each month went from more than seven days to two. The time to close the books at the end of the year went from two weeks to less than a week. And the problem of managing the payment for materials became one of the novel solutions. It was very visual.

The Payment process was flow charted so that everyone was doing the work the same. The finance manager came in each morning and allocated the work as she had always done.

The difference was when any of her staff ran into a problem, they would raise a red flag, and yes a real red flag like the one you would have on a bicycle. This meant they had run into an issue that was taking more time than allocated for the payment process. The manager would then re-allocate the work and help in handling the payment processing.

The visual nature of the problem also allowed the other staff personnel to volunteer help when they were ahead.

Late payments went to zero, the office area camaraderie increased, and the suppliers became more satisfied. This is a true, win, win, and win result.

How was it solved?

By using the Seven Steps of *Stress Free*^{TM} *Work Process Solutions.*

2. **Parent Roll Centering** - put it in the center of the road

Paper hand towels and toilet tissue have a very complicated production process. Additionally, the equipment is very large. The parent roll centering problem was a chronic problem in the converting process. This process takes a huge roll of paper called a parent roll and transforms it into the familiar paper towel rolls and the bathroom tissue rolls. The problem had been experienced from the first day the converters of this kind were installed.

The problem as stated was that papermaking was making bad rolls and passing them on to converting. The converting folks were convinced the converter could not convert the loosely wound parent rolls.

The improvement team went out to the floor to observe the problem. A "bad" roll was brought to the line and mounted as per the standard loading procedure. The converter could not convert the roll because the parent roll telescoped as it ran.

The line leader was asked to mount another bad roll.

"It will do the same thing." was the line leader's response.

"I believe you, but the improvement team needs to see it again," was my reply.

The improvement team was instructed to read the standard loading procedure as the process was being executed.

Bad roll number two was loaded as per the standard and it telescoped and the web broke.

"Does the team understand the problem," was my next question?

In the work process improvement team meeting room, the team put together their cause and effect diagram and came up with only a few causes.

One process cause was so obvious they immediately went out to run one more trial for understanding. They stopped by the machinist shop to pick up a magnet held red laser.

"I know, you want to load another bad roll," was the line leader's comment as the team came back out.

This time with the improvement team guided the loading of the bad roll; the converter converted the entire roll. They had the operator position the roll so that the laser mounted on the frame illuminated the end of the parent roll when it was in the optimum position.

The roll was positioned so that the strategically aimed laser turned edge of the parent roll a bright red. The operator was to keep the red on the end of the roll maximized.

The roll ran flawlessly.

"You guys were lucky," was the comment of the line leader.

The team was so confident of their solution they did two more "bad" rolls.

The work process of loading and centering the roll was modified. Every operating team was trained on the new procedure. The line performance increase significantly.

The line leader became the best advocate for the solution.

The solution was achieved on day 1 of a three-day problem-solving session. It is highlighted here because it was a combination of work process and equipment problem solving. This is often the case.

How was it solved?

By using the Seven Steps of *Stress Free^{TM} Work Process Solutions.*

Work Process Solutions Process

Step 1: Business Need

Step 1.1 Understand the Work Area

- Material Transformation Analysis (MTA)
- System Diagram
- Top Level Flow Diagram
- Physical Layout Diagram

Step 1.2 Problem Aiming and Stratification

Step 1.3 Understand the Customer

Step 1.4 Area Self-Assessment

Step 1.5 Observe Selected Priority Area

Step 1.1 Understand the Work Area Material Transformation Analysis (MTA)

Material Transformation Analysis is an adaption from industrial engineering that originally focused on people and their actions. Only two elements do work: equipment and people. Equipment ages and declines in its work ability. People when nurtured grow and become more valuable. They think, they do, they take care of the equipment. Enough cannot be said about developing the individual to the point where the individual becomes the catalyst for continuous improvement.

The benefit of MTA is how quickly it is done. A complex system quickly becomes understandable. Entire production lines fit on an 8.5 by 11 piece of paper. Training is improved. Problems are quickly identified. Improvement priorities are visible to every associate on the line.

Standard Symbols used in constructing the material transformation diagram

These symbols are standard for the Industrial Engineering area. Transformation is used in the broad sense for data and raw materials. Transport is used in the same broad sense. Data is transported electronically, where materials are transported physically. Inspection can be done for the material transformation and as well for a data transformation into information.

the symbol for a transformation

the symbol for transport or movement

the symbol for inventory

the symbol for inspection

the symbol for delay

the symbol for rework

Symbol for an Associate

Example 1 : Hamburger Making Line (MTA)

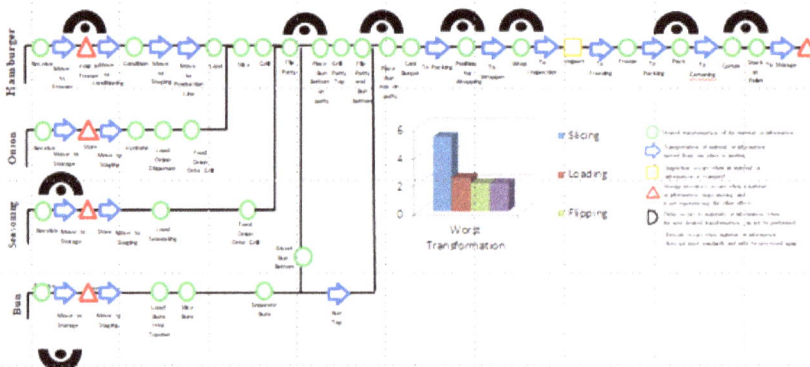

Hamburgers were prepared, frozen and boxed for shipment. The production line had a variety of problems. Each Associate team member had set of problems they felt were most important.

Each line associate was asked to create a list of their problems. This list got discussed and prioritized. Improvement occurred on a daily basis.

At least one major improvement was accomplished at every station. The production line up time and throughput went up approximately 20%.

This was accomplished in a five day workshop.

Example 2: Custom Hand Pack line (MTA)

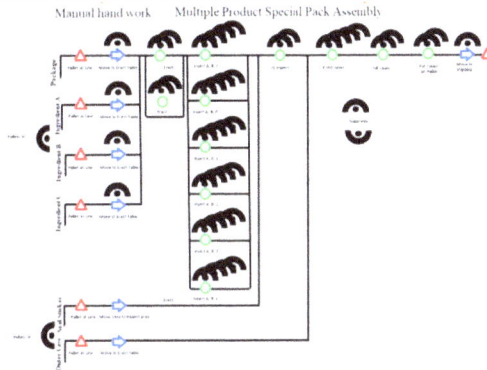

This custom hand pack line was maxed out in its capacity. It was not keeping up with demand. Additionally there was a demand of the customization of additional product.

In this case, the forty or so associates were often a different group mix as they went day to day and week to week. The manaagement team were permanent employees. The initial transformation analysis was done by the management team.

The key improvements were to make permanent shift teams and to train members at each station. Each member qualied at three stations.

This was accomplished in a five day workshop.

Example 3: Accounting / Finance Area. (MTA)

Primary Processes

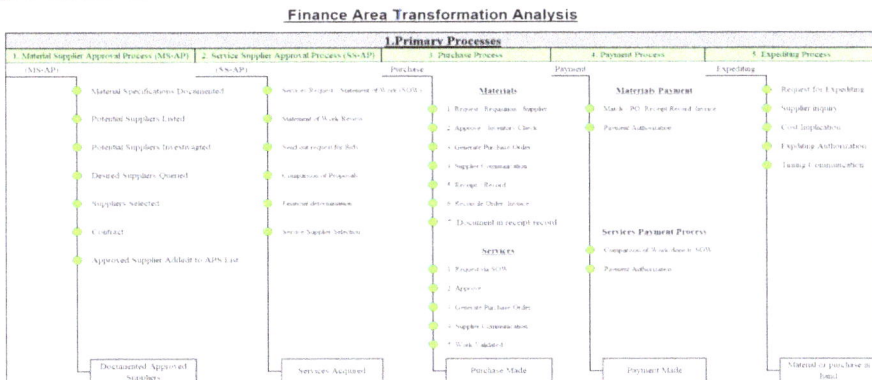

Notice that the transformation analysis is now listed vertically with fewer symbols. The transformation is highlighed but the action or steps in between are simplified. This could use all the symbols used in the previous two examples but this simpler approach proves sufficient for many office work processes.

The value add flow analysis is also very effective in the office environment and is often used to complement the MTA.

The steps 2-4 For the work porocess listed are shown in detail in the Excel Workbook.

- Record Keeping
- Auditing
- Additional Work Processes

This Transformation analysis provided the information to standardize common repetitive work. This in turn made it easy for the finance personnel to support each other and make work, flow smoothly. Blocked payments went from being the number on problem to zero.

Improvement was accomplished in a five day workshop

Use of the System Diagram)

The system diagram can be very simple as shown here or it can get much more detailed and complex. Start simple and add more detail if it is needed.

This is the hamburger making line shown as a simple flow diagram.

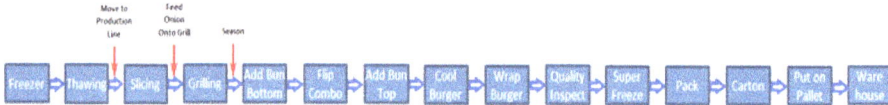

Top Level Flow Diagram for the financial area.

This is a financial area flow diagram of the work done in that office.

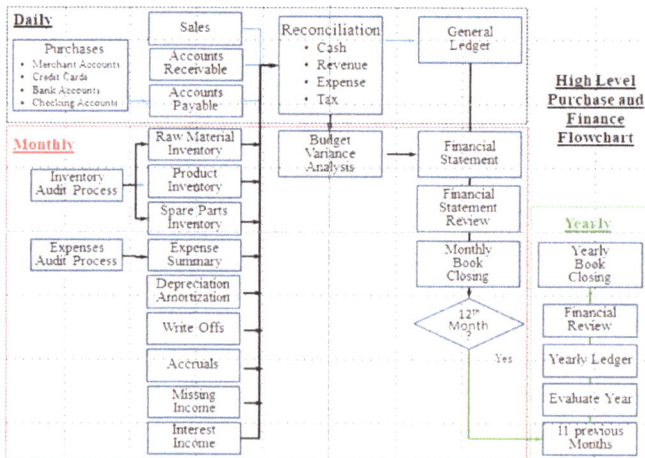

Step 1.1 Understand the Work Area (Physical Layout Diagram)

The physical layout out diagram provides another important way to understand the work area.

This is the layout of the customization area.

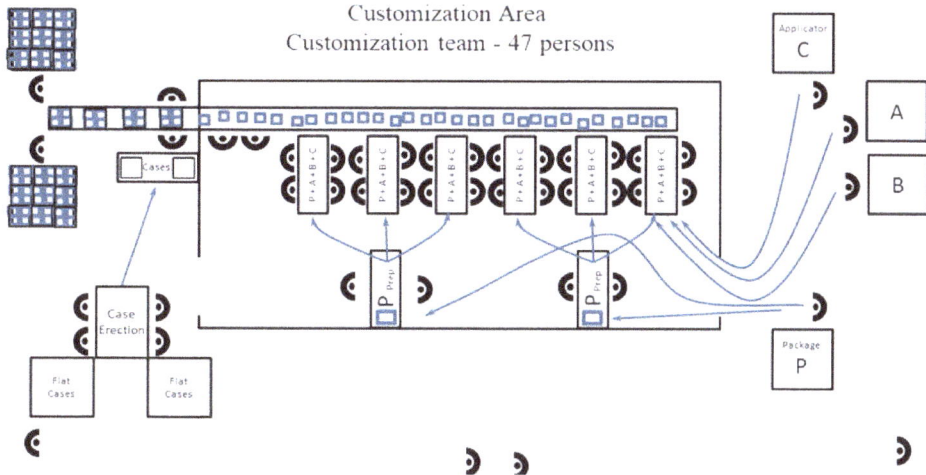

A rearrangement of he work flow changed the manual assembly in a manner that the number of people required to do the same amount of production went from fourty-seven to Fourteen.

The rearrangement of the manual work decreased the effort required. It also eliminated the need for a planned expansion that was to cost two million dollars.

This was accomplished in a five day workshop.

Summary: Understand the business

The material transformation analysis, the system diagram, the top-level flow diagram and the physical layout diagram each provide a level of understanding that provides all improvement participants a deep level of understanding that gets used to stratify and aim the improvement effort.

Step 1.2 Problem Aiming and Stratification

Production Systems and Work Processes experience many problems. Often various leaders and work associates have differing opinions about which problems should be addressed and in what order.

Step 1.1 provides a common understanding to the improvement team. However, the deeper understanding and team discussion normally leads to the identification of more improvement items than is possible.

There is a very quick and accurate way to utilize the knowledge of the individuals doing the work to get to the actionable elements of the problem and the "Hard Work".

Pareto Interview Process (PIP)

Step 1: On a chart pad draw the first bar of a Pareto.
Step 2: Ask: What is the second worst problem?
Step 3: Ask: What is next worst problem?
Step 4: Repeat the process for each of the three Pareto bars in step three.
Step 5: Select the problem at the lowest level that the people in the room choose.

The **Pareto Interview Process (PIP)** works very well for Identifying the "Hard Work". The hard work is known by those doing it. However, the main problem is zeroing in on the actionable elements of the problem. Every participant will have a slightly different view and will normally mix in fixes for the problems they see.

The **Pareto Interview Process (PIP)** for a specific problem is an interview technique that relies on the knowledge of the people in the room. Five knowledgeable people will correctly aim the improvement focus more than 85% of the time.

The facilitator has the simple task of asking two questions,

1. What is the worst problem you experience?
2. What is the next worst one and how does it compare to the worst one that ranks higher?

This initiates the aiming process.

Pareto Interview Process (PIP) (example)
Step 1: On a chart pad draw the first bar of a Pareto.

- By definition this problem is the worst and gets a 100% value.

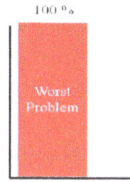

Step 2: Ask: What is the second worst problem?

- Ask: Relative to the first how bad is the second problem?

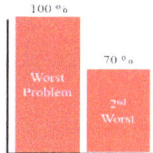

- Draw this out on the chart pad.

Step 3: Ask: What is next worst problem?

- Often the third problem is a significantly lower issue.

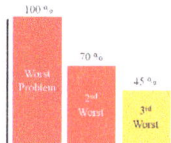

There may be problems beyond the fourth or the fifth bar but normally they are of even lower value.

Step 4: Repeat the process for each of the three Pareto bars in step three.

- Go down another two levels if possible.

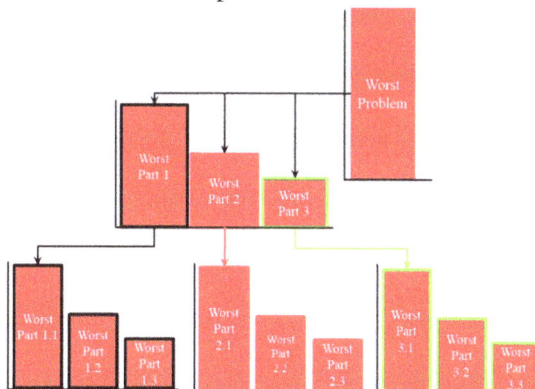

Step 5: Select the problem at the lowest level

Here is the resulting Excel worksheet showing the stratification

A verbal description of the situation is included. This clarifies the problem, its value and how the resulting solution will be evaluated.

Step 1.2 Problem Stratification

Organization	Hamburger Making and Packing Line
Need:	Identify and Resolve key line operational support issues
Problem Situation:	Periodic disruption and break down of normal workflow.

Description of situation:
Work normally flows smoothly but consistently a problem arise and like a surge on the highway it causes a cycle of back ups that can then go on for days. It is not always the same problem but it is a problem that disrupts the flow of work among the staff.

Value of solving the problem:
The OEE of the line is at 55% due to the cycle of down time experienced by seemingly random but continuous cycle through problems at various operational locations. An increase of 5% OEE would prevent the investment in additional production capacity. This would be a multimillion dollar savings.

How problem solution will be verified:
- Elimination or reduction of specific problems at the selected work stations.
- An increase in Line OEE from the base of 55%

Aiming of the Problem

Step 1: What is your worst problem?

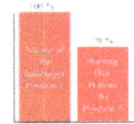

Step2: What is the second worst problem?

Step3: What is the third worst problem?

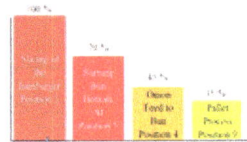

Step4: What is the fourth and fifth worst problems?

Step5: Select the problem to solve

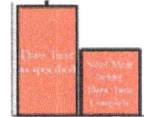

Step 1.3 Understand the Customer

The customer is the next in line to receive transformation output. The customer may be internal or may be external. The customer in this case is the line operating team. The supplier is the improvement team.

The same Pareto Interview Process (PIP) used with the organization is once again used but this time with the customer of the improvement. The problem of getting the material to the line on time, on quality and at the right quantity is the defined need.

Step 1.4 Area Self-Assessment

People with drive overcome hard work. They however look to lessen or eliminate the hard work. They look to eliminate the grind. The part of the work that makes it hard. How you handle the grind is often what separates the winners from the quitters. If hard work is to be worthwhile it must meet certain standards and measures that matter to those performing the work.

Creating an improvement plan gives everyone involved an opportunity to contribute, or object to aspects of the change. Hard work is a day by day issue. The improvement needs to address the work and how it contributes to the need of the business.

Why does this work need to be done?

Is it value added work?

Is the current struggle worth it?

Identifying the improvement and making it happen quickly is important. Doing the "right thing" must be easier than doing the "less than the right thing". Everyone with an oar in the water must pull together. When one thinks of oneself it is of the person that we were when forty or thirty or twenty. When you look in the mirror you are often surprised at the person looking back.

The work of the organization has a similar analog. Everyone sees the work in a different way and will usually be surprised at the variations by which the work gets done.

And finally, when the work is monitored and freshly documented the surprise is that it is different than almost everyone expected.

The ***Stress Free^{TM} Work Assessment*** process facilitates the organization to get a good qualitative understanding of the current work situation.

Thirty-five questions covering the customer, the work processes, the material flow, the people, the support systems, the environment, and leadership provide a comprehensive qualitative assessment of the current work situation.

Work Area Self-Assessment Questions

Work Area Assessment Questions		No	Not Sure	OK	Mostly	Good	Best in Class
Customer							
1	Customer Satisfaction is the primary focus of the work				a		
2	Customer quality expectations are exceeded			a			
3	Customer input is sought and utilized					a	
4	Customer Satisfaction is rated after every interaction				a		
5	Frequent customers are utilized to improve the business				a		
Work Processes		No	Not Sure	OK	Mostly	Good	Best in Class
6	Work Processes are easy to learn and do.				a		
7	Work Processes are visualized and mistake proofed			a			
8	Each major work process has been optimized				a		
9	Work design ensure easy to maintain practices				a		
10	Work processes get periodical review and improvement focus				a		
Material		No	Not Sure	OK	Mostly	Good	Best in Class
11	Material Quality Characteristics have units and tolerances defined.				a		
12	The supplier is certified and the material meets the required specifications					a	
13	Incoming materials are verified to correctness, quality and quantity.					a	
14	Damaged incoming materials are not accepted				a		
15	In process material handling issues are rare and easy to recover from				a		
Human		No	Not Sure	OK	Mostly	Good	Best in Class
16	Expert problem prevention skills are the norm.				a		
17	Advanced condition management skills are the norm.			a			
18	Adherence to Standards and following Standard Operating Procedures is the norm				a		
19	Mistake proofing has eliminated mistakes	a					
20	Our people are highly motivated, continuous improvement leaders				a		
Systems		No	Not Sure	OK	Mostly	Good	Best in Class
21	Systems exist and are well documented.				a		
22	Systems ensure Cpk>1.33 and no defects				a		
23	Systems ensure required production rate is maintained.				a		
24	Systems are explained and trained using the lastest techniques				a		
25	Systems are easy to learn requiring less than five days to get qualified.			a			
Environment		No	Not Sure	OK	Mostly	Good	Best in Class
26	Support Organizations accept our solutions and integrate it into their design.				a		
27	Purchasing adjusts its buying based on the problem solution.					a	
28	Material specifications are adjusted based on specific problem solutions					a	
29	Operational conditions are changed as required to maintain improvements				a		
30	Logitics are adjusted to support specific problem resolution.					a	
Leadership		No	Not Sure	OK	Mostly	Good	Best in Class
31	Leaders review the root cause of all key problems.				a		
32	Key problem resolution always get public recognition.			a			
33	Leaders schedule root cause validation time.			a			
34	Leadership goes to the root cause to see and get understanding				a		
35	Leaders participate in stress free problem evaluation			a			

The discussion among the participants as they try to agree to a specific rating is probably as valuable as the focus their agreed to rating provides.

Visual Stress Free[TM] Evaluation

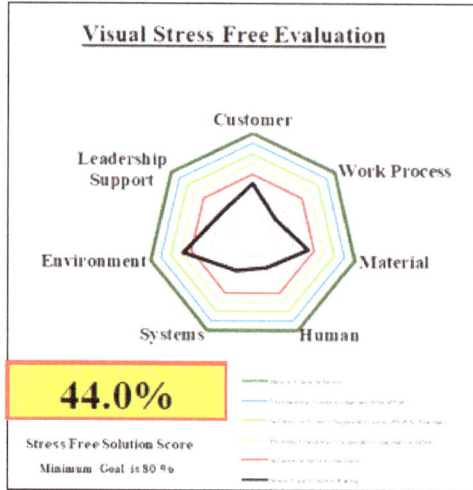

The answers provide a visual spider diagram that portrays the gaps in the organizations work.

The ideal would be to have each area at the outer boundary. The heavy black line in the center represents an organization scoring itself at a 44% out of a possible 100%.

The gaps are obvious, but they may not be equal in importance, or priority.

Priority Rating

	Prioritization			
	GAP	1-5 Business Need	1-5 Easy to do	1-5 Have Resources	Priority
Customer	4.8	5.0	4.0	4.0	384.0
Work Process	7.2	5.0	3.0	4.0	432.0
Material	4.6	3.0	3.0	3.0	124.2
Human	6.8	5.0	3.0	4.0	408.0
Systems	6.4	4.0	3.0	4.0	307.2
Environment	3.2	4.0	3.0	3.0	115.2
Leadership Support	6.2	5.0	3.0	4.0	372.0

The assessment continues with a priority rating exercise.

1. The business need for closing the assessed gap is rated on a one to five scale.

2. Next how easy will it be to close the gap and

3. Finally, are there resources that can make the improvement?

These three consideration ratings are multiplied together with the assessed gap.

Opportunity Pareto

Opportunity Priority

The priority is graphed to produce the Opportunity Priority Pareto. In this example the number one bar is the Work Process. But the skills of the people come in a close second.

Stress Free^{TM} Work Process Improvement will solve the work process problem while at the same time greatly improving the problem-solving skills of those making the improvement.

The participants of the evaluation now have much greater alignment and understanding of the improvement possibilities and the problems that may be solved. They are still at the thirty-thousand-foot level and need to get much closer to the problem.

Step 1.5 Observe Selected Priority Area

Material Transformation Analysis (MTA), System Diagram, Top Level Flow Diagram, Physical Layout Diagram used in step one provided a great deal of understanding. A more detailed observation of the specific problem will now take the learning in Step 1.1 and create a more detailed granularity. This much closer look with new understanding results in a dramatic increase the ability to "see".

The following tools provide this additional granularity that leads to root cause solutions.

- Travel Chart
- Time and Travel Observation Chart
- Cycle Chart
- Individual Hourly Effort Chart
- Individual minute by minute or second by second Effort Chart
- Team Effort Balance Chart

Each increases the level of problem granularity and results in a root cause solution in record time.

Travel Chart

This is used to understand the walking and the path the associate takes while doing the work. It is intended to be a pencil hand sketch of what the associated is doing.

It:

- Will visualize the movement of people
- May include a plant layout, a department or area layout.
- It will show movement of one person or multiple people.
- It may detail the movement of products or components.
- Can be a tool to suggest layout design changes.

Example:

Before Improvement

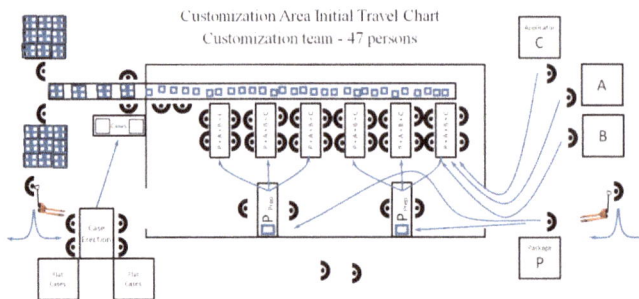

Customization Area Initial Travel Chart
Customization team - 47 persons

After Improvement

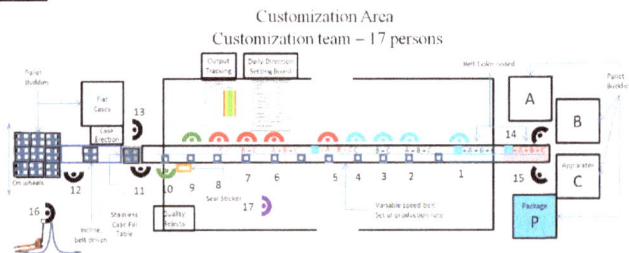

Customization Area
Customization team – 17 persons

Note that only the person removing finished product and bringing materials has any travel.

In both situations the detailed motion chart for each individual is an important tool to evaluate the physical work situation of each individual.

The same conveyor was used, and a ten-foot extension added.

Step 1.5 Observe Selected Priority Area

Time and Travel Observation Chart

This is similar to the Travel Chart but intended to be more structured and less visual but with more precision.

Time and Travel Observation Process

- For the Associate being observed, record the actual time taken for each task,
- Use stopwatches. In today's world the I-phone can be used to time and record the actions of the person doing the work,
- Observe all work area team members individually.
- Repeat the observation as many times as necessary to get an accurate value.
- Determine the accurate value and record.

Example 1: Time and Travel Observation Chart

Used to:

- Understand actual on the floor work facts and data
- Clarify the work process
- See and understand the Hard and Non-Value Add work – See Waste
- Understand how long each task takes to do
- Identify improvement opportunity
- Standardize work

Work Cycle Chart

The work cycle chart provides a step by step visual presentation of the length of time for each step. This provides a visual signal for potential improvement areas.

Example 1: Work Cycle Chart - Card Loading

Work Cycle Time Steps

1. State the job to be studied
2. Pick a tasks' starting and ending point.
3. Write a brief description of each detail.
4. Fill in the time it takes to do each task.

Example 2: Cycle Chart

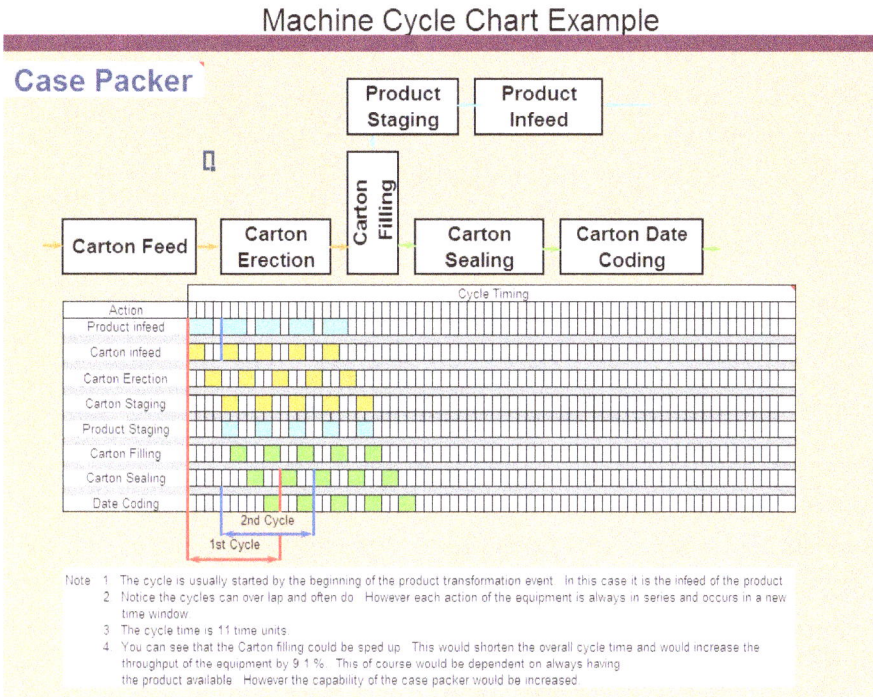

Machine Cycle Chart Example

This is a time-based cycle chart that relates the events in the process of packing a case of product.

A similar chart can be made studying the position of various equipment components.

The level of the study is determined by what needs to be learned or understood.

Step 1.5 Observe Selected Priority Area
Example 3: Time based Circular Cycle Chart

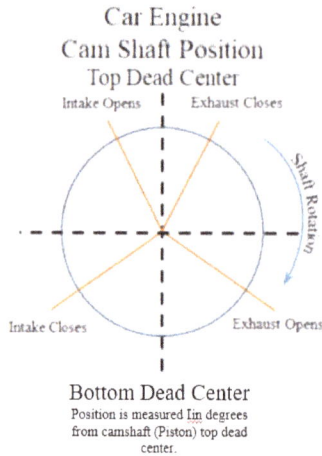

Car Engine
Cam Shaft Position
Top Dead Center
Intake Opens | Exhaust Closes
Shaft Rotating
Intake Closes | Exhaust Opens
Bottom Dead Center
Position is measured Iin degrees
from camshaft (Piston) top dead
center.

1. Note that the intake valve opens 13.5 degrees before top dead center, and it closes 55.5 degrees after bottom dead center.
2. The exhaust valve opens 55.5 degrees before bottom dead center and the exhaust closes 13.5 degrees after top dead center.

This means the energy transfer of the piston is happening between 13.5 degrees after top dead center and 55.5 degrees before bottom dead center. Or said another way the energy transfer from the gasoline explosion happens in only 30.1 % of the piston cycle.

Cycle Charts provide a wealth of understanding of what is happening in the work or transformation production cycle. It often is the first point of improvement discovery. It is also a visual way for all involved to gain a deeper way of understanding their work.

Individual Effort Chart - Hourly

Initially used to get a quick step by step understanding.

Example: Individual Effort Chart - Hourly

Individual Effort Chart
- Hourly Increments
Hamburger Making Steps

1.0 Load Meat
2.0 Meat Cutter Synchronization
3.0 Meat cut inspection
4.0 Meat frying screen brushing
5.0 Meat and Onion Fry
6.0 Meat patty flip
7.0 Bun Bottom Flip
8.0 Meat on Bun Bottom
9.0 Onions on top of meat
10.0 Bun Top placement
11.0 Quality Check

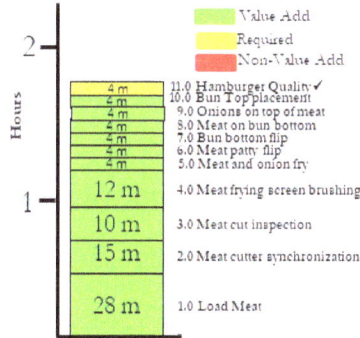

Value Add	
Required	
Non-Value Add	

Time	Step
4 m	11.0 Hamburger Quality ✓
4 m	10.0 Bun Top placement
4 m	9.0 Onions on top of meat
4 m	8.0 Meat on bun bottom
4 m	7.0 Bun bottom flip
4 m	6.0 Meat patty flip
4 m	5.0 Meat and onion fry
12 m	4.0 Meat frying screen brushing
10 m	3.0 Meat cut inspection
15 m	2.0 Meat cutter synchronization
28 m	1.0 Load Meat

The individual effort chart captures each work or action done by an individual in either an eight-hour workday (480 minutes) or a twelve-hour workday, (720 minutes). This specific example uses hour by hour increments. This is only useful to get the overall material transformation. The visualization of the improvement opportunity occurs by going down to the minute versus the hourly increment.

The bar chart begins at the bottom at zero time and builds sequential to cover the entire workday. In this example the operator will execute three work cycles of the shown work sequence.

Value Add is the effort put into delivering the product desired by the customer.

One customer is the one that is paying for a product. This customer is external to the company.

However, many intermediate products get made for internal customers. In this example the next in line customer is the person that executes a quality inspection (required time), wraps and weighs the burger and moves it to the next station.

The work to satisfy either external customers or the internal customer is considered as Value Add.

Non-value is time lost to such things as waiting for materials or approval. Rework is non-value add.

Required is time spent on such work as inspection to assure good quality or waiting for line clearance documentation before new product can be produced.

The build increments get finer each time an analysis is done. The one-hour effort stack is often immediately followed by the minute effort chart.

Once the entire bar for day's work is stacked, the red areas are examined to see if there is a way to eliminate or greatly reduce them.

The yellow bar is next to being scrutinized and improved.

Green is often where the most improvement opportunity is found. Material quantities, feed procedures, material placement and handling arrangements, equipment startup, and information preparation all are example improvement areas.

Individual Effort Chart Minute Scale

Each individual in the work area is tracked and all work action times are documented. A stacked bar chart provides a visual display that is easily examined for work improvement opportunities.

Example: Individual Effort Chart – Minute

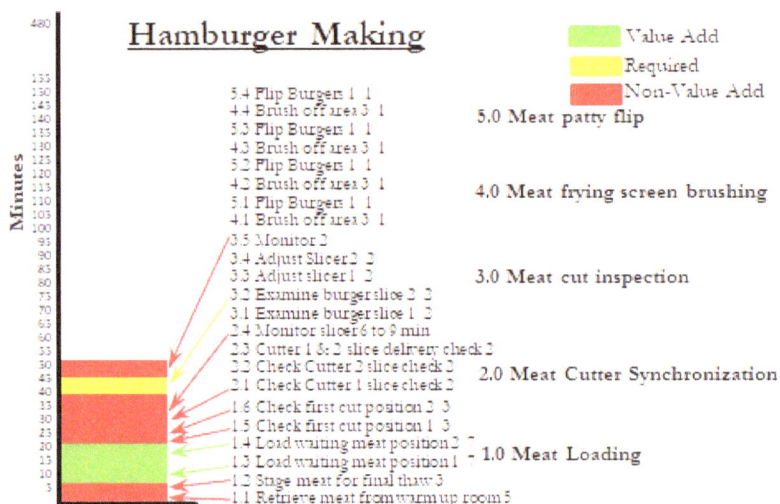

Red is the non-value add effort. Yellow is the required work that does not add value to the product such as quality inspection, or record keeping. Green is the material transformation work that adds value.

Team Effort Balance Chart

Once all individual effort charts are done they are transferred to an effort balance chart. Here the work balance among all the associates can be compared and the work adjustments made.

The variability of the work done in each of the work positions or roles is also documented. This means that multiple associates are timed at each work position. Variability must be reduced to ensure that any associate will perform equally in any position. The variability reduction comes from both training and practice.

Team Effort Balance Chart Example

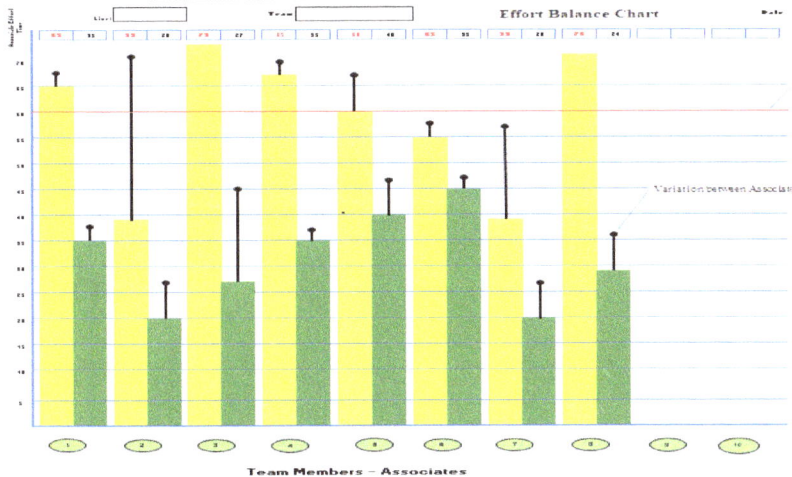

After using many or all of these ways to understand the problem the team is ready to define the improvement - Step 2: Define the Improvement.

Imagine how the initial improvement focus may have changed! It almost always is different, more focused and immediately achievable.

Step 1: Tips on Understanding the Situation

1. Spend as much time as it takes to use the suggested tools.
2. Listen to the associates doing the work. Listen for understanding.
3. Accept the different views. Have competing views work together to resolve the situation.
4. Go to the "Floor" observe the actual situation.
5. Utilize photographs and video to better see the problem.

Step 1: Tools for Understanding and Aiming

1. Material Transformation Analysis (MTA)
2. System Diagram
3. Top Level Flow Diagram
4. Physical Layout Diagram
5. Pareto Analysis
6. Travel Chart
7. Time and Travel Observation Chart
8. Work Cycle Chart
9. Individual Effort Chart - Hourly
10. Individual Effort Chart - Minute
11. Team Effort Balance Chart

Step 2: Define Improvement

The goal is to define the improvement in such a way that it becomes the desired way, the easy to do way for the work. The five sub steps of step 2 provides the guidance.

Step 2.1. Identify hard work

Step 2.2. Reduce Movement

Step 2.3. Improve material flow, location, amount

Step 2.4. Mistake proof the Work.

Step 2.5. Define the VA, NVA, Required work

Step 2.1: Identify hard work

We work because we have a desire to be contributing, value adding, self-reliant members of society. The anatomy of hard work often looks similar to value added work.

People with drive overcome hard work. They however look to a plan that lessens or eliminates the hard work. They look to eliminate the grind, the part of the work that makes in hard.

How you handle the grind is often what separates the winners from the quitters. If hard work is to be worthwhile it must meet certain standards and measures that matter to those performing the work.

Motivation sets the person up to overcome the grind of hard work. Identifying the positive elements of the motivation sets the improvement effort up for success.

Internal motivation, such as passion, self-satisfaction, personal desire is the most powerful. External Motivators such as financial reward, work security and professional recognition are also powerful. Countering these positive motivators is the fear of failure. The resentment towards those controlling the financial aspects of our lives.

Creating an improvement plan gives everyone involved an opportunity to contribute, or object to aspects of the change. Hard work is a day by day issue. The improvement needs to address the work and how it contributes to the need of the business. Why does this work need to be done? Is it value added work? Is the current struggle worth it? Identifying the improvement and making it happen quickly is important. Doing the right thing must be easier than doing the less than right thing. Everyone with an oar in the water must pull together.

The improvement plan is critical. Without it the organization will tread water.

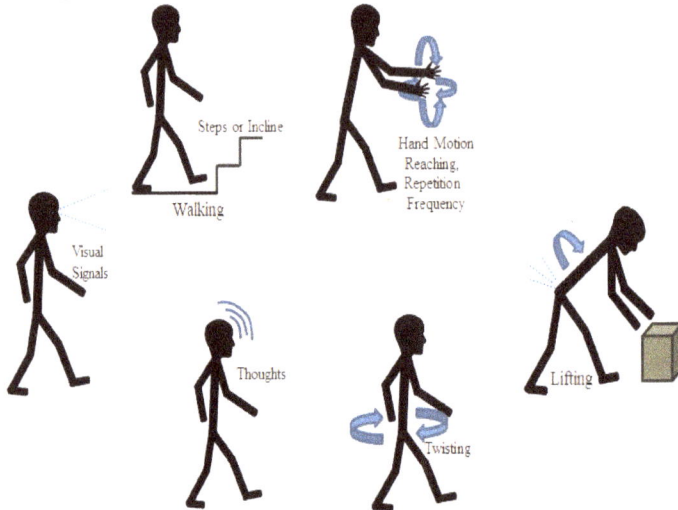

How do you identify the hard work? Use the interview technique.

Step 2.2: Reduce **Movement**

Physical movement, especially repetitive movement is an area to investigate. In assembly operation the same movement over and over, even when little strength is needed is an area of concern. In this case it is the number of times the same action is taken during a working period. In lifting it is the number of times, the weight and the type of movement required. In twisting to get materials the twist degree, the weight, and the frequency are factors to consider.

Motion Chart

Material positioning is critical in all these cases. Assembly aids that reduce movement are another factor to consider. Work balance and rotation provides another tool to ensure hard work is reduced or shared equitably.

Walking from one side of the line to the other, going to get a tool, going to get parts or materials are all examples of movement that should be greatly reduced or eliminated

Step 2.3: Improve material flow, location, amount

Material flow to the transformation area is crucial. The right amount, at the right time, put in the optimum position is the goal. This often requires work process change.

More frequent, smaller quantity deliveries with a just in time approach is key. The ideal situation is for the material to exactly meet the production or work process material requirement. No material take-away at Change Over time!

Step 2.4: Mistake proof the Work

Make it impossible to do an unsafe act. Make each work process step doable in only one way. Make assembly possible only when 100% quality is assured.

Mistake proofing can be accomplished in many ways. Checklists, pictures, size gauges, dimensional guides are a few examples of mistake proofing.

Examples of common Mistake Proofing

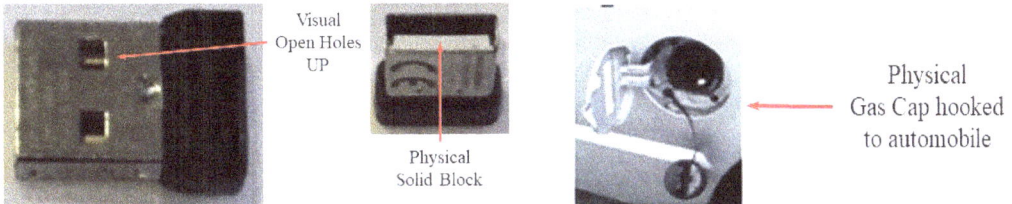

Visual Open Holes UP

Physical Solid Block

Physical Gas Cap hooked to automobile

Mistake proofing is all around us. Usually, it is very simple. It manifests itself in the physical world, but it is also built into software and visual environments.

Step 2.5: Define the VA, NVA, Required Work

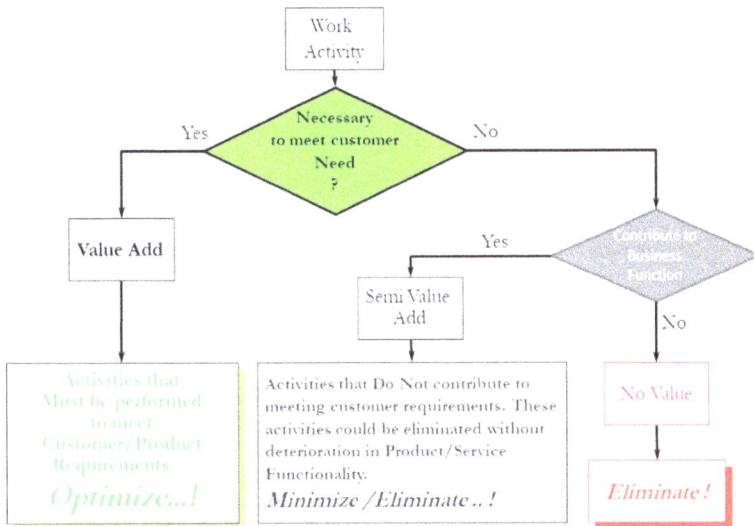

183

This step should constantly be on one's mind. Then as the work process is in its final stages, it is again time to evaluate the nature of the work and the various steps in the production process. Value Add, Non-Value and Required work should once again be considered. Value should be optimized. Non-Value eliminated or minimized.

Required work should be minimized and optimized.

Work Process Solutions Step 2: Tips on Defining the Improvement

1. Listen to those doing the work to identify "hard work"
2. Understand that high repetition, even when it takes little strength is "hard work".
3. Detailed motion studies are critical, do them.
4. Mistake proof. It makes work easier.
5. Eliminate the red from the minute by minute work analysis.

Step 2: Tools

1. Detailed Motion Chart
2. Value Add Analysis
3. Mistake proofing

Step 3 Improve

This is the take action step. Try a new approach. Think differently. Make things easy to do.

Step 3.1: Eliminate the hard work

Step 3.2: Eliminate Variation

Step 3.3: Eliminate Non-value-added work.

Step 3.4: Simplify - ECRS

Work Process Solutions Step 3.1: Eliminate the hard work

In every case make the human the one that benefits. The equipment and the infrastructure should be adjusted to make it easy for the human. I have walked up to production lines where the human was expected to climb over the production line. Why not raise the production line so the human can stay on the level floor? The human is expected to work twenty, thirty, maybe forty years in this negative situation. The equipment will get modernized and renewed multiple times.

Give the human a break!

This is one example of many,

- Material adjustment points where the human is expected to climb several steps.
- The equipment is low, and the human is expected to climb several steps.
- Material feed where the human is expected to lift and place.
- Finished product where the human is expected to pick up and stack.

Utilize the Work Combination chart to evaluate the points where the human and the equipment interact. Make the production process human friendly.

Work Combination Chart Example:

Salami Slicer Example:

This shows the interaction of the associate responsible for sliced salami ready for packaging. The cycle time is thirty-six minutes. The time spent on each physical action is recorded. Much of this information will be available if a minute scale individual effort chart has been done.

Step 3.2: Eliminate Variation

Variation of work between different associates is a key source of work process loss. The ability to balance the work across the associates that make up the team is dependent on the ability of each associate to do the work at each workstation. This means the development of every associate is important and critical to optimize and balance the workload.

Training, cross training and qualifying of all associates becomes important. Invest in the people. They will take care of the equipment. Invest in peoples' skills and they will invest their capability in improving the business results.

Training the associates in how to improve their work processes and how to solve problems to root cause are two fundamental capabilities that pay out immediately.

Training on the operation of the equipment, how work is to be done is the fundamental responsibility of the business organization.

The concept of *mistake proofing* is the basis of making sure that the quality of the work supports the required quality of the product. It is a partner of making work easy to do. Easy to do, mistake proofing visual instruction makes training an investment with immediate payout. Mistake Proofing makes it easy to maintain the required Product Quality.

Mistake proofing prevents,

- Setup errors
- Processing errors
- Missing parts
- Wrong parts being used
- Processing omission
- Processing the wrong work piece
- Adjustment errors
- Wrong equipment setup
- Wrong tools and preparation

Step 3.3: Eliminate Non-value-added work.

The time and travel chart is a tool very similar to the travel chart. At this point the elimination of non-value work is a key part of the analysis. Additionally, variability of time between associates is also of interest. The goal is minimum variability and travel distance and time.

Time and Travel Observation Example

This cycle is 40 minutes in duration. In this example John Henry walks 17, 220 paces a day! Is that value added? Does the company really want to pay for the walking? How might this be improved in an economic way?

Step 3.4 Eliminate, Combine, Reduce, Simplify (ECRS) Evaluation

Eliminate, Combine, Reduce, Simplify, (ECRS) analysis is an additional tool that is to be applied.

ECRS Mindset Questions

- Purpose
- what is done?
- why is it done?
- what else could do it?
- what else should be doing it?

- People
- who does it?
- why does he or she do it?
- who else could do it?
- who should do it?

- System
- Is the computer support system 'Easy to"?
- Is the Work System Supportive?

- Place
- where is it done?
- why is it done?
- where else could it be done?
- where should it be done?

- Sequence
- when is it done?
- why is it done at that time or order?
- when could it be done?
- when should it be done?

- Method
- how is it done?
- why is it done so?
- how else could it be done?
- how should it be done?

Step 3: Improvement Tips

1. Focus on making it easy for the person.
2. Utilize all the analysis observations.
3. Do the inexpensive improvements first.

Step 3: Tools

1. Work Combination Chart
2. Time and Travel Observation
3. ECRS

Step 4: Evaluate

Ensuring the desired and targeted results were achieved is a critical step in making any improvement change. These evaluation measures should be defined before any improvement effort has been attempted. Alignment to the success measures is a critical leadership habit that needs to be cultivated.

The evaluation of successful efforts is a point in time where improvement praise is meaningful to those who have achieved the improvement.

Step 4.1: Easy To

Step 4.2 Improvement Measures

Step 4.3: Materials - Data - Information

Step 4.4: Process

Step 4.5: Systems

Step 4.1: Easy To

Making the work easier to do means that it will most likely be appreciated and followed. A red flag should quickly be raised when a work process is not readily followed by those doing the work. People always gravitated to the easiest way to accomplish a task. There should be no objection to doing work the easiest way possible as long as it meets quality and throughput criteria.

Is the work easier to do?

Step 4.2 Improvement Measures

Have the critical and predefined measures of the improvement seen a measurable improvement?

Some of the measures are,

- Safety
- Quality
- Productivity
- Cost
- Distribution
- Worker Satisfaction
- Throughput
- Overall Equipment Efficiency (OEE)
- Scrap reduction
- Customer Satisfaction

Have the critical measures improved?

Step 4.3: Materials - Data - Information

189

Getting the right quantity of materials, to the right place at the right time is of key importance. Often the timing and quantity is determined not by the process need but by the storage unit, delivery method and work balance issues. The placement of materials is often of secondary design concern.

Are materials in the right location and easy to utilize?

Are the material amounts about right?

Is Material delivery in the right time and quantities?

Is pitch synchronized? Here we define pitch as the standard Quantity of product produced with each scheduled run of the SKU.

Step 4.4: Process

Individual effort and effort balance in the work team is of critical importance. Has the work been simplified and improvements that make work easier to do implemented? Record keeping automation, visual aids, work to standards and standardized work implementation all provide process improvement.

Is duplication of effort eliminated?

Has work balance been achieved?

Step 4.5: Systems

Technology has progressed to the point that it is sophisticated and relatively inexpensive. Operational readings can now be achieved with remote reading, wireless system application. The high quantity of radio frequency interfering structures and equipment add technical challenges but walk by or proximity reading techniques are barrier busters.

Simpler system designs, slower in rate but sufficient in quantify often provide an alternate way to address multiple SKU's.

Lay out adjustments often provide ways to streamline production and improve work environment issues.

Have the systems been modified to provide better support?

Step 4: Tips

1. The earlier the success measures are identified the better. Clarity on the evaluation measures aids in the proper guidance of the improvement effort. This a key point for anyone leading the process.

Step 4: Tools

1. Measure definition
2. Field Observation
3. Control Charting of the Results

Step 5 Repeat Steps 2-4

A first cycle of improvement has been executed. Clear improvements have been achieved. The energy of the work team is high.

Don't stop.

Make the next improvement now!

The team members should have additional insights and fresh ideas. Have associates from other areas or other sights review and input their ideas.

This step often results in a break-through. Something unexpected often surfaces and makes the first four steps the foundation for the breakthrough.

Step 5.1 Brainstorm

Step 5.2 Re-examine, re-evaluate.

Step 5.3 Summary Report

Step 5.1 Brainstorm

This is one of the few times that brainstorming to solve a problem is recommended. The intent is to get a different approach, a new approach to surface.

- Brainstorm improvements!!!
- Select the best ones and try them out. It is OK to try ideas and have them fail.
- Have an expert buddy watch for additional improvement opportunities.

Don't allow yourself to be the frog in hot water.

Step 5.2 Re-examine, re-evaluate.

Look over everything that has been done. Check for omission, complication, missed simplification. The work combination chart is useful for closely examining each interface.

Work Combination Chart

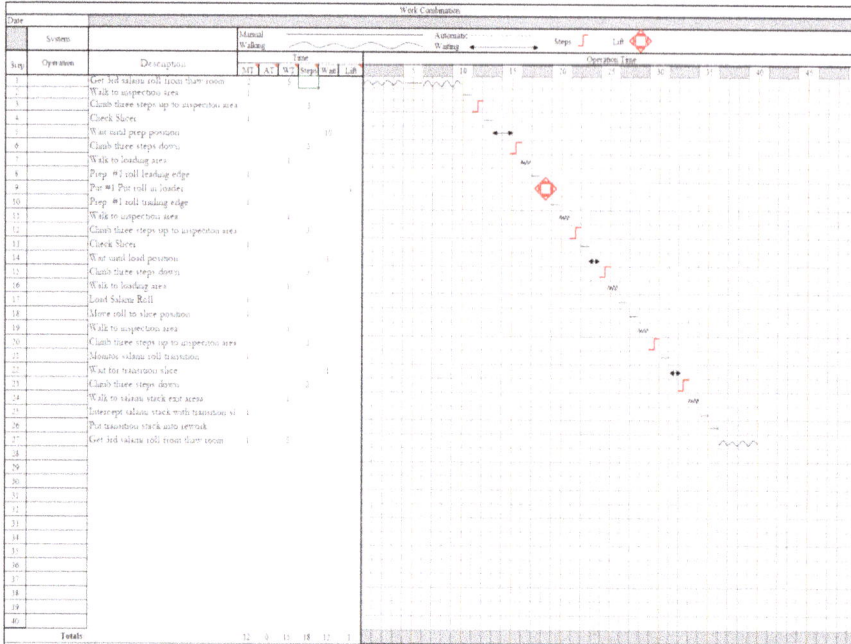

Step 5.3 Summary Report

At this step a report to the supporting leadership is appropriate and meaningful. Use the report as the transition to step 6.

Summary Report Example:

Salami at its Best	Date: Today
	Associate: John Henry

Topic:	Salami Slicing Improvement	Improvement $ Value: $ 75,000

1. Purpose and Link to the business

The work in this area can be improved to be easier to do and more efficient. Productivity will be increased by twenty percent.

2. Current situation.

The associates in this area spend: 40 % in value add and required work

32 % waiting

and   28.% walking

3. Improvement Key Points:

- Relocated Salami thaw room. - walk time reduced by 80%

- Reduced waiting with visual controls by 57%

- Optimized Salami roll prep and loading - reduced time by 30%

– Added Quality inspection and documentation to role

– Added Autonomous Maintenance to role

4. Result Data	**5. Standardize**
- Walk time = 5% of work time	
- Waiting time = 14 % of work time	**6. Reapplication Recommendation**
	Evaluate other work positions and
- Value Add and Required time = 81% of work time	improve
	Reapplication Approval
	John Henry

193

Step 5: Tips

1. Try for two or three immediate cycles of improvement.
2. Strive for more granularity and detail on each cycle.
3. Take the time to document.
4. Study each previous improvement cycle's documents.

Step 5: Tools

1. All the tools described in previous chapters.
2. Summary Report

Step 6: Integrate

The improvement has been made but the decay begins immediately. Integration means making the improvement part of the work culture and practice. Maintaining the improvement must be made "easy to". Maintaining the improvement is often as challenging as making the improvement.

Step 6.1: Visualize

Step 6.2: Integrate

Step 6.1: Visualize

Visual control provides a very public way for an improvement to be maintained. Create Visualized Step by step document showing size, location, orientation of information aids in the maintenance of the improvement.

Visual instructions that show each work step makes it easier to utilize the process and quicker to train new people to do the task. The discipline to visualize the work steps creates yet a final opportunity to make improvement.

Visual Instruction Example

Step 6.2 Integrate
Training and Qualification process

Every associate with and uses the improved work process must qualify in the flawless delivery of the product of the improved work. New members must be trained and qualified. Periodically all associates may need to requalify. All of these situations should be addressed by the training and qualification system.

Support Systems

- Safety
- Quality
- Spare Parts
- Maintenance
- HR
- Engineering
- Finance and Accounting
- Purchasing

Step 6: Integrate Tips

1. Enroll affected personnel in the evaluation.

Step 6: Tools for Integration

1. Statistical Analysis

Step 7: Utilize

Step 7.1 Track Variation

Step 7.2: Daily Management System (DMS)

Step 7.3: Schedule Improvement Evaluation

Step 7.1 Track Variation

Plot the variability between team members and investigate problems/issues. Track the production output and note any variation. The goal is to stay to the hour by hour production target. Either too low or too high is unacceptable.

Output Tracking Example:

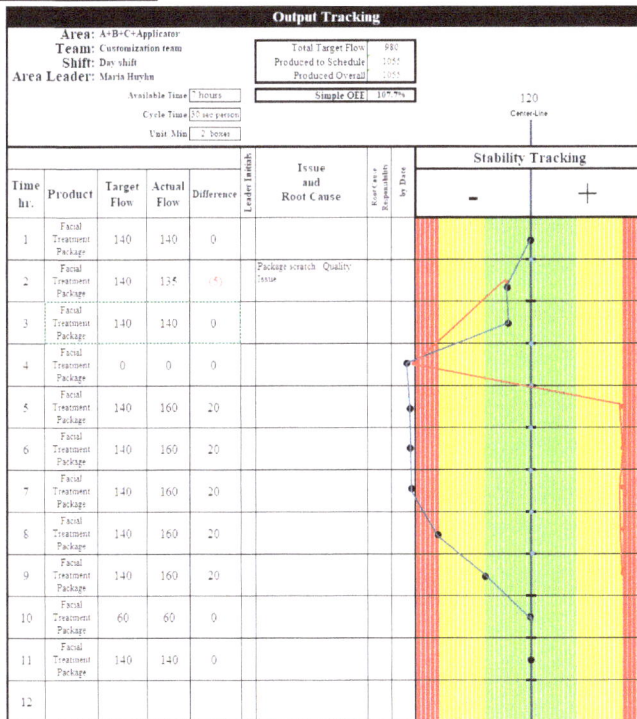

Step 7.2: Put into the Daily Management System (DMS)

- **Practice**

  Have all the required team members practice the work process.

- **Coach and Review**

  Provide coaching for those having trouble with the process

Daily Management System Diagram Examples:

Production Area

Daily Management - Production Area

System:	Production Organization Daily Management	Requirements: Output Tracking and performance metrics.	Measures: In-Process: See column below	Date
Customer:			
System Process Description: The Production organization transforms raw materials into the desired customer product. It is a mix of equipment, materials and people that in concert deliver on quality product safely.			Output Measures: External Customer 98% satisfaction Rating	Picture of Area Leader

System / Process Flow Diagram

	Step Name	In process measures	Action Limits	Who
Physical Work — **Production Line Organization Daily Management**	1. Safety	Home	Any Incident	Safety Leader
		Car	Any Incident	Safety Leader
		Work Area	Any Incident	Safety Leader
	2. Quality	# of defects	> 2%	Quality Leader
		Rework	any	
		scrap	> 2%	
	3. Delivery	As per plan	< 100% Adherence	Individual
	4. Productivity	< 80% Loading	Any Overtime	Area Leader
		# of load changes		
	5. Budget	On Planned Trend		Area Leader
	6. Learning	One OPL / day		Individual
	7. Next Twenty Four	Plan Adjustments Root Cause Countermeasures		Everyone
	8. Support Request	Ability to Resolve		Everyone

Op Team / Line / Department / Operation / Site / Supply Chain

- 7:30 am — Out Going Ldr Review Staff / Out Going Line Ldr Review Line / Review Open Support Requests / Review Open Support Requests / Review Open Support Requests / Review Open Support Requests
- 7:45 am — Update Support Request / ID continuing Issues
- 7:45 am — In Coming Ldr ID needs for Shift / Line Walk / Dept Ldr Walk Through / Operation Ldr Walk Through / Site Ldr Walk Through / Supply Chain Ldr Walk Through
- 8:00 am — Line DDS
- 8:15 am — Support Need? Yes / Dept DDS
- 8:30 am — Execute Against Plan / Support Need? Yes
- 8:45 am — Execute Against Plan / OP DDS

Daily Direction Setting Meeting
1. **SAFETY**
   - Home
   - Driving   Visual
   - Line
2. **QUALITY**
   - Equipment Issues   Visual
   - Material Issues
3. **DELIVERY**
   - Adherence to Plan   Visual
4. **PRODUCTIVITY**
   - Work Balance
   - Through Put   Visual
5. **Cost / Scrap**
6. **Learning**   One Point Lesson
7. **Next Twenty Four items**
8. **Support Request**

- Support Need? Yes
- Execute Against Plan / Site DDS / SC DDS
- Support Need? Yes / Support Need?
- Execute Against Plan / Execute Against Plan

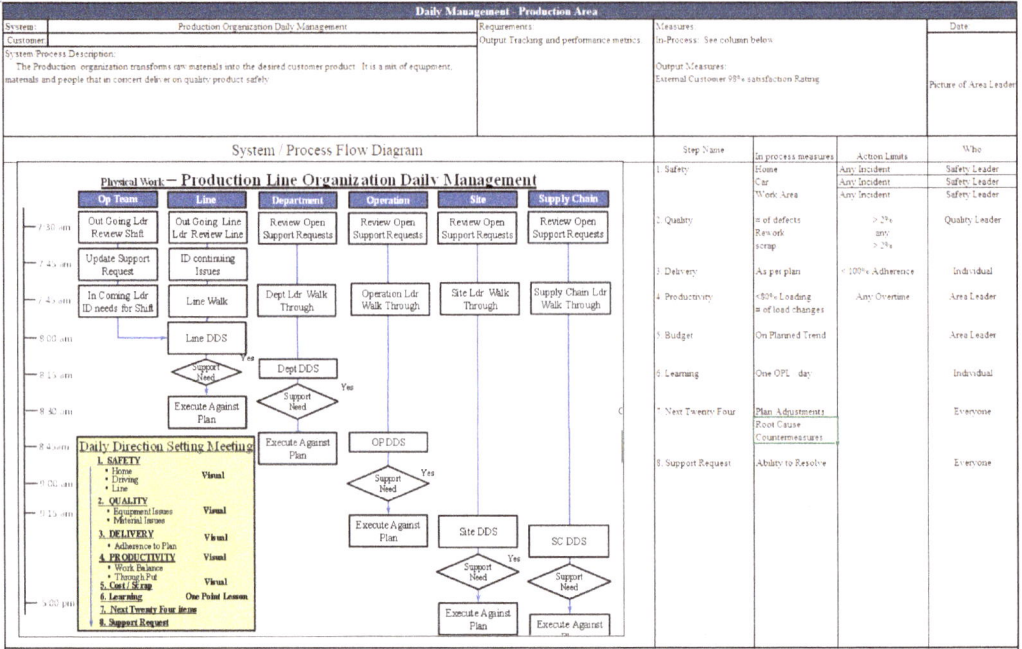

Manual Assembly Area

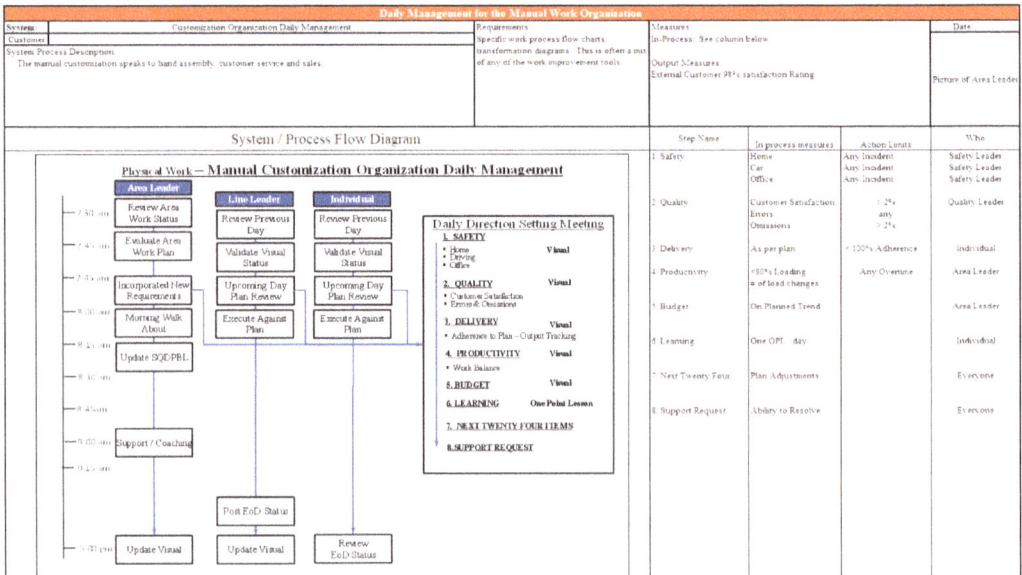

Daily Management for the Manual Work Organization

System:	Customization Organization Daily Management	Requirements: Specific work process flow charts, transformation diagrams. This is often a mix of any of the work improvement tools	Measures: In-Process: See column below	Date
Customer:			
System Process Description: The manual customization speaks to hand assembly, customer service and sales.			Output Measures: External Customer 98% satisfaction Rating	Picture of Area Leader

System / Process Flow Diagram

	Step Name	In process measures	Action Limits	Who
Physical Work — **Manual Customization Organization Daily Management**	1. Safety	Home	Any Incident	Safety Leader
		Car	Any Incident	Safety Leader
		Office	Any Incident	Safety Leader
	2. Quality	Customer Satisfaction	> 2%	Quality Leader
		Errors	any	
		Omissions	> 2%	
	3. Delivery	As per plan	< 100% Adherence	Individual
	4. Productivity	< 80% Loading	Any Overtime	Area Leader
		# of load changes		
	5. Budget	On Planned Trend		Area Leader
	6. Learning	One OPL / day		Individual
	7. Next Twenty Four	Plan Adjustments		Everyone
	8. Support Request	Ability to Resolve		Everyone

Area Leader / Line Leader / Individual

- 7:30 am — Review Area Work Status / Review Previous Day / Review Previous Day
- 7:45 am — Evaluate Area Work Plan / Validate Visual Status / Validate Visual Status
- 7:45 am — Incorporated New Requirements / Upcoming Day Plan Review / Upcoming Day Plan Review
- 8:00 am — Morning Walk About / Execute Against Plan / Execute Against Plan
- 8:15 am — Update SQD/PBL
- 8:30 am
- 8:45 am
- 9:00 am — Support / Coaching
- 9:15 am

Daily Direction Setting Meeting
1. **SAFETY**
   - Home
   - Driving   Visual
   - Office
2. **QUALITY**   Visual
   - Customer Satisfaction
   - Errors & Omissions
3. **DELIVERY**   Visual
   - Adherence to Plan – Output Tracking
4. **PRODUCTIVITY**   Visual
   - Work Balance
5. **BUDGET**   Visual
6. **LEARNING**   One Point Lesson
7. **NEXT TWENTY FOUR ITEMS**
8. **SUPPORT REQUEST**

- Post EoD Status
- 5:00 pm — Update Visual / Update Visual / Review EoD Status

Knowledge Work – Office Area

Step 7.3: Schedule Improvement Evaluation

It is critical for the organization to periodically evaluate the effectiveness and efficiency of all work processes. Evaluate what has changed. What new ideas could improve the work process?

Utilize the Stress FreeTM Work Area Self-Assessment and begin the next round of defining the improvement opportunities.

Step 7: Tips on Utilize

1. Use the hand edited field paperwork immediately. The formal paperwork may take longer to get through the system. Assign an owner to update all documents.

Step 7: Tools for Utilize

1. Maintenance Calendar
2. Retraining Schedule

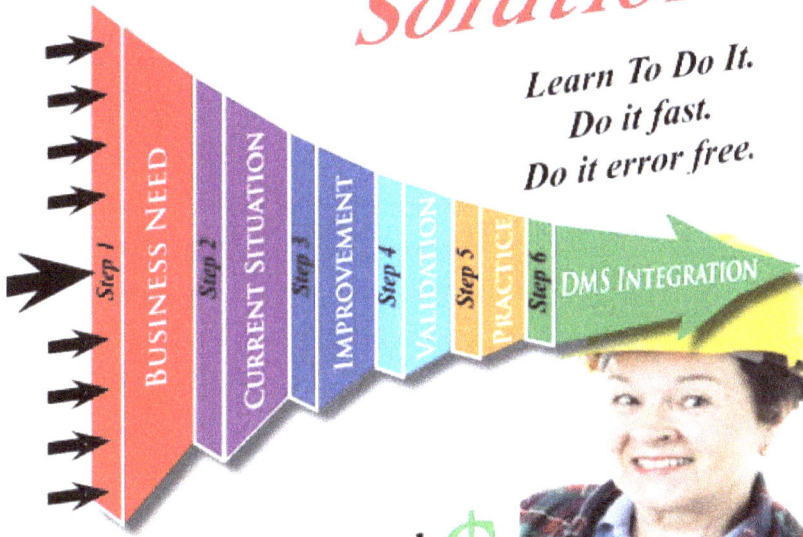

Stress Free^{TM} Changeover Solutions
Throughput Optimization

By: Ron Mueller

Around the World Publishing LLC
4914 Cooper Road Suite 144
Cincinnati, Ohio 45242-9998

ISBN 13:
ISBN 10:

Distributed By Ingram
Cover Picture By: Lisa F. Young, Dreamstime.com
Cover Design By: Ron Mueller

TECHNICAL EDITOR:

Gordon Miller P. E.

DEDICATION

To all those who want to make it
fast,
easy to do
and
error free.

Table of Content

ACKNOWLEDGMENTS

The people put in a lifetime of hard work.

Making Changeover, easier and faster to do makes

this work a little easier.

Everyone doing the work deserves this break.

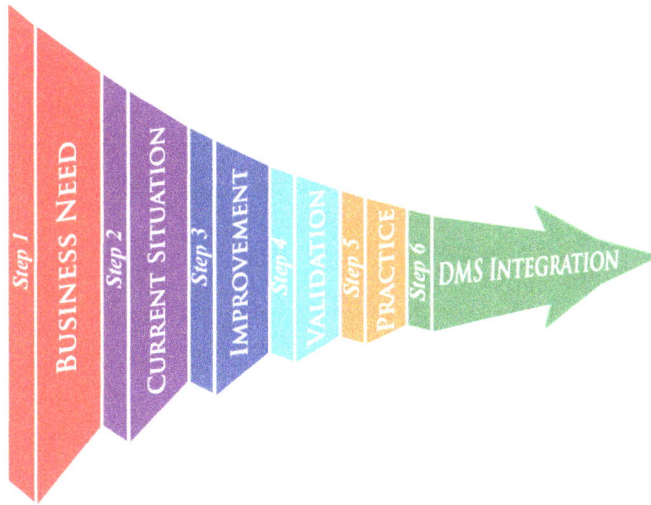

Change Over Solutions Introduction

The concept of rapid changeover is very well demonstrated in car racing's pit row rapid tire changes and refueling. The coordination, teamwork, equipment and wheel preparation with the car is exceptional. The gravity feed gas resupply is faster than can be achieved with a pressurized system. These processes are done by very talented people, who have practiced to the point of perfection. They minimize the pit time and maximize the run time and thus directly affect the outcome of the race.

This concept can be applied along the entire supply chain; at the customer, at the truck loading area, at the finished product warehouse, at the production line, and for raw material transport and receiving. It can also be applied in many other repetitive work processes.

The race is about meeting the customer product demand as fast and as cost effective as possible. The time and the quantity of raw materials and finished product that is either in transit or in storage along the supply chain affects the profit margin for the product and if possible must be reduced.

The supply chain usually has multiple material flows and multiple finished products being produced. The supply chain in fact is made up of multiple supply chains that flow the physical material to product(s) transformation system(s). This parallel, multi-product supply system has a direct impact on the profit for the company.

In manufacturing, changeover is the process of converting a line or machine from running one product to another. Changeover times vary based on the design of the production equipment. The goal is to make it as short as economically possible.

Reducing changeover time creates more productive (value-added) time for production. Additionally, reducing changeover time allows reduction of production batch sizes, work-in-process (WIP), and inventory.

Changeover is the amount of time taken to change a piece of equipment from producing the last good piece of a production run to the first good piece of the next production run.

Changeover focuses on:

- Improving the timeliness of response to customer orders.
- Quality on the first next product.
- Improving the flow of the supply chain.
- Reducing inventory allowing the recovery of operating cash and manufacturing space.
- Increase production flexibility
- Increasing Throughput
- Eliminating setup adjustments

The required or target changeover time is determined by:

- What it takes to satisfy the customer.
- The available time and number of products to be produced on the same line.
- The cost of the changeover
- By the product family value stream capability.

Financially it comes down to the choice of spending capital to gain more capacity or storing more finished product to be able to ship to order or to optimizing the current capital investment by producing multiple products on one production line.

This generates questions such as,

- How much inventory is required for each product?
- How many changeovers are required to meet the customer demand?
- Would investing in more capacity be a better choice?
- Do I need to move inventory from DC to DC?

These are questions that determine the required changeover time. These are questions that leaders will answer at they set the changeover time targets.

The goal is to achieve a low variability, cost effective flow product to the customer.

What Flows?

"ITEMS" flow through a value stream

- In manufacturing, materials and finished product are items.
- In design & development, designs are the items.
- In service, external customer needs are the items.
- In administration, internal customer needs are the items.

Changeover Process

Changeover is focused on improving the supply chain flow.

Stress Free*[TM] *Changeover Solutions (COS) is presented in Six steps.

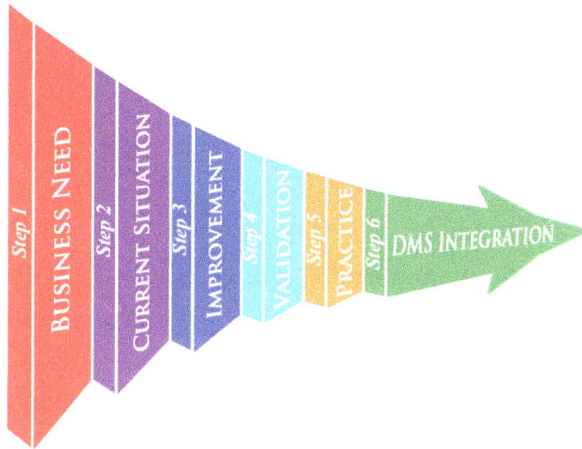

Change Over Process

Step 1: Business Need
- Opportunity Dimensions
- Changeover Focus Scope
- Preparing Changeover Improvement Participants

Step 2: Understand the Current Situation
- External changeover preparation
- Shutdown preparation
- Internal changeover
- Startup
- External Completion

Step 3: Make Improvement
- Separate Internal from External
- Streamline the internal
- Streamline the external

Step 4: Validate the Improvement
- Organizational Improvement
- Equipment Improvement

Step 5: Practice the Changeover

Step 6: Integrate into daily management system.

Step 1: Business Need

Leadership

Changeover improvement must be tied to a specific business need. The drivers for improving the time it takes to move from the production of one product to the production of the next product are:

1. The need to produce a greater number of products on the same line.
   The ability to produce multiple products on the same line helps reduces the capital that must be spent to build multiple lines.
2. The desire to free cash trapped in inventory.
   The ability to make the product on multiple smaller volume production runs allows the inventory to be kept at a lower level.
3. The desire for better on time delivery.
4. The ability to respond rapidly to an order enhances the organizations ability to meet variations or sudden requests that take the inventory level to zero.

Establish Changeover goal

Need Statement Steps

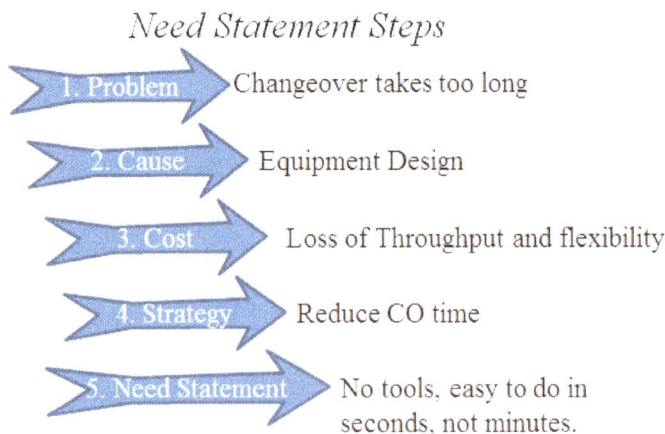

1. Problem	Changeover takes too long
2. Cause	Equipment Design
3. Cost	Loss of Throughput and flexibility
4. Strategy	Reduce CO time
5. Need Statement	No tools, easy to do in seconds, not minutes.

What does the business need?

Be aggressive – an improvement effort should yield 80% improvement

What do the operators need? The changeover improvement should make it easier for them.

Value of the Changeover

The value of improving the changeover is determined by several factors,

1. The dollar value of the finished product inventory.
2. The value of in-process materials
3. The value of the raw materials inventory
   These three are also referred to as trapped cash. This is money that could be freed up and potentially used to invest in growing the business or paying for improvement efforts.
4. The impact on customer service
   The ability to quickly respond to changing customer demand with no financial impact enhances the business performance.
5. The impact in the ability to be flexible and responsive to change.
   This is mentioned again for emphasis. A business that has the ability to respond with no loss is able to partner with their customers and improve the supply chain for all participants.

Business Linkage

This changeover concept is utilized in the product production area to facilitate the changeover from one product to the equipment or process set up for a second and different product. This changeover capability allows the reduction of finished product inventory and leverages the existing capital tied up in the equipment.

It is important to understand that changeover improvement comes from a variety of areas.

Organization Connection

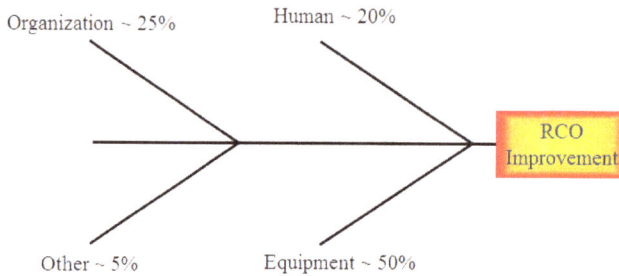

Organization ~ 25%   Human ~ 20%

RCO Improvement

Other ~ 5%   Equipment ~ 50%

Leaders define and set the behavior and culture of the organization. The organization design determines how it responds to the required work and to the variations that impact the work. Leaders must understand their supply chain as well as their business processes.

A leader's number one focus is to take the actions that ensure their customer's needs are met and exceeded. This customer focus drives the design of the entire organization.

The people involved in the work to satisfy the customer need to be enabled by a developmental, skill growth culture. The design of such a culture is detailed in *"Stress Free^{TM} Organization and Leadership Solutions*. This book will focus on optimizing the work of changing over from a specific series of work and equipment processes to another in as short a time as possible.

Human Connection

Humans and equipment do work. Equipment is used in the broad sense that includes computers and other data processors as well as the equipment that transforms raw materials into finished products.

Humans grow in capability over time. Equipment and processes must be developed by the humans. The growth of the human is determined by the leaders of the organization as well as the human's own drive and interest. The organization that stalls and fails, often does so because of leadership's failure to cultivate and grow the human capability.

This book focuses on developing both the human capability as well as simplifying the equipment and process to improve the speed of the changeover.

Equipment Connection

Changeover time is determined by equipment design and installation lay out. Reducing change over time requires that the human to equipment interaction be improved by making each task easier to do. Changeover time is reduced, when the work required to do it is reduced.

System Changeover

The changeover cycle is defined as the time it takes to go from "going to going". The changeover time begins when the production stop button is pressed. The changeover ends when the product is being produced at the target production rate.

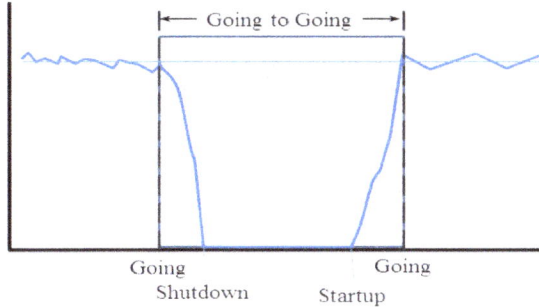

The system changeover may be going on in many places along the supply chain. These changeovers need to be synchronized to insure they are not affecting each other.

The going-to-going time is the focus for the improvement effort. Ideally it would be close to a zero gap in the production process.

System Layout

Changeover (CO) capability improvement is important when implementing statistical inventory replenishment. CO allows for the reduction of production pitch or production quantity orders. This in turn facilitates the reduction of inventory and improves the ability to serve the customer on time with at least a 99.7% customer delivery.

The concepts in *Stress Free^{TM} Changeover Solutions* are successful because of the second by second granularity of timing and analyzing the process of changing the equipment over. This increased granularity from hours and minutes to seconds provides new insights to improvement opportunities.

This approach builds on concepts presented in *Stress Free^{TM} Work Process Solutions.*

In Changeover improvement results in,
1. Reduced work effort.
2. The ability to reduce inventory
3. The ability to increase throughput.
4. Increase of on time product delivery

This provides a reward to everyone doing the work and a significant gain for the business.

Improvement Value Evaluation

Tying changeover improvement to a specific business need or goal ensures the effort will be valued. This value should be judged on the basis of a business investment. The required changeover improvement choices can then be judged the same as any other business investment.

The specific business linkage drives the changeover strategy. The cost of changeover helps to set this strategy.

Value Measurement

Optimal Changeover Time
(OCT)

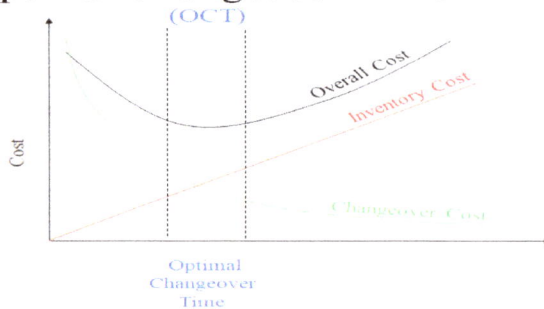

$$OCT = \sqrt{\frac{2 \cdot CO \frac{cost}{year}}{Inventory \frac{Cost}{Year}}}$$

Yearly CO cost = Changeover #/year · cost per changeover

Changeover Cost = [(Average Changeover time) x (Line Speed)(y products/min)] x [Cost per y product ($/product)]

Cost

The changeover cost coupled with the number of required changeovers and the inventory carrying costs can then be utilized to determine the value of making any improvement.

Being able to reduce the changeover time and therefore the cost of changeover moves the changeover curve on this diagram.

Changeover Preparation

The value to the business has been determined. Leadership is clear that an improvement to the changeover process will be important. An improvement team has been selected.

The team should be comprised of those doing the changeover and the people that will participate in improving the changeover. The changeover team should be paired with a person that will be observing and documenting the changeover action.

The team will need training that will include the changeover process and how success will be measured. This measure will be on value. Value to the person and value to the business.

Preparation insure, the success of the changeover improvement.

The Preparations Focuses on:
People
Each person on the team will have key roles that they must fulfill.

Safety Leader: must ensure all participants know and follow the safety requirements.

Change agent: Also known as the "devil's advocate" for constantly asking why or why not?

Support agent: This is the person who knows how to get stuff when needed.

Timing agent: Anyone in the observation role.

Documentation agent: the person willing to document each step of the process.
Often one person will fill several roles or people will partner up.

Role Clarification: Everyone needs some specific training. This is provided by the workshop trainer.

Role Walk Through: The trainer will also do an on the floor walk through of standardized Change Over Tasks

Role Floor Check
Proper parts in place

Needed Tools in place

Extraneous materials out of the way

Materials
Quantity – minimum required

Floor Location

Tools
Needed tools

Organized

Placed in the proper location

Change Parts
- Right parts
- Right condition
- Right Place
- Easy to verify

Walk-Through
Review Changeover each individual at their changeover location

It is important to get to the floor and watch the actual changeover in progress. The line team each have an observation partner. The line team member and the partner do a simulation of what the changeover entails. Production continues undisturbed.

External Changeover Preparation

This is the first part of the walk through. Each changeover location may have slightly different preparation. The cleanup procedure, the change part staging is described.

Shutdown preparation

The details of the shutdown process are described. Safety procedures are a key part of this preparation. Control system, mechanical, electrical, hydraulic and pneumatic lock out procedures are reviewed.

Internal Changeover

A step by step description of the changeover procedure is given by the changeover person. The changeover partners for the improvement process ask any clarifying questions.

The description is done with the production system running.

The end of a production line changeover is a point in time where extraordinary safety consideration needs to be observed.

Startup

Startup must be designed in a mistake proof fashion. Every individual on the changeover team has their personal lockout. Each individual must have a foolproof way to let the line leader know that it is safe to startup.

External Completion

The clean up around the production line and of the change parts is an important step but may not be as time dependent as the internal changeover duration.

Make final preparation

Initial improvements may already have been identified. These initial ideas may be tried and evaluated. These initial ideas need to be documented and the modified procedures talked through.

Change Over Limitations

Equipment

The intent is to experience the first changeover trial with no equipment change. Subsequent changeovers may require minor changes, but they will be those changes that can be made immediately such as,

- Change parts location
- Tool location
- Safety cover bolt number reduction
- Quick disconnect application.

Any changes must be reviewed for safety and approved as safe to do.

Material

Material placement and movement out of the way are often important to consider. Safely handling material movement away from the change area and then returning prior to startup should be considered where the space is tight.

System

Any control system changes that are required to run the next product are a part of the changeover process. Often these changes must be documented as a way to verify the changeover.

Legal/Cultural

Some businesses have legal changeover requirements. These must be specifically adhered to. However even the legal requirements should be examined to ensure they were properly interpreted.

There are often environmental or work process limitations. The changeover teams are often limited by the number of available people and the workspace around the production line.

Additionally, there may be a variety of legal requirements that impact the changeover process or speed.

Define the required Changeover time.

Calculation of the
Required Changeover Time

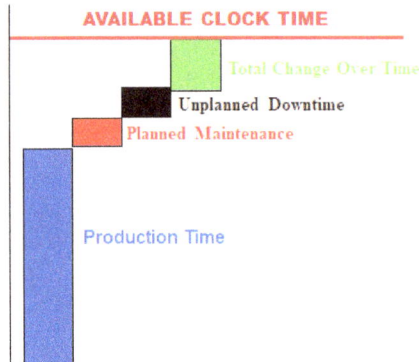

AVAILABLE CLOCK TIME

Total Change Over Time

Unplanned Downtime

Planned Maintenance

Production Time

1. Determine Available Clock Time
   a. Begin with total Time
   b. Remove Lunches and Breaks
   Note: CO, PM and Unplanned Time is include in the available time.
2. Determine the time to produce the customer required product (Production Time)
3. Subtract Production Time from the Available Clock Time.
4. Subtract Planned Maintenance from the Available Clock Time.
5. Subtract Unplanned Downtime from the Available Clock Time.
6. What Remains is the Total Change Over Time.
7. Divide the Total Change Over Time by the Target time for Changeovers.
   • This result is the **TOTAL NUMBER OF CHANGE OVERS THAT CAN BE SCHEDULED.**
8. Divide the Total Change Over Time by the number of changes required to run the scheduled production.
   • This result is the Required Change Over Time.

Defining the required changeover time is key step in determining if Changeover improvement is warranted. This required changeover time can then serve as a lens by which to evaluate all transformation points along the supply chain. This ensures the improvement at one point along the supply chain can be properly supported and maintained.

Chapter 1 Tips and Tools:

1. Use Case Study File / Workbook
2. Determine the changeover value
3. Determine the changeover success measure
4. Do a mental, verbal and on the floor walkthrough

Step 2 Current Situation

Now it is time to do it. Each step will be studied and documented.
The following documents will all be used,

- Time Observation Sheet
- Travel Diagram
- Detailed Motion Chart
- Task Chart (alias Zigzag) chart
- Brainstorm Fishbone
- Change Over Observation

Each document will peel back the cover and expose the root cause solution.

Time Observation Sheet

This will provide detailed times for each movement the changeover requires.
The external steps will be documented separately from the internal steps.

TIME OBSERVATION SHEET

Tasks	Step	Steps	Observed Step Times - sec	Lowest Repeat time	Lowest Time	Highest Time	Range	Travel Distance	Travel Time	Notes
1 Start		Log-out		0			0			
2		Lockout					0			
3		Electrical					0			
4		Mechanical					0			
5		Pnuematic					0			
6		Control System					0			
7		Remove Safety Guard					0			
8 Collator		Vacuum equipment					0			
9		Examine equipment					0			
10		begin change					0			
11							0			empty automatically
12		unbolt tray					0			
13		- remove tray and put					0			
14 Tampon chain		remove pusher					0			

Operator: *Date*   *Observer*

Preparation of the Time Observation sheet

Have the changeover person describe every task and the steps of that task that they will be taking. This listing will be adjusted during actual observation if additional actions are necessary.

Step 2 Current Situation
Travel Diagram
Initial Travel Diagram

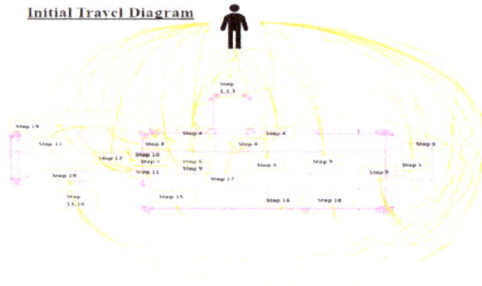

Improved Travel Diagram

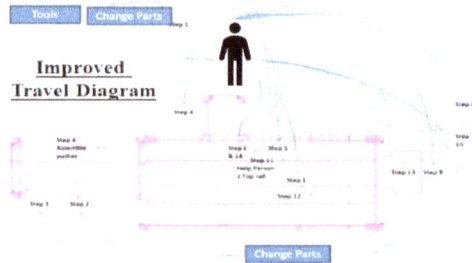

Final Travel Diagram

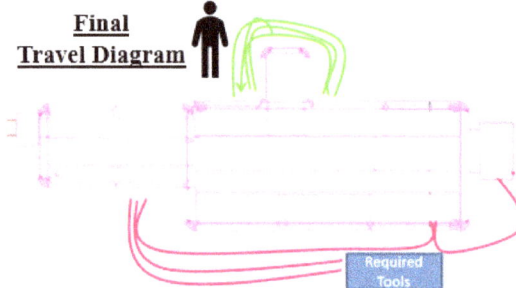

The travel diagram is used to understand the human movement at the high level. The travel diagram is very visual and allows for the immediate identification of improvements.

Detailed Motion Chart

The detailed motion diagram is the tool for the motion when the person is standing or sitting in one place doing the work.

1. Observe the work being done
2. Capture the body motion of the individual doing the work
3. Show the type of motions and the number of repetitive ones.
4. Identify hard work or highly repetitive work
5. Note improvements, issues on task and time and motion chart

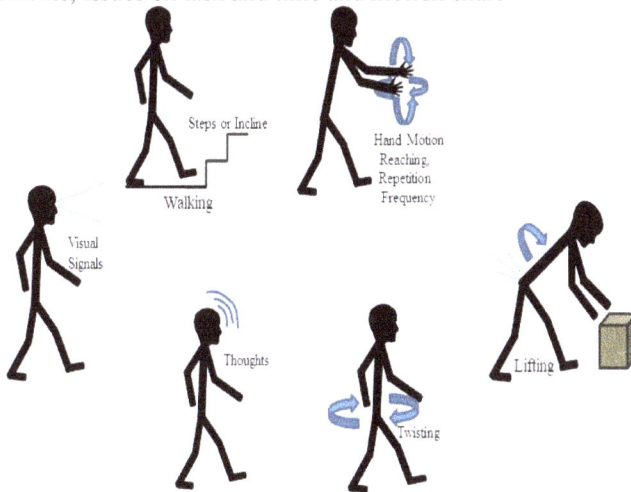

Task Chart (alias Zigzag) chart

This provides a visual of the value add and required steps. It is more often used in the office area or in a document management area.

Task Chart													
Work Process		Date											
			○	✚	➡	△	▣	D	◇	▭	ft	Min	Min
Steps	Step Description	Value Add	NVA but reqd	Travel	Storage	Inspection	Delay	Rework	NVA	Distance	Time	Effort	Comments

Brainstorm Fishbone

Brainstorm Fishbone

Changeover is one of the few places that I recommend brainstorming. The fishbone helps to organize the element of the brainstorm.

Change Over Observation

The changeover will be slowly executed, and detailed documentation created or updated. This slow execution is a time when the process is examined for its ease of execution or any issues. It is a time that is rich with improvement discovery.

Use a separate detailed observation chart for each section.

If there are enough resources have one person timing each step, in seconds, one person capturing the motion, one person immediately documenting. It is very common to have three persons teaming up to document the changeover.

- **External Preparation**
  This preparation will be done for the entire production line. Use the detailed observation chart.

- **Shutdown**
  The changeover improvement teams will synchronize their actions and shut down the line as one group. Safety procedure will be strictly followed, and lockout will include all elements.
  Once the lockout is complete the internal changeover begins.

- **Internal Changeover**
  Each section of the line has a specific team to address the changeover. One team member will do the physical part of the changeover while the other documents the action.
  Once all teams have completed the changeover the line will be restarted by the operating team. All safety procedures are strictly adhered to

- **Startup**
  The all clear must be declared by each changeover improvement team. The line leader points to and acknowledges the clear signal from each improvement team.

- **External Completion**
  The changeover teams continue their improvement work until all the external work complete.

This initial look may seem detailed. It is done this way in order to develop a deeper understanding of the changeover processes. It is executed slowly and should be studied thoroughly.

Chapter 2 Tips and Tools

1. Observe the Changeover

Step 3 Identify & Improve

Create Changeover Timing Chart

Document the action of each changeover person (measure to seconds)

a) Time Observation Chart (example actions observed)

1. Walk to electrical lockout   _____ sec
2. Lock out electrical   _____ sec
3. Walk to pneumatic   _____ sec
4. Lock out pneumatic   _____ sec
5. Walk to operator side   _____ sec
6. Open guard.   _____ sec
7. Turn around and go to table   _____ sec
8. Select specific Allen wrench   _____ sec
9. Go back to filler   _____ sec
10. Open three locking screws   _____ sec

   Etc. usually between 50 to 100 steps

This timing chart would be the focus for the entire changeover. After the completion of the changeover this information would be analyzed by plotting it on a stacked bar chart.

b) Plot the results on a stacked bar chart.

Example: Observation Stacked bar

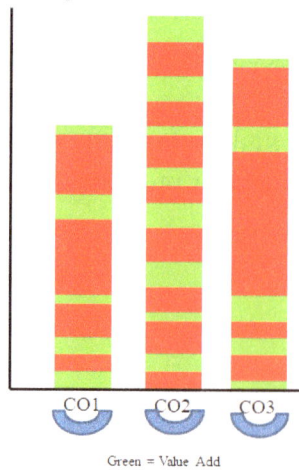

CO1   CO2   CO3

Green = Value Add

(scale it in seconds, do in pencil, one bar for each person)

1. First action at the base of the bar

2. Each subsequent action above it.
3. Color value add action – Green
4. Color non-value add action in RED
5. Estimate the potential improvement and if the work could be done with fewer people.

c) Review with CO Team

1. Pick an immediate go do improvement
2. Ask operations team to do, a go do after each change over
3. Pick the focus for a full RCO Improvement

Step 3 Identify Improvement Opportunities

Look at the red and:

- Eliminate all unnecessary tasks, motions, movement, steps, or parts that need changing.
- Look for ways to have universal parts.
- Question if something needs changing at all.
- Simplify Make things simple to do.
- Eliminate the need for precise measurement by using jigs, fixtures, stop blocks, gage blocks, detents, etc.
- Improve methods to do tasks by examining the functional requirement and simplify.

Try the Improvements

Establish New Changeover Process

The analysis yields a great number of improvements that require several changeover cycles to validate the improvement. Up to three changeovers should be target during the changeover improvement week.

Schedule and Execute full CO practice for line team

Once all activities of the changeover are documented and displayed on a timing chart more ideas to improve the changeover are identified following a four-step approach:

1. **Maximize External effort**
   - Observe each Internal Action a second time
   - Analyze the Internal Action a second time
   - Brainstorm Improvement to allow more external work
   - Identify a third improvement to try

2. **Optimize the Internal**
   - Observe each Internal Action a second time
   - Analyze the Internal Action a second time
   - Brainstorm Improvement to speed up internal
   - Identify a third improvement to try

3. Optimize the External
- Observe each External Action a second time
- Analyze the external Action a second time
- Brainstorm Improvement to reduce the work
- Try Improvement

4. Eliminate Adjustments
- Observe each Adjustment
- Brainstorm Improvement
- Apply Poke Yoke
- Implement Improvements

5. Brainstorm Improvement
- No Time-Eliminate time wasters from changeover.
- No Tools-Eliminate wherever possible the use of a tool.
- Make use of simple, hand-operated devices.
- No Talent-Make it so simple anyone can do it.

Try the ideas and incorporate the ones that work. Do these trials in rapid but controlled evaluation trials.

Step 3 Tools and Tips
1. Develop Initial Timing Chart
2. Clarify Internal and External Actions
3. Brainstorm Improvements

VALIDATION
Step 4

Step 4: Validate Selected Changeover Improvements

True Statistical validation takes several weeks to several months. That level of validation is part of the changeover process, but immediate validation comes during the improvement period. The immediate validation is done in the same week when the improvement is achieved. The longer-term validation is done as part of the Daily Management System. The short-term validation should be based on the measures that will be used to maintain the changeover process.

The proof of improvement rewards those doing the improvement and the business is assured of effort and money well spent.

Organizational Validation Elements

Integration of the changeover progress into the daily management process ensures longer term survival for the improvement.

Training materials, engineering documents, and equipment operation instructions all need to be updated.

Equipment Validation Elements

Equipment operation and maintenance should be closely scrutinized to ensure the changeover improvement has not cause any production issues. Safety and Quality are the two main elements to validate.

Chapter 4 Tips and Tools

1. Get an analyst to specify the long-term validation statistics.
2. Work with the maintenance members to ensure mechanical integrity and ease of maintenance.
3. Do a second quality validation design with the product quality owners.
4. Do a safety evaluation of all actions of the changeover.

Step 5: Practice Selected Changeover improvements

Practice of the changeover should be scheduled as part of the production process. The only difference between a normal changeover and a practice one is that the practice one has some additional observers watching and timing the changeover. Their observations and feedback are incorporated into keeping the changeover at its peak performance.

Step 5 Tips and Tools

1. Use Observation timing sheet.
2. Have experts from other lines be the observers.
3. Plan and schedule practices out into the future.

Step 6: Integrate into Daily Management System (DMS)

- Identify Leadership Actions to Maintain RCO Capability
- Identify a sustaining leader changeover partner
- Periodically check changeover time
- Dept Manager Participates 1 time per week
- Operations Manager observes CO 1 time per month
- Evaluate Reapplication of improvement

Step 6 Tips and Tools

1. Make the changeover evaluation and time achievement part of the DMS review.

Stress Free™
Daily Management
Solutions

Ron
MUELLER P. E.

Stress Free[TM] Daily Management Solutions
Zero Defect, Twenty-Four Hour, Management

By: Ron Mueller

Around the World Publishing LLC
4914 Cooper Road Suite 144
Cincinnati, Ohio 45242-9998

ISBN 13:
ISBN 10:

Distributed by Ingram
Cover Picture By: Drazen Zigic, Shutterstock.com
Cover Design By: Ron Mueller

TECHNICAL EDITOR:
Gordon Miller P. E.

Dedication
To all the people that want to make it
a stable, organized execution of daily work
and to make work life manageable

Acknowledgments
To all the people that want a stable and well-organized workday and
want to make their work life more manageable.

Daily Management Contents

Daily Management Introduction

Daily Management

Daily management is by definition the management of the work done by people on multiple teams and by multiple organizations engaged at several organizational levels in the transformation of materials and information into products desired by the customer and the production of organization reports desired by the organization leaders.

Maintain and Improve

There are two sides to Daily Management.

There is Daily Work Management (D.W.M.) and there is the Daily Continuous Improvement (D.C.I.).

Daily Work Management (D.W.M.) focuses on Maintaining the work environment at a zero loss, zero waste condition. It is always focused on ensuring that the next twenty-four hours are at standard.

Daily Continuous Improvement (D.C.I.) focuses on the creation of new skills, improvement of the supply chain transformation elements and improving the customer's satisfaction by providing what is desired when it is desired and where it is desired.

What is Stress Free™ Daily Management Solutions?

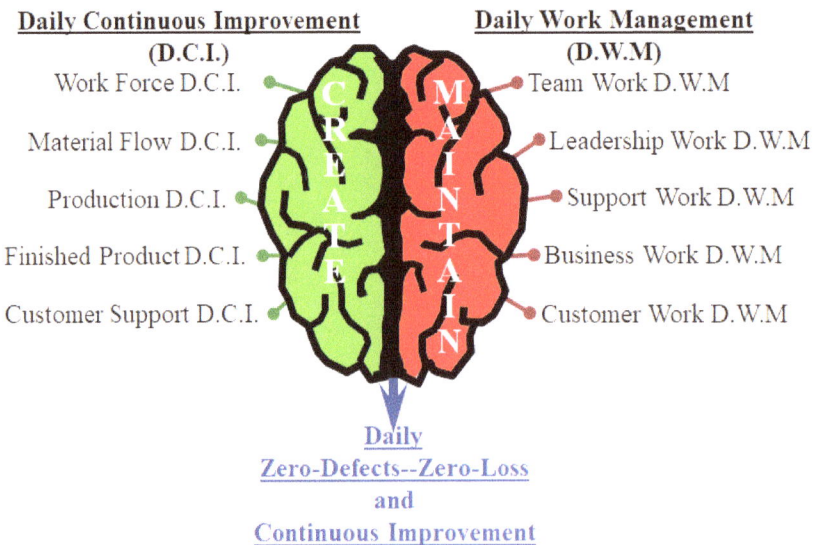

Daily Continuous Improvement (D.C.I.)

Work Force D.C.I.
Material Flow D.C.I.
Production D.C.I.
Finished Product D.C.I.
Customer Support D.C.I.

Daily Work Management (D.W.M)

Team Work D.W.M
Leadership Work D.W.M
Support Work D.W.M
Business Work D.W.M
Customer Work D.W.M

Daily
Zero-Defects--Zero-Loss
and
Continuous Improvement

Daily Management Goal

The goal of zero product defects, zero material waste and zero lost time for the next twenty-four hours is achieved by utilizing an organized daily management method detailed in Stress Free^{TM} Daily Management Solutions.

This daily management is based on the participation of the entire organization. It requires leadership coordination and adherence to standards.

Leadership begins on the line operating team. Each operating team member has a secondary role along with their line operation role. Operating team members assume a secondary role such as Safety coordinator, Quality coordinator, Throughput tracker, Maintenance coordinator, OEE tracker, Team leader.

The Operating team leaders, one per shift, utilize the output production tracking sheet to understand the operational situation and communicate with the next shift and the department manager.

The use of a standard agenda and the use of the Production Output Tracking sheet supports effective and efficient meetings up through the organization's leadership.

Daily Management Value

The stability generated by an organization practicing daily management generates zero losses for each 24-hour operating period, resulting in millions of dollars savings all along the entire supply chain.

Value Elements

The primary purpose of business is to make money. The specific elements of time, materials, production, finished product and consumer satisfaction are all involved in creating the business value or generating the desired profit. A stable production system supports these business goals.

Time

Time is an element in all the actions and transformations that occur along the supply chain. It is the metric that allows the measurement of consistency. Think of time as the universal element: the time to bring in raw materials, the time to handle the raw materials, the time to transport the raw materials to the point of transformation, the time to transform the raw materials into a finished product, the time to move the finished product to a temporary holding area, the time to retrieve and load the finished product onto the transport vehicle, the time to transport the finished product to the buying customer, the time to put the finished product into the hands of the final consumer.

Time is the fundamental unit.

Materials

The materials to make a product need to come together in an orchestrated way that meets the flow of each material moving into the production realm. It is important to synchronize each material with the flow required by the transformation process. The application of the Incoming Material Tracking tool highlights issues with key materials needed for production.

Production

The transformation of materials at the customer product pull rate results in the ability to hold a cost-effective inventory level. It also supports stable and consistent production work practices.

The primary tools are Production Output Tracking, Standard Daily Management meeting agendas, use of visual signals and a clear split of production and maintenance responsibilities.

Finished Product Handling

Holding a three-sigma level (this level assures that 99.7% of the time there will be enough inventory) of finished product inventory and handling the inventory a minimal number of times contributes to finished product stability. This stability reflects the condition of all the work processes and actions up stream in the supply chain.

The ability to deliver the finished product to the customer, on time, in the quantity desired, at the point desired completes the business cycle.

Finished Product Output tracking aids in creating a stable controllable system.

Customer Satisfaction

A satisfied customer is the goal of every business. The Stress Free^{TM} approach asks the customer what they want and then it meets the customer requirement and generates customer satisfaction and a desire for continued partnership.

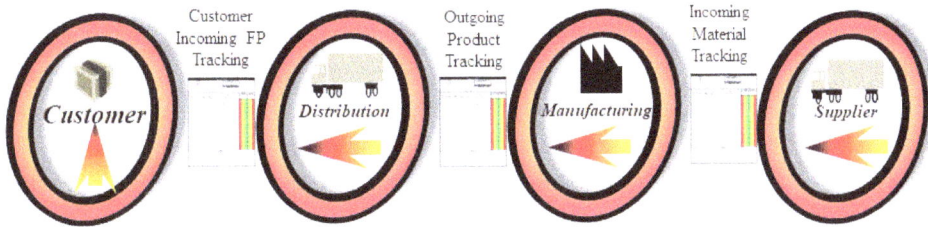

Output and Input tracking utilized at partner boundaries provides a simple, common language way to understand the flow issues.

Output tracking is explained in detail in chapter eight.

Achieved Value

The Stress Free^{TM} approach, tools and techniques consistently deliver the desired results. Time, material, and finished product inventory is reduced. Production throughput and finished product handling is synchronized to the customer pull. The customer in all cases is more satisfied and develops a closer working relationship with you, their supplier.

Daily Management Tools (See chapter 8)

The tools used to create and maintain Stress Free^{TM} Daily Management Solutions are a set of simple techniques, meetings, team, and leadership practices. These elements used in a specific way and managed in a specific time sequence result in a supply chain flow that experiences minimum loss and achieves high stability. The people implementing the techniques and tools all experience work process stability and error free work that results in an environment that invigorates them.

Daily Management Implementation

Some key considerations when implementing Stress Free^{TM} Daily Management Solutions are; the organization design, team-oriented work processes, just in time and mistake proof practices, no over production and meeting the customer expectations.

The Production Area Personnel at the top.

Daily Management begins with the production line operating teams. The production operating teams ensure that the material transformation leading to the product desired by the purchasing customer is defect free at the minimum loss possible for the current system. These teams take part in Daily Work Management (D.W.M) and in Daily Continuous Improvement (D.C.I.)

What is Stress Free™ Daily Management Solutions?

Each production line team is supported by the production line team leader. This team leader is an integral member of the production line team but has earned the role of leading the team. He or she makes sure the team works to standard and the team continues to develop their skills.

Daily Management Organization Structure Example

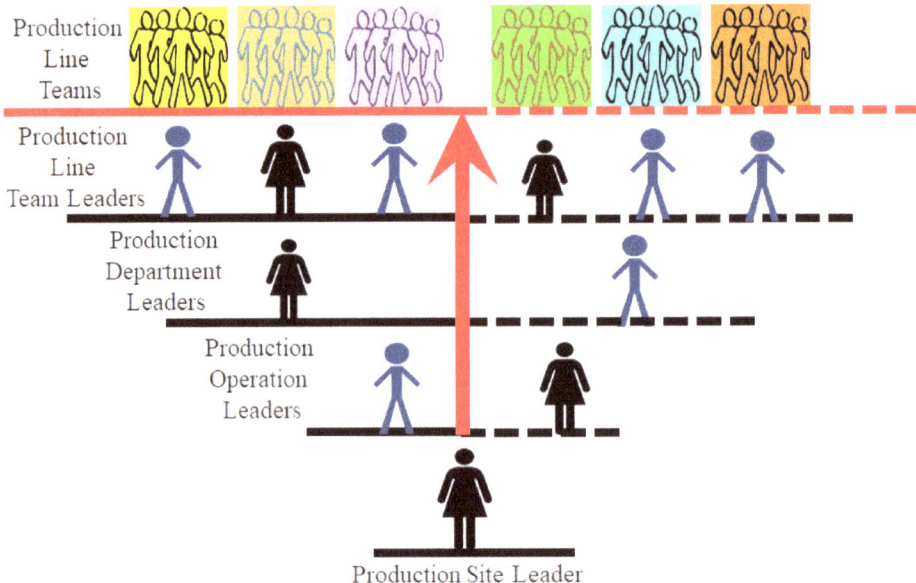

Production line teams are in turn supported by the Production Department Leader. The Production Department Leader normally represents the first organizational level that manages a spend budget. This budget is largely focused on maintaining the production transformation processes. This leader is often the first level responsible for the entire line for every twenty-four-hour period.

Production Department Leaders are supported by Production Operations Leaders. The Production Operations Leader manages personnel assignment and often directly ensures the Daily Continuous Improvement (DCI) for the work force, the material flow and finished product flow.

The role of supporting Finished Product Handling is normally a logistics role at the Operation level and includes handling the storage and the shipment of the finished product.

The Customer Support is most often handled by the production site leader in conjunction with a customer sales representative.

Support organizations: Safety, Quality, Engineering, Accounting participate in the Daily Production Management activities in a support role and then hold their own Daily Management meeting.

The size of the organization determines the number of organizational levels and the responsibilities of each level. The five levels described will fit all medium to large production facilities. Smaller organization normally still required a solid daily management system. The main difference is that the people in the smaller organization wear multiple responsibility hats.

The application of Stress Free^{TM} Daily Management Solutions applies to all organization sizes.

Chapter 1: Line Shift Team Daily Management

The shift operating team operates and maintains the production line. They are responsible for a flawless shift. It is important for the operating team to have a successful, flawless shift and to ensure that the next shift is set up to continue the flawless operation and maintenance of the production line.

Daily Management Activities

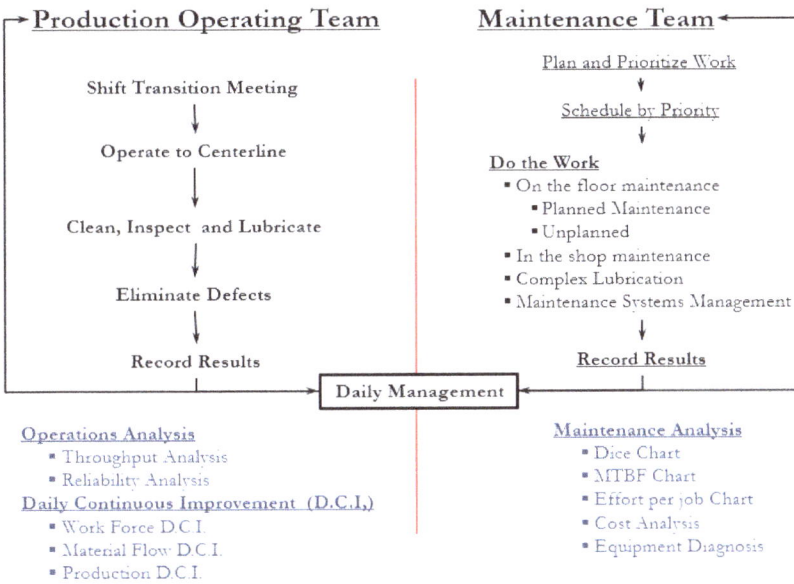

Production Operating Team

Shift Transition Meeting

↓

Operate to Centerline

↓

Clean, Inspect and Lubricate

↓

Eliminate Defects

↓

Record Results

Maintenance Team

Plan and Prioritize Work

↓

Schedule by Priority

↓

Do the Work
- On the floor maintenance
  - Planned Maintenance
  - Unplanned
- In the shop maintenance
- Complex Lubrication
- Maintenance Systems Management

↓

Record Results

[Daily Management]

Operations Analysis
- Throughput Analysis
- Reliability Analysis

Daily Continuous Improvement (D.C.I.)
- Work Force D.C.I.
- Material Flow D.C.I.
- Production D.C.I.

Maintenance Analysis
- Dice Chart
- MTBF Chart
- Effort per job Chart
- Cost Analysis
- Equipment Diagnosis

Production Line Operation Team

Daily Management Sequence

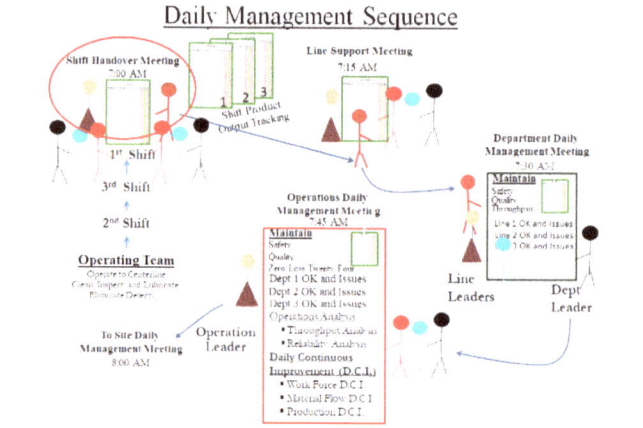

Shift Hand Over meeting

OBJECTIVE: Understand gaps from previous shift to support setting the right priorities for the next shift
Peer to peer information handover to get basic understanding of the previous shift

	Focus	Who	Information Needed
Safety	Incident	Shift line leader	Incident forms
	Unsafe condition & behaviour	Shift line leader	Verbal information
	Behavior Observation Plan	Shift line leader	
Quality	Quality Issues	Shift quality operator owner	Incident forms & sample
	Finished product sample for oncoming team to check	Shift quality operator owner	one bag of product
Throughput	Planned production	Shift line leader	Upcoming shift production plan
	Production output	Shift line leader	Previous shift output tracking
	Top Loss - Unplanned Stops	Shift line leader	Previous shift output tracking
	Changer Over (C/O) plan	Shift line leader	Upcoming shift production plan
Stability	Clean Inspect and Lubricate (CIL) plan	Shift CIL operator owner	CIL history
	Current Team CIL Completion	Shift CIL operator owner	CIL history
	Equipment touches (ET)	Shift (ET) operator owner	Equipment Touches history and goal
	Defect elimination (DE)	Shift (DE) operator owner	Defect elimination history and goal
	Support need	Shift line leader	

PARTICIPANTS

1 On coming shift line leader	4 Shift Process Technician
2 Off going shift line leader	6 Shift maintenance technician
3 On coming line operators	7 Shift E&I technician

Shift Hand Over Meeting

The shift handover meeting is the beginning of a sequence that flows up to the production operation level. Each organizational level utilizes a similar agenda. This supports a common language and similar culture throughout the organization.
The shift hand over meeting is focused on the off going shift updating the oncoming shift. The meeting is intended to be focused and short. Output tracking puts all the information on one sheet. Technology is changing how the output tracking sheet is shared. It is now feasible to do this via the i-phone.

This meeting format is followed up to the Operation level. Each organizational level will add items to the agenda for which they are responsible.

The oncoming team leader reviews the previous two shifts output tracking. This provides context for what happened during the time the shift team had been off.

The outgoing production operating team leader conducts a transition meeting with the oncoming production operating team. The exchange focuses on any safety and quality issues as well as the production system reliability and throughput achieved. If improvements have been made this is also communicated

.The shift production output tracking chart is the focus of this discussion. The output tracking chart shows the hour by hour scheduled and achieved production volume. Hourly notes capture the production system performance. The line reliability is tracked on an hour by hour basis.

It is critical that each of the meetings is focused and in the fifteen-minute range.

Output Tracking

The output tracking sheet is a comprehensive hour by hour presentation of the line production.

Output Tracking

Area: A+B+C +Applicator
Team: Customization team
Shift: Day shift
Area Leader: Maria Huyhn

Total Target Flow	980	
Produced to Schedule	980	
Produced Overall	980	

Available Time: 7 hours
Cycle Time: 40 sec person
Unit Min: 2 boxes

Simple OEE: 100.0%

Time hr.	Product	Target Flow	Actual Flow	Difference	Leader Initials	Issue and Root Cause	Root Cause Responsibility	By Date	Stability Tracking −	+
1	Facial Treatment Package	140	140	0						
2	Facial Treatment Package	140	135	(5)		Package scratch Quality Issue				
3	Facial Treatment Package	140	140	0						
4	Facial Treatment Package	0	0	0						
5	Facial Treatment Package	140	140	0						
6	Facial Treatment Package	140	140	0						
7	Facial Treatment Package	140	140	0						
8	Facial Treatment Package	140	145	5						
9										
10										
11										
12										

Shift Summary

Five quality defect. Made up at last hour 8.

Shift ended with complete scheduled production

Output Tracking forms the basis of communication along the supply chain and up through the organization. The daily meeting agenda and format utilizes output tracking as a basis for a common discussion.

Output or input tracking should be utilized at every supply chain boundary. Output tracking is a simple form that provides the participants on two sides of an organizational or supply chain boundary to communicate clearly. It provides the information that results in reducing the problems at every boundary.

Products of Chapter 1:
1. Aligned focused operating team
2. Safe operation
3. Stability and product produced at Quality
4. Zero Loss next twenty-four hours.

Chapter 1 Tips and Tools
1. Use Standard Meeting Agenda
2. Use output tracking
3. Use Next Twenty-Four Task List
4. Schedule Support help

Chapter 2: Line Team Leader Daily Management Support Meeting

The line leader meets with the line support members to review the issues facing the operating team and to determine if the line support personnel agree that they are able to handle the identified issues. The intent is to make sure that the line has the required support for the next upcoming shift.

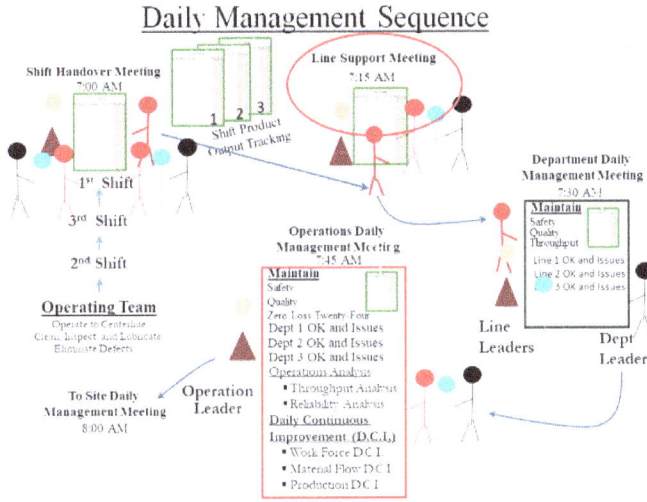

Daily Management Sequence

The agenda that is followed is the same as the line shift team used. This makes for a quick transition for the line leader in the discussions with the support team.

The Line support meeting allows the line leader to marshal the resources needed to address any of the current issues facing the line.

Critical Item Task List

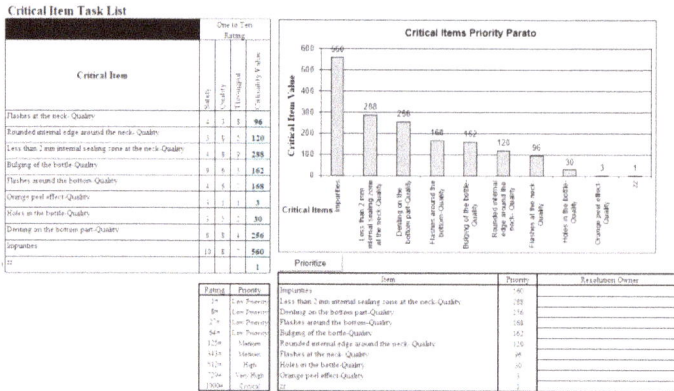

A key product is the Critical Item Task list. The critical items are listed, and resolution owners assigned. This focus is aimed at producing a zero loss for the next twenty-four-hours. The items are rated as to criticality and then action is taken based on priority.

The coordination and sharing of information with the support personnel eliminates surprise situations. It also determines if the any item on the critical list requires resource beyond the line support team.

Daily Management Maintenance Support

The maintenance organization is a critical partner with the line operating team. They provide equipment training, equipment maintenance and critical lubrication and coach the operating team how to do the less difficult lubrication when the line is down for cleaning.

The maintenance organization supports the operating team when significant maintenance is required. The degree of maintenance support is determined by the experience of the shift operating team and the condition of the production equipment. An example maintenance plan is shown.

The goal is to maintain the line at its peak operating condition. For this to occur maintenance work needs to be closely coordinated with the operation. It is important to schedule major maintenance work, just as it is important to schedule product production.

The maintenance goal is to manage maintenance time in such a way as to optimize the production time.

The production line operator skills are improved to the point that they do the normal line lubrication and minor repairs. This is a key part of growing the production line skills. This operator hands on approach to line maintenance dramatically improves production line performance.

Output tracking captures this performance on an hour by hour basis.

The goals for the maintenance area are,

- To achieve a 100%, line operation request response.
- To plan and schedule 90% of maintenance tasks thirty days in advance.
- To have 95% of maintenance tasks
- To have a maintenance strategy for all equipment
- To have a visual annual maintenance schedule.

The maintenance department has multiple responsibilities. There are eleven mentioned in this book. This list is not all inclusive.

Daily Management

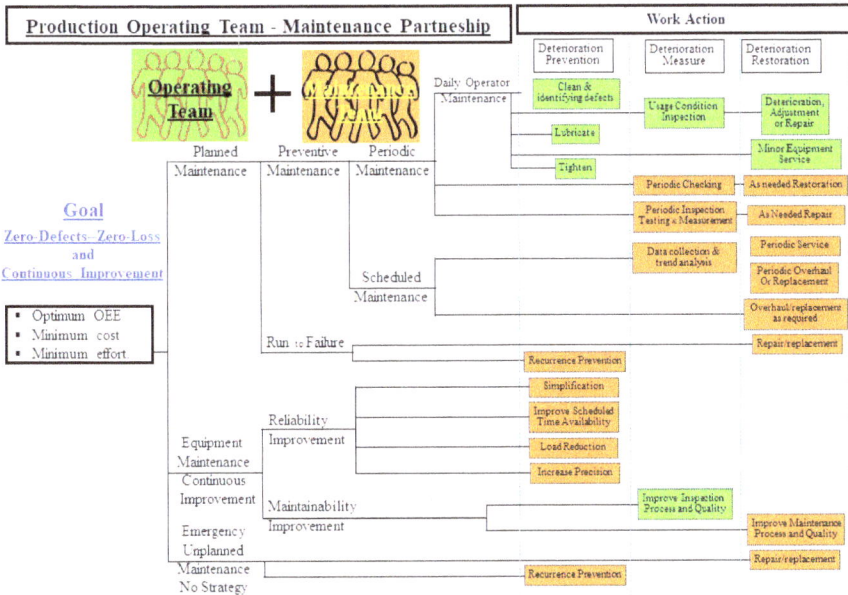

Products of Chapter 2:

1. Aligned focused operating team
2. Safe Operation
3. Stability and Product produced at Quality
4. Zero Loss Next twenty-four hours.

Chapter 2 Tips and Tools

1. Use Standard Meeting Agenda
2. Use output tracking
3. Use Next Twenty-Four Task List
4. Schedule Support help

Chapter 3: Department Daily Management

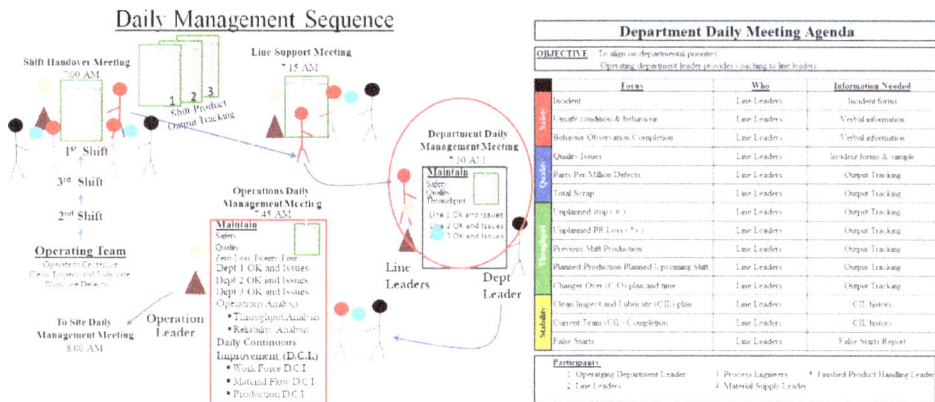

Daily Management Sequence

The department daily meeting comes after the operating team leaders support meetings. All the Line leaders are done reviewing the previous shift performance utilizing the Production Output Tracking Charts. They understand the condition of their line. They are clear about their needs. They have evaluated the ability of the line to meet the upcoming shift's needs.

Safety is the first item to address. The person responsible for Safety leads this session. This person asks each line leader for comment. Use of red, green, and yellow cards allows for quick indication of the safety status. Only those showing a yellow or red card need to talk.

The person responsible for Quality follows a similar process.

The person responsible for identifying throughput issues follows as similar process.

Throughput is addressed by the department manager. The department manager announces the expected product production by line and highlights any special line action that will be required.

Again, only the line that has a problem signals in red. The rest show a green.

251

The logic to get resources for a specific problem focuses first on the line operating team solving their own problem. If the team does not have the skill or have other issues that prevent them from solving the problem, the resource request follows the logic.

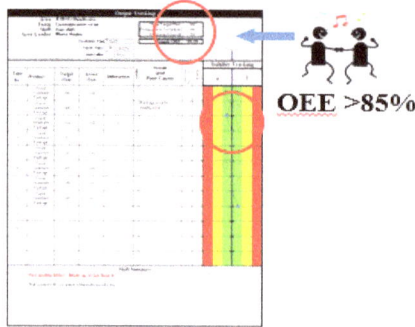

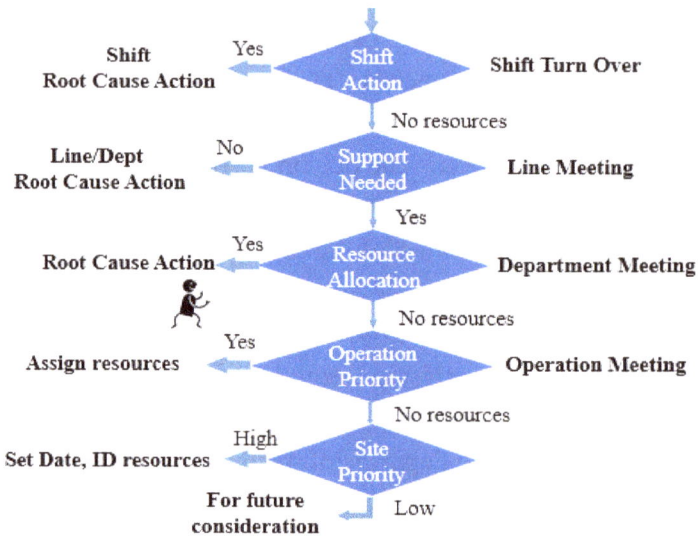

This resource need logic flows up to the site priority level.

Individual, Team and Department Skill Evaluation
Individual Skill Summary

Equipment and people do work. It takes maintenance to keep equipment in good condition. Equipment needs constant maintenance. It never improves.

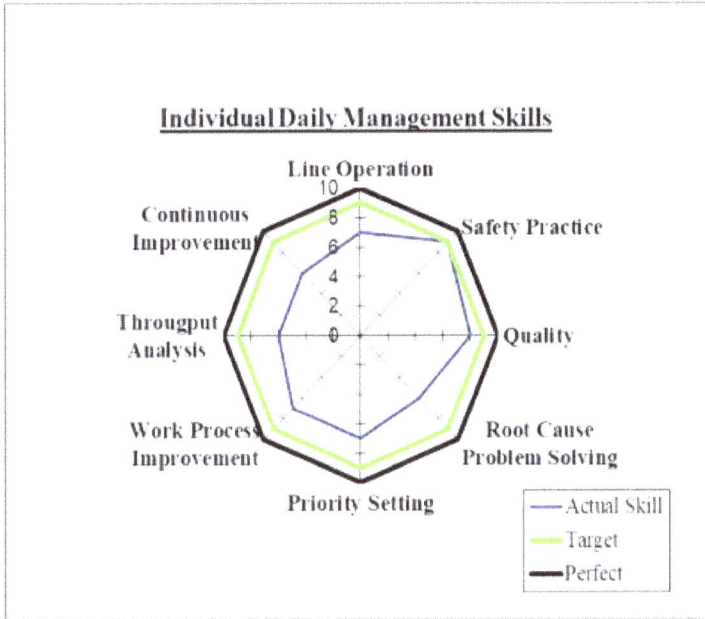

Individual Daily Management Skills

People do work and if nurtured grow and continuously improve. They take care of it and improve it.

Monitoring the skills of every individual and helping them set skill improvement goals ensures that the individual is improving in the currently needed skills. It also allows setting of skill growth that will be needed in the future.

Using a visual display of the individual's skills provides a way for leadership to coach the individual.

Line Team Skill Summary

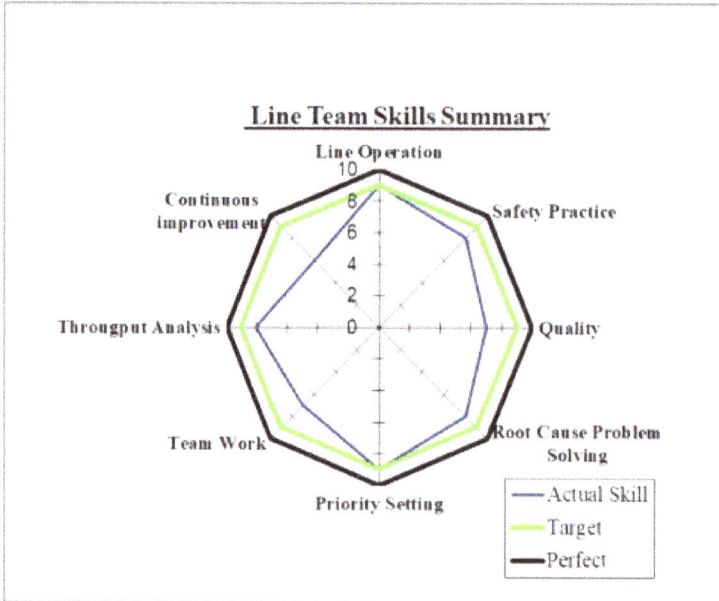

A visual line team, composite skill summary is a good way for line leader and department manager to understand what skills need to be further developed in the operating team. It also allows line team members to select the skill growth that best helps the team.

The lowest score for this team is in their continuous improvement area. However, they could also improve in how they handle quality issues and they also have an opportunity in improving their teamwork.

Department Skill Summary

The composite skill profiled for the department guides the department manager in choosing the areas to focus the coaching and provides guidance in the selection of the training to give the department member.

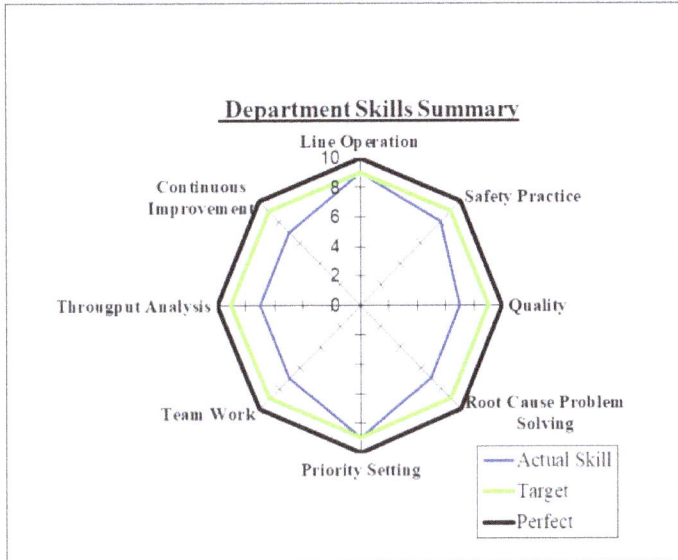

This diagram would guide me to select root cause problem solving training for the department. Root Cause training would most likely improve the throughput analysis capability and improvements coming out of solving some problems at root cause may improve the quality rating.

Products of Chapter 3:

1. Aligned, focused department
2. Safe Operation
3. Stability and Product produced at Quality
4. Zero Loss Next twenty-four hours.

Chapter 3 Tips and Tools

1. Use Standard Meeting Agenda
2. Use output tracking
3. Use the resource allocation logic.
4. Use Next Twenty-Four Task List
5. Schedule Support help

Chapter 4: Operation Daily Management

The daily management process began with the operating line team and its leader. The line leader met with the line support team to discuss needs of the line team and to understand support actions that might impact the line operation. It then brought together all the operating team leaders in a meeting with the department leader. The department leader gained a detailed understanding of the line needs and then proceeded on to the Operations daily meeting.

Daily Management Sequence

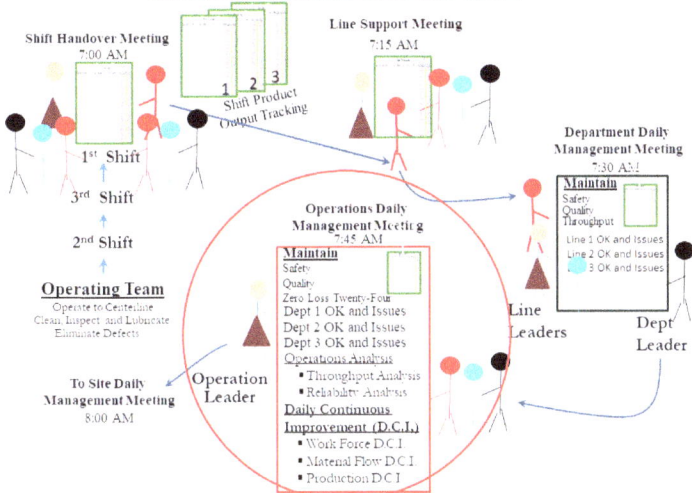

The Operations Daily Management Meeting has two parts; the **Maintain** and **Continuous Improvement**.

Maintain

The Maintain part of the agenda is a duplicate of all previous agendas. The maintain items are addressed by each department and support area as needed.

Each department leader brings their Safety, Quality and Throughput priority needs. These needs are visually displayed in a Pareto format. The goal is to clearly communicate what resources will be needed to maintain continuous improvement.

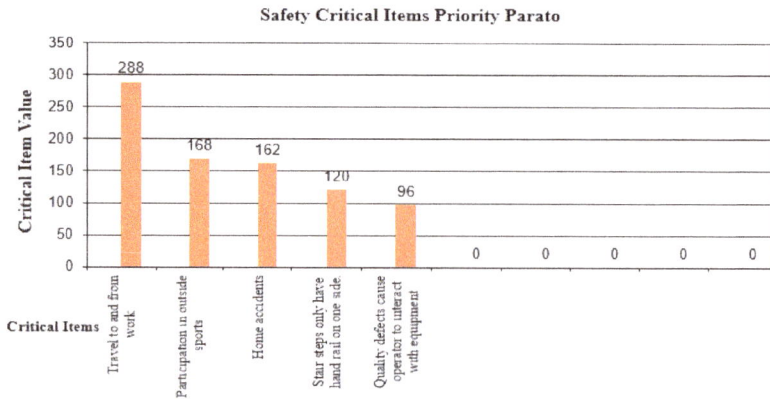

Safety Critical Items Priority Parato

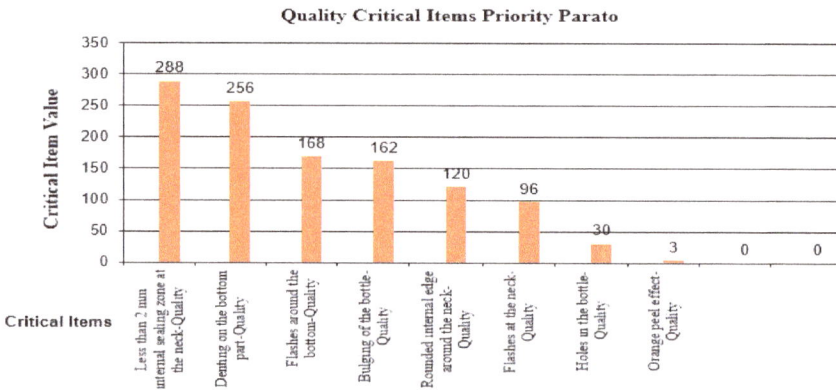

Quality Critical Items Priority Parato

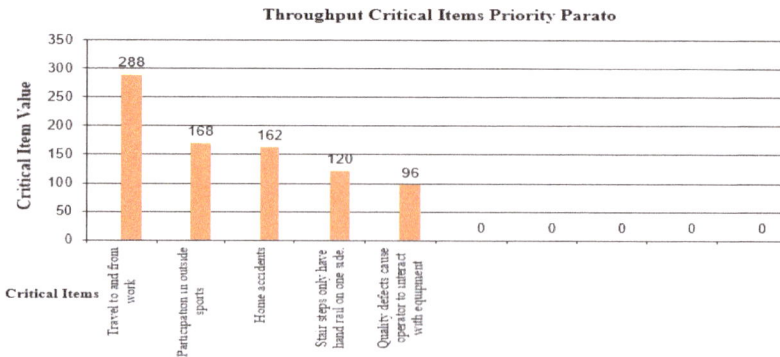

Throughput Critical Items Priority Parato

Continuous Improvement

The continuous improvement items are briefly discussed.

Continuous Improvement	Work Force Continuous Improvement	Operating Department Managers	Specifics based on Improvement
	Material Flow Continuous Improvement	Operating Department Managers	Specifics based on Improvement
	Production Continuous Improvement	Operating Department Managers	Specifics based on Improvement
	Environment Continuous Improvement	Operating Department Managers	Specifics based on Improvement

Work Force Continuous Improvement

Skill and capability assessment of individuals and teams are used to determine the training support required to ensure the entire organization is improving and prepared for new organization challenges. The goal is to develop and organization capable dealing with the change that technology and the marketplace creates.

Material Flow Continuous Improvement

Maintaining the minimum inventory of all raw materials but having them available for all production volume cycles is the goal of material flow improvement work. Output tracking and quantity flow control provides the basis for maintaining a minimum material required for production.

Production Continuous Improvement

There are small improvements such as reducing product to product changeover time, to larger improvements such as increasing production throughput on two lines so a third production line can be retired. In most production systems there are a large number of small but significant improvements. The big improvements normally present themselves when the product is being improved and in turn causes the production system to be changed.

Environment Continuous Improvement

Improved lighting, a leak proof roof, a better floor skid proof coating, improvement in the break area, an improved lunch area, are all examples of environment continuous improvement. These improvements impact the individuals in the work area. They may impact all the maintain metrics and in some cases they make the work area more pleasing.

Conclusion

The goal is for daily progress to occur. Each department leads on one item and if the improvement they lead is successful the other departments are responsible for reapplication,

Upon completion of the Operations Daily meeting the operations leader moves on to the site leadership daily meeting.

Products of Chapter 4

1. Aligned, focused operating department
2. Safe Operation
3. Stability and Product produced at Quality
4. Zero Loss Next twenty-four hours.
5. Continuous Improvement

Chapter 4 Tips and Tools

1. Use Standard Meeting Agenda
2. Use output tracking
3. Use of Priority Matrixes
4. Use Next Twenty-Four Task List
5. Schedule Support help

Chapter 5: Site Daily Management Meeting

Site Leadership
Daily Management Meeting

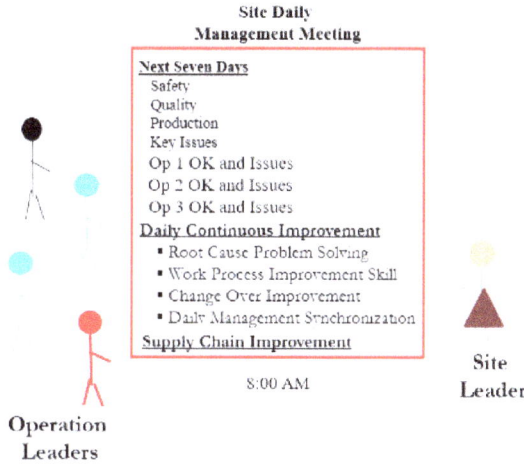

**Site Daily
Management Meeting**

Next Seven Days
Safety
Quality
Production
Key Issues
Op 1 OK and Issues
Op 2 OK and Issues
Op 3 OK and Issues
Daily Continuous Improvement
- Root Cause Problem Solving
- Work Process Improvement Skill
- Change Over Improvement
- Daily Management Synchronization

Supply Chain Improvement

8:00 AM

**Site
Leader**

**Operation
Leaders**

Site Leader's Meeting		
OBJECTIVE: To prioritise support across all operations To ensure clear site wide priority is clear To ensure continuous improvement is executed To understand the supply chain barriers and improvement opportunities		
Focus	**Who**	**Information Needed**
Safety	Site Safety Owner	Site Safety Issues Summary
Quality	Site Quality Owner	Site Quality Issues Summary
Production	Site Production Plan Leader	Site Output Tracking Summary
Key Issues	Site Leader	Key Issues List
Root Cause Problem Solving	Problem Solving Owner	Individual Skill Cards
Work Process Improvement Skill	Work Process Improvement Owner	Individual Skill Cards
Change Over Monitoring	Operations Managers	Change Over Monitoring Process
Daily Management Synchronization	Operations Managers	Daily Mgmt Monitoring Process
Supply Chain Improvement	Site Manager	Boundary Output Tracking
PARTICIPANTS 1. Site Leader 2. Operation managers 3. Support organization leaders		

There are **two forms** for the site leadership meeting. **The one described in this chapter is referred to as the common version. The one described in Chapter 7: Daily Management Leadership Walk is more interactive and on the floor approach.** It requires close coordination among all the leaders.

The site daily management meeting agenda has **three** parts.

Part One

The first part is similar to all the agendas coming up from the line and addresses remaining issues for Safety, Quality, Throughput, and any issues still requiring resources. This is the Maintain part of the agenda.

Part Two

The second part of the agenda focuses on Daily Continuous Improvement:

- Root cause problem solving is a critical skill for every individual. *Stress Free*^{TM} *Manufacturing Solutions* addresses this capability in detail.
- Work process improvement is the next item that provides the organization a way to stabilize the work activities. *Stress Free*^{TM} *Work Process Solutions* addresses this capability in detail.
- Many production lines produce more than one product. The ultimate goal is to have a push button change over from on product to the next.
  However, a common situation is that production line equipment parts need to be changed out. The changeover from one product to the next costs time. The goal is to make the change over as short as possible. *Stress Free*^{TM} *Changeover Solutions* addresses this capability in detail.
- Synchronizing Leadership action from the production line up through the Site Leadership forms the basis of a production operation that performs in an optimum, safe, productive way. Getting the organization leaders synchronize is covered in this book; *Stress Free*^{TM} *Daily Management Solutions*

Part Three

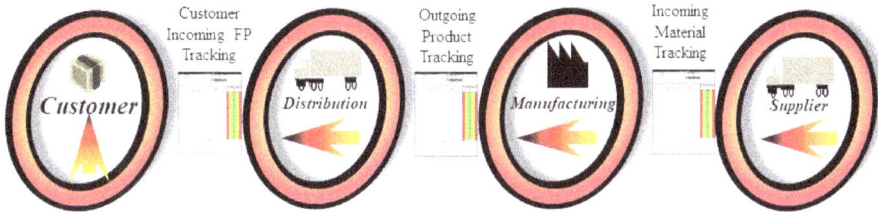

The final part of the agenda focuses on the site supply chains. The operations leaders and the site leaders discuss the issues from the suppliers of materials, the manufacturing issues affecting flow, the distribution issues and the flow of finished products to the customers.

The customer is the primary focus, but productivity, quality and cost all are important.

Note that the Output Tracking sheet is used between each of the supply chain interfaces to identify the critical issues and losses.

Outside the site participants

On a monthly basis and a rolling three-month focus, the supply chain leaders participate with other participating supply chain members. The goal is to address supply chain boundary issues and prioritize problem resolution.

Supply Chain Meeting			
OBJECTIVE: To evaluate category performance / To identify common category problems			
	Focus	Who	Information Needed
Quaterly Performance	Safety Performance	Site Safety Leader	Site Safety Report
	Quality Performance	Site QualityLeader	Site Quality Report
	Production Performance	Site Production Leader	Production Report by SKU
	Inventory Performace	Site Production Planning Leader	Site Inventory Report by SKU
	Supply Chain Interface Issues	Supply Chain Partners	Supply Chain Output Tracking Sheets
Next Quarter focus	Safety Performance	Site Safety Leader	Category Safety Goal
	Quality Performance	Site QualityLeader	Category Quality Goal
	Production Performance	Site Production Leader	Production Performance Goal
	Inventory Performace	Site Production Planning Leader	Category Inventory Goal
	Supply Chain Interface Issues	Supply Chain Partners	Supply Chain Issues List
PARTICIPANTS			
1. Category Leader	4. Participating Suppliers		
2. Site Leaders	5. Participating Customers		
3. Category Support Organization leaders	6. Participating Transport and logistic partners		

Periodically the participants on the leadership team utilize a zero-loss assessment to better understand the supply chain situation.

Organization Zero Loss Assessment

The losses along the supply chain fall into five loss categories: Human Effort Losses, Organization Design Losses, Supply Chain Losses, Process and Equipment Losses and Other Losses.

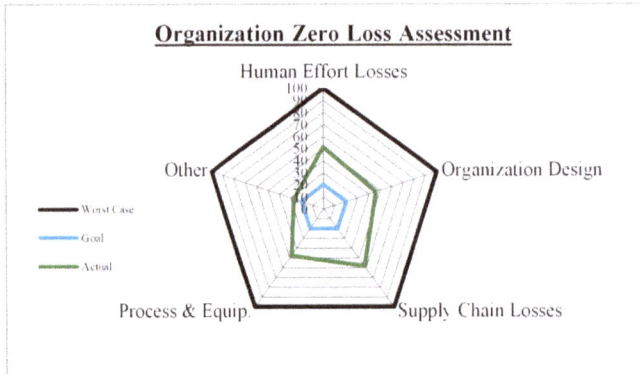

Human Effort Losses
Human effort losses have two elements
1. **Leadership Losses**

   Leadership losses consider having a zero-loss vision, a master plan with key strategies and objectives. It considers the leaders actions, such as building trust and staffing for excellence,

2. **Personal Mastery Losses**

   Personal mastery losses consider that the organization has a goal to have every individual achieve mastery. It considers if the skills to maintain the business at zero loss have been chosen and that the needs of the business have been integrated into each individual's skill development plan.

   It also considers if education and training effectiveness is measured and if losses due to lack of skill are measured and trending down.

Organization Design Losses
Organization design losses have two loss elements
1.Organizational Culture

It checks to see if there are documented principles, strategies and objectives that are clear to all employees.

Employees are asked if they can link their efforts to the business goals.

It checks to see that the organization encourages and assists individuals to develop their skills.

It checks whether effective, capable teams exist to address interdependent work.

2. Organizational Design

This area looks at recruiting practices, team-oriented work design, flexible resource allocation, the reward and recognition system and if proper staffing is the norm for most work areas.

Supply Chain Losses

Five supply chain loss areas are considered

1. Incoming materials logistics

Incoming raw materials and parts losses are reviewed.

Incoming raw materials and parts quality validation are reviewed.

The number of times each raw material or part is handled is checked.

The material delivery timeliness and quantity to the production line is evaluated.

The material and parts handling damage is considered.

2. Outbound finished product logistics

Outbound finished product handling losses, grouping losses, staging losses, truck loading losses and customer receiving losses are all evaluated.

3. Production area losses

Line startup losses, material and quality losses, line operational losses, line shutdown losses and line maintenance losses are evaluated.

4. Yield losses

Material use losses, remnant losses, minor stop losses, destructive quality testing losses and finished product handling losses are all considered in this category.

5. Production flow losses

Raw material flow, material handling effort losses, flow maintenance, finished product and handling flows are examined.

Process and Equipment Losses

Process and Equipment Losses

Three elements are examined in this category

1. Equipment down time losses

Maintenance losses, equipment setup, startup and failure are evaluated.

Waiting for materials of product tests losses are evaluated.

2. Equipment performance losses

Minor stops, rate variability, equipment idling, reduced speed operation and safety related losses are evaluated.

3. Quality defect losses

Raw material defect losses, product defect losses, quality testing, product rework and product handling quality losses are part of this area's evaluation.

Other Losses

Other Losses

Production Scheduling losses, energy related losses, utilization of equipment and facilities losses, employee health, housing and transportation to work losses and environmental losses are under the other category.

Supply Chain Critical Item Task List

The supply chain losses have been reviewed. The supply chain participants now have an understanding about the condition of the supply chain and having used output and input tracking at each supply chain boundary they are prepared to list and rank the critical items.

This activity provides a way for the participants to discuss the issues that affect each of them.

The rating and the subsequent selection of the improvement action to take provides focus.

This process is one of the more useful supply chain activities.

Products of Chapter 5

1. Aligned, focused Site
2. Aligned focused supply chain leaders
3. Supply Chain Stability

Chapter 5 Tips and Tools

1. Use Output and Input Tracking sheet
2. Use Organization and Supply Chain Loss Assessment
3. Use Critical Items Task List

Chapter 6: Support Area Daily Management

The Support Areas are:

- The Safety Department
- The Quality Department
- The Engineering Department
- The Finance Department
- The Office Support group.

Each of these organizations hold a morning meeting. Because the people in these organizations participate in the production daily management meetings, the timing for these meetings follow immediately after the line daily management meetings.

Quality Daily Management Flow

Quality Support Area Daily Meeting

OBJECTIVE: To prioritise Quality support across all operations.
To ensure Zero Losses due to Quality

	Focus	Who	Information Needed
Finished Product	Safety as related to Product Quality	Site Safety Owner	Site Safety Issues Summary
	Product Quality	Site Finished Product Quality Owner	Site Product Quality Issues Summary
	Finished Product PPM Defect Rate	Site Finished Product Quality Owner	Product Defect Tracking List
	Key Finished Product Quality Issues	Site Finished Product Quality Owner	KeyFinished Product Qulity Issues List
Raw Materials	Safety as related to Materials Quality	Site Safety Owner	Site Safety Issues Summary
	Materials Quality	Site Materials Quality Owner	Site Materials Quality Issues Summary
	Materials PPM Defect Rate	Site Materials Quality Owner	Product Defect Tracking List
	Key Materials Quality Issues	Site Quality Owner	Key Materials Quality Issues List
Critical Items	Critical Item 1	Site Quality Owner	Quality Critical Items List
	Critical Item 2	Site Quality Owner	Quality Critical Items List

PARTICIPANTS

1. Site Quality Leader   4. Department Representatives*   * Attendance as needed
2. Product Quality Owners   5. Site Safety Owner*
3. Materials Quality Owners

All support areas practice a similar daily management flow.

This is an example of the Quality department daily meeting. The Quality Department focuses on; current production line issues, finished product quality issues and raw material quality issues.

Current Production Quality Issues

The previous shift and the upcoming production shift quality issues are discussed. Support for getting the production to 100% quality production is discussed and resources are assigned to support the problem area.

Finished Product Quality Issues

The finished product from each line is tested and evaluated. Additionally, the outgoing product is tested to assure no handling and transport damage is occurring.

Raw Materials Quality Issues

Each raw material is checked to ensure it meets the quality criteria and has no damage. This checking is done by the person receiving the material.

The quality may have been certified by the material provider or it may undergo random quality checks upon receipt. The goal is to have defect free material flowing to the production line.

Quality Critical Items List

This is the overall list of critical quality issues whether raw, finished product quality or quality related safety issues.

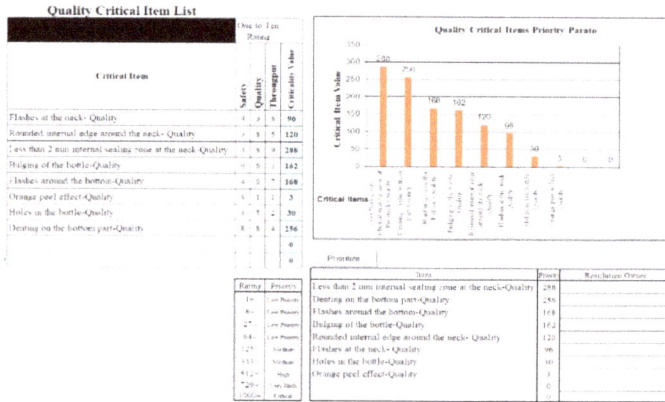

Issues are listed and then rated as to impact on Safety, Quality and Throughput on a one to five scale, where five is the most critical. The priority is visualized with a graph and the items can be assigned to a resolution owner.

The rating value is compared to a rate and priority scale to better understand the how critical an item may be.

All issues are important but an issue that is rated high or above is must receive

Products of Chapter 6

1. Aligned, focused support areas
2. Critical Items identified

Chapter 6 Tips and Tools

1. Use Standard Meeting Agenda
2. Use output tracking
3. Use of Priority Matrixes
4. Use Next Twenty-Four Task List
5. Set support help Schedule

Chapter 7: Leadership Daily Management Walk

The daily leadership walk is a dynamic on the floor way for leadership to interact at each level of the organization. It allows leadership at every level to interact with each other and it affords top leaders to interact and coach at every level.

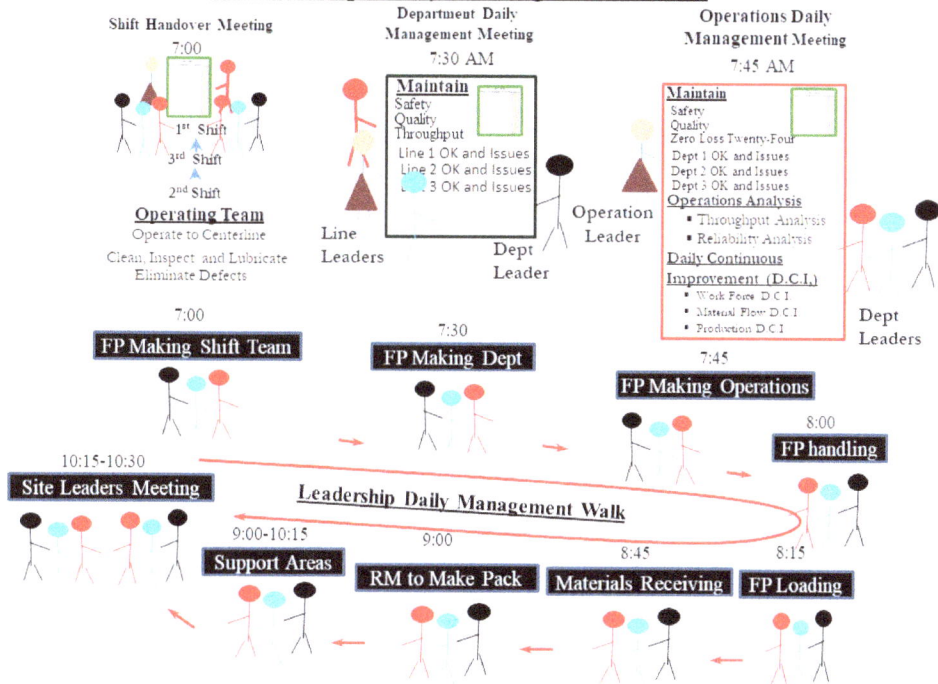

Leadership Daily Management Walk

The walk begins at the line team level. Since there are many line teams, a schedule is set so that every line team is visited during one complete leadership walk cycle. That logic is applied to every level of the organization,

The site leader or a designated replacement leads the team. This team is met by the leader for the area being visited. They listen to the area's daily meeting. They have a predetermined standard set of questions for each area.

Synchronized Daily Management Walk Support Questions

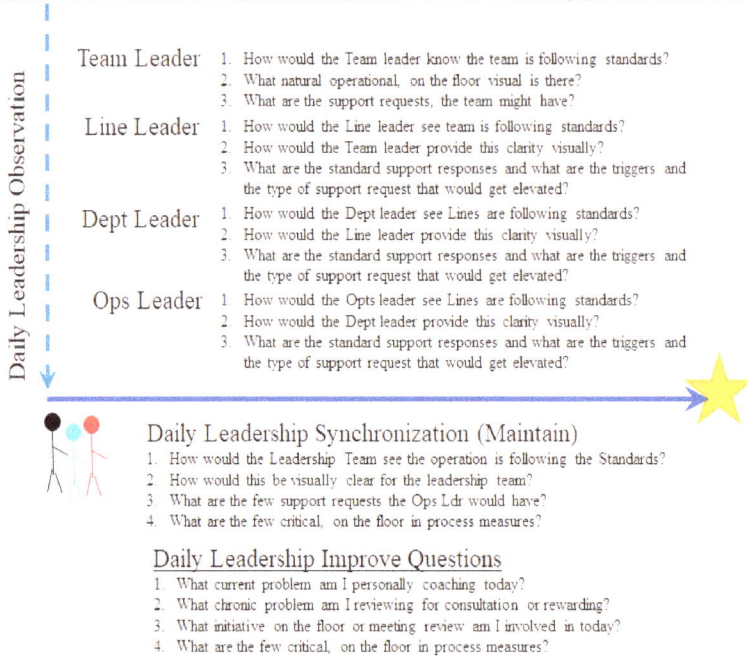

Daily Leadership Observation

Team Leader
1. How would the Team leader know the team is following standards?
2. What natural operational, on the floor visual is there?
3. What are the support requests, the team might have?

Line Leader
1. How would the Line leader see team is following standards?
2. How would the Team leader provide this clarity visually?
3. What are the standard support responses and what are the triggers and the type of support request that would get elevated?

Dept Leader
1. How would the Dept leader see Lines are following standards?
2. How would the Line leader provide this clarity visually?
3. What are the standard support responses and what are the triggers and the type of support request that would get elevated?

Ops Leader
1. How would the Opts leader see Lines are following standards?
2. How would the Dept leader provide this clarity visually?
3. What are the standard support responses and what are the triggers and the type of support request that would get elevated?

Daily Leadership Synchronization (Maintain)
1. How would the Leadership Team see the operation is following the Standards?
2. How would this be visually clear for the leadership team?
3. What are the few support requests the Ops Ldr would have?
4. What are the few critical, on the floor in process measures?

Daily Leadership Improve Questions
1. What current problem am I personally coaching today?
2. What chronic problem am I reviewing for consultation or rewarding?
3. What initiative on the floor or meeting review am I involved in today?
4. What are the few critical, on the floor in process measures?

These questions are meant to provide a common interchange at every level of the organization.

The stop at each level is meant to be brief but effective. The goal is to be done by the first half of the day.

One key impact of the walk is that resources get allocated quickly and many meetings that normally happen throughout the day are no longer needed. The content of these meetings was resolved during the morning daily management walk.

The walk path is designed to have a representative mix of leaders visit each level of the organization. The support area members are always on each walk. This provides a firsthand exposure of problems to the support area.

Daily Management Organization Structure Example

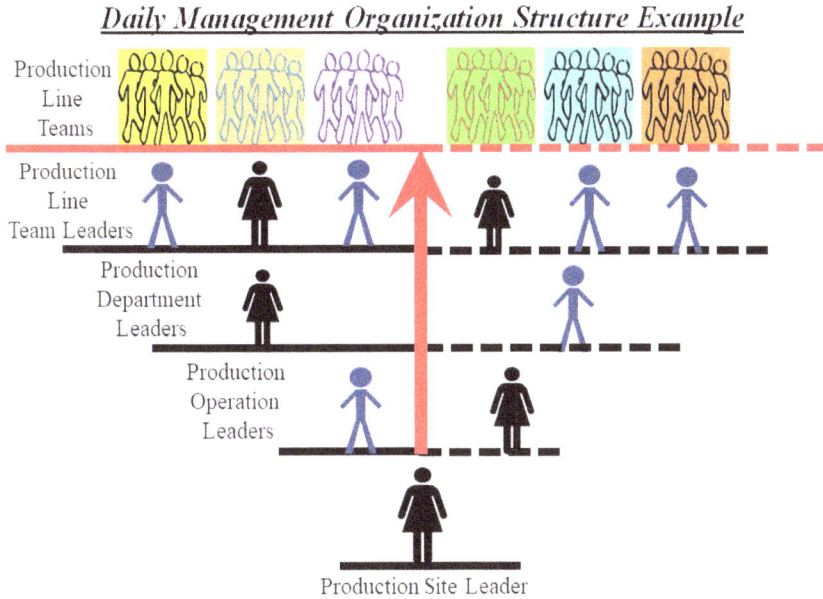

Production Line Teams

Production Line Team Leaders

Production Department Leaders

Production Operation Leaders

Production Site Leader

The leader at each level guides and manages the walking visitors. This approach gives each level leader exposure to the leadership team.

The entire organization benefits from this on the floor style of daily management,

Products of Chapter 7

1. Aligned, focused operating department
2. Safe Operation
3. Direct on the floor coaching
4. Zero Loss Next twenty-four hours.
5. Continuous Improvement

Chapter 7 Tips and Tools

1. Examine the use of Standard Meeting Agenda
2. Examine the use of output tracking
3. Examine the use of Priority Matrixes
4. Examine the use of Next Twenty-Four Task List

Chapter 8: The Building Blocks of Daily Management

Daily Morning Meeting Agenda's

Using a common set meeting agenda from the line to the site level provides a basis for a common interaction at every level of the organization

Shift Hand Over Meeting

The shift hand over meeting is the first of the series. The four main topics are Safety, Quality, Throughput and Stability

Shift Hand Over meeting

OBJECTIVE: Understand gaps from previous shift to support setting the right priorities for the next shift
Peer to peer information handover to get basic understanding of the previous shift

	Focus	Who	Information Needed
Safety	Incident	Shift line leader	Incident forms
	Unsafe condition & behaviour	Shift line leader	Verbal information
	Behavior Observation Plan	Shift line leader	-
Quality	Quality Issues	Shift quality operator owner	Incident forms & sample
	Finished product sample for oncoming team to check	Shift quality operator owner	one bag of product
Throughput	Planned production	Shift line leader	Upcoming shift production plan
	Production output	Shift line leader	Previous shift output tracking
	Top Loss - Unplanned Stops	Shift line leader	Previous shift output tracking
	Changer Over (C/O) plan	Shift line leader	Upcoming shift production plan
Stability	Clean Inspect and Lubricate (CIL) plan	Shift CIL operator owner	CIL history
	Current Team CIL Completion	Shift CIL operator owner	CIL history
	Equipment touches (ET)	Shift (ET) operator owner	Equipment Touches history and goal
	Defect elimination (DE)	Shift (DE) operator owner	Defect elimination history and goal
	Support need	Shift line leader	

PARTICIPANTS
1. On coming shift line leader
2. Off going shift line leader
3. On coming line operators
5. Shift Process Technician
6. Shift maintenance technician
7. Shift E&I technician

The topic is discussed in detail only if there is an issue. If there are no issues for a topic a green card is held up or "green" is declared.

Line Support Meeting

This agenda is used to communicate between the line leader and the line support personnel. The intent is to make sure that the line has the required support for the next upcoming shift.

Line Support Meeting		

OBJECTIVE: - Review last 24 hrs results to identify top 3 losses, determine immediate actions and root cause actions.
    - Determine and additional actions for shift team.
    - Verify that the support resources are able to address any outstanding issues

	Focus	Who	Information Needed
Safety	Incident	Line Leader	Incident forms
	Unsafe condition & behaviour	Line Leader	Verbal information
	Behavior Observation Completion	Line Leader	Verbal information
Quality	Quality Issues	Line Leader	Incident forms & sample
	Parts Per Million Defects	Line Leader	Output Tracking
	Total Scrap	Line Leader	Output Tracking
Throughput	Unplanned stop (#)	Line Leader	Output Tracking
	Unplanned PR Loss (%)	Line Leader	Output Tracking
	Previous Shift Production	Line Leader	Output Tracking
	Production Planned for the upcoming shift	Line Leader	Output Tracking
	Changer Over (C/O) plan and time	Line Leader	Output Tracking
Stability	Clean Inspect and Lubricate (CIL) plan	Line Leader	CIL history
	Current Team (CIL) Completion	Line Leader	CIL history
	False Starts	Line Leader	False Starts Report
	Maintenance Requirements	Line Leader	Maintenance Schedule

PARTICIPANTS
1. Line Leader
2. Maintenance Technician
3. E&I Technician
4. Process Technician
5. Department Safety Owner (as needed)
6. Department Quality Owner (as needed)

Department Meeting Agenda

The department meeting provides an across the production lines view of the condition and any conflicts in support needs.

Department Daily Meeting Agenda

OBJECTIVE - To align on departmental priorities
- Operating department leader provides coaching to line leaders

	Focus	Who	Information Needed
Safety	Incident	Line Leaders	Incident forms
	Unsafe condition & behaviour	Line Leaders	Verbal information
	Behavior Observation Completion	Line Leaders	Verbal information
Quality	Quality Issues	Line Leaders	Incident forms & sample
	Parts Per Million Defects	Line Leaders	Output Tracking
	Total Scrap	Line Leaders	Output Tracking
Throughput	Unplanned stop (#)	Line Leaders	Output Tracking
	Unplanned PR Loss (%)	Line Leaders	Output Tracking
	Previous Shift Production	Line Leaders	Output Tracking
	Planned Production Planned Upcoming Shift	Line Leaders	Output Tracking
	Changer Over (C/O) plan and time	Line Leaders	Output Tracking
Stability	Clean Inspect and Lubricate (CIL) plan	Line Leaders	CIL history
	Current Team (CIL) Completion	Line Leaders	CIL history
	False Starts	Line Leaders	False Starts Report

Participants
1. Operatging Department Leader   3. Process Engineers   5. Finished Product Handling Leader
2. Line Leaders   4. Material Supply Leader

Resource conflicts are resolved. If there is a resource shortage or issue the department leader will take it to the Operations level meeting,

If there are specific problems that require outside support then the pertinent people are asked to attend the meeting.

Operations Meeting Agenda

The operations meeting brings together all the department managers and all support area leaders as needed.

Operations Meeting		
OBJECTIVE: To maitain next 24 hour production across the departments To review the progress of the continuous improvements		
Focus	**Who**	**Information Needed**
Safety	Operating Department Managers	Safety incident forms
Quality	Quality Leaders	Quality incident forms
Throughput Analysis	Operating Department Managers	From Output Tracking form
Production Plan	Finished product planners	Production Plan
Critical SKUs and qualifications	Finished product planners	Production Plan
Stop Plan for next 24 hrs	Operating Department Managers	Production Plan
Production Line Constraints	Operating Department Managers	Verbal information
Through Put Analysis	Operating Department Managers	From Output Tracking form
Reliability Analysis	Operating Department Managers	From Output Tracking form
OEE Review	Operating Department Managers	From Output Tracking form
Inventory Performance	Warehouse leader	From WHS. Output Tracking form
Delivery	Operating Department Managers	Output Tracking Summary
Operation Organiztion Skill Spider Diagram Evaluation	Operating Department Managers	Line and Composite Spider Diagrams
Work Force Continuous Improvement	Operating Department Managers	Specifics based on Improvement
Material Flow Continuous Improvement	Operating Department Managers	Specifics based on Improvement
Production Continuous Improvement	Operating Department Managers	Specifics based on Improvement
Environment Continuous Improvement	Operating Department Managers	Specifics based on Improvement

PARTICIPANTS
1. Operation Manager
2. Department Managers
3. Raw Materials Planners*
4. Finished product planners *
5. Warehouse leader *
6. Quality leader*
7. Material supply leader*

*Invited based on situation

The agenda follows the pattern set up by the organizations below this level. The new items are those focused on continuous improvement. The department managers each have a specific improvement for which the take the lead. Once an improvement is made the other department managers are responsible for the reapplication of the improvement.

Site Meeting Agenda

The site daily meeting has a longer-term flavor. It looks at safety, quality, production and other key issues with a seven-day forward look. The goal is to make sure that these three areas are in total control.

Site Leader's Meeting		
OBJECTIVE: To prioritise support across all operations. To ensure clear site wide priority is clear To ensure continuous improvement is executed To understand the supply chain barriers and improvement opportunities		
Focus	**Who**	**Information Needed**
Safety	Site Safety Owner	Site Safety Issues Summary
Quality	Site Quality Owner	Site Quality Issues Summary
Production	Site Production Plan Leader	Site Output Tracking Summary
Key Issues	Site Leader	Key Issues List
Root Cause Problem Solving	Problem Solving Owner	Individual Skill Cards
Work Process Improvment Skill	Work Process Improvement Owner	Individual Skill Cards
Change Over Monitoring	Operations Managers	Change Over Monitoring Process
Daily Management Synchronization	Operations Managers	Daily Mgmt Monitoring Process
Supply Chain Improvement	Site Manager	Boundary Output Tracking
PARTICIPANTS 1. Site Leader 2. Operation managers 3. Support organization leaders		

Continuous Improvement in Root Cause Problem Solving, Work Process Improvement, Change Over and Daily Management Synchronization are each address. The goal is to make steady progress. Each area has an owner at the top leadership level responsible in sponsoring and coaching the continuous improvement.

Supply Chain Improvement is the site manager's responsibility. There may be other members on the leadership team involved. The goal is to create a smoothly flowing stream of materials and finished product with only a three-sigma inventory level.

Supply Chain Meeting Agenda

The supply Chain "daily" management meeting is usually scheduled once per month. It always looks back at the last three months and then looks forward for what issues to resolve.

	Focus	Who	Information Needed
Quaterly Performance	Safety Performance	Site Safety Leader	Site Safety Report
	Quality Performance	Site QualityLeader	Site Quality Report
	Production Performance	Site Production Leader	Production Report by SKU
	Inventory Performace	Site Production Planning Leader	Site Inventory Report by SKU
	Supply Chain Interface Issues	Supply Chain Partners	Supply Chain Output Tracking Sheets
Next Quarter focus	Safety Performance	Site Safety Leader	Category Safety Goal
	Quality Performance	Site QualityLeader	Category Quality Goal
	Production Performance	Site Production Leader	Production Performance Goal
	Inventory Performace	Site Production Planning Leader	Category Inventory Goal
	Supply Chain Interface Issues	Supply Chain Partners	Supply Chain Issues List

Supply Chain Meeting

OBJECTIVE: To evaluate category performance
To identify common category problems

PARTICIPANTS
1. Category Leader
2. Site Leaders
3. Category Support Organization leaders
4. Participating Suppliers
5. Participating Customers
6. Participating Transport and logistic partners

The use of the output tracking sheet between each organizational boundary provides specific performance information allows the partnering organizations to address specific problems. The Supply Chain Issues list prioritizes the action that should be taken during the coming month. This approach makes all supply chain participants partners in creating a minimum loss, flowing supply chain,

Support Area Meeting Agendas

The support areas use a similar agenda being used throughout the organization. The support organization meeting takes place immediately after the line daily management meetings end. This allows them to have fresh information as to the condition the work they need to do in support of the organization.

Quality Support Area Daily Meeting

OBJECTIVE: To prioritise Quality support across all operations.
To ensure Zero Losses due to Quality

	Focus	Who	Information Needed
Finished Product	Safety as related to Product Quality	Site Safety Owner	Site Safety Issues Summary
	Product Quality	Site Finished Product Quality Owner	Site Product Quality Issues Summary
	Finished Product PPM Defect Rate	Site Finished Product Quality Owner	Product Defect Tracking List
	Key Finished Product Quality Issues	Site Finished Product Quality Owner	KeyFinished Product Qulity Issues List
Raw Materials	Safety as related to Materials Quality	Site Safety Owner	Site Safety Issues Summary
	Materials Quality	Site Materials Quality Owner	Site Materials Quality Issues Summary
	Materials PPM Defect Rate	Site Materials Quality Owner	Product Defect Tracking List
	Key Materials Quality Issues	Site Quality Owner	Key Materials Quality Issues List
Critical Items	Critical Item 1	Site Quality Owner	Quality Critical Items List
	Critical Item 2	Site Quality Owner	Quality Critical Items List

PARTICIPANTS

1. Site Quality Leader   4. Department Representatives*   * Attendance as needed
2. Product Quality Owners   5. Site Safety Owner*
3. Materials Quality Owners

Critical Items Task List

The critical items task list provides a convenient way to visually display the priority issues. This for can be customized to fit specific organization or specific focus.

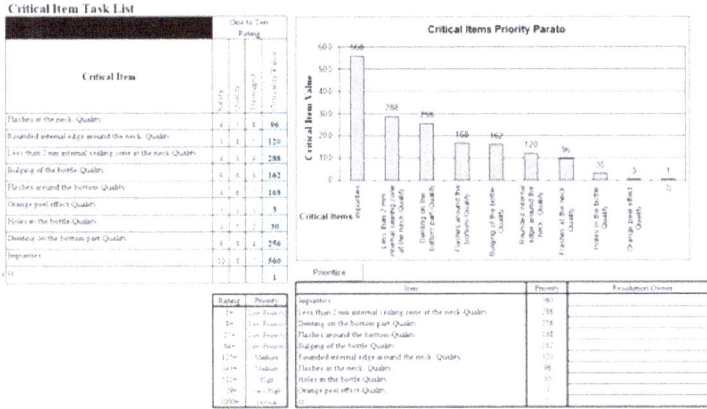

Safety Critical Items List

This is the critical items list as it might be applied to safety issues.

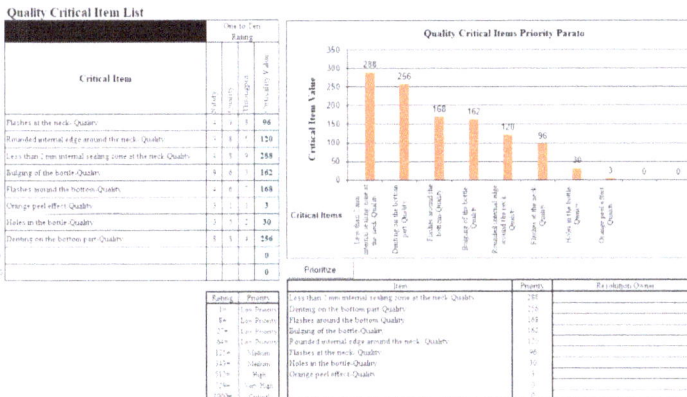

Quality Critical Items List

This is the critical items list as it might be applied to Quality issues.

Quality Critical Item List

	Critical Item	Safety	Quality	Throughput	Criticality Value
1	Flashes at the neck- Quality	4	3	8	96
2	Rounded internal edge around the neck- Quality	5	8	5	120
3	Less than 2 mm internal sealing zone at the neck-Quality	4	8	9	288
4	Bulging of the bottle-Quality	9	6	3	162
5	Flashes around the bottom-Quality	4	6	7	168
6	Orange peel effect-Quality	3	1	1	3
7	Holes in the bottle-Quality	5	5	2	30
8	Denting on the bottom part-Quality	8	8	4	256
9					0
10					0

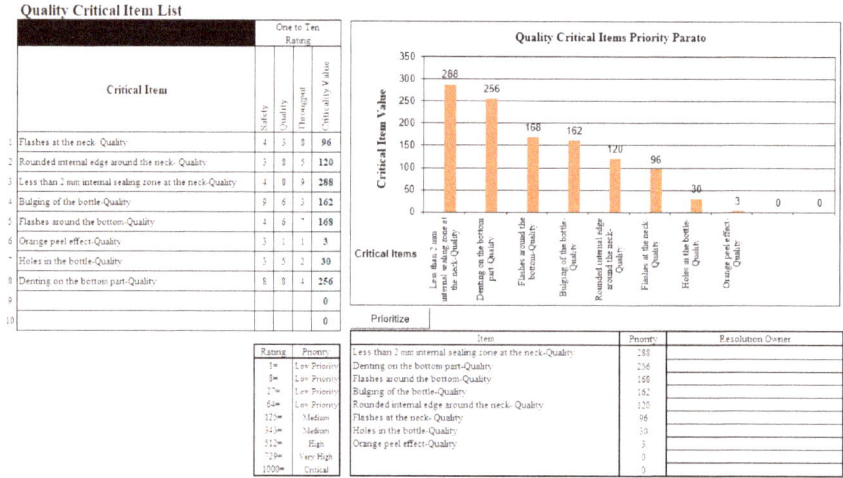

Quality Critical Items Priority Parato

Rating	Priority
1=	Low Priority
8=	Low Priority
27=	Low Priority
64=	Low Priority
125=	Medium
343=	Medium
512=	High
729=	Very High
1000=	Critical

Prioritize

Item	Priority	Resolution Owner
Less than 2 mm internal sealing zone at the neck-Quality	288	
Denting on the bottom part-Quality	256	
Flashes around the bottom-Quality	168	
Bulging of the bottle-Quality	162	
Rounded internal edge around the neck- Quality	120	
Flashes at the neck- Quality	96	
Holes in the bottle-Quality	30	
Orange peel effect-Quality	3	
	0	
	0	

Throughput Critical Items List

This is the critical items list as it might be applied to production throughput issues.

Throughput Critical Item Task List

	Critical Item	Safety	Quality	Throughput	Criticality Value
1	Quality defects	4	5	8	160
2	Major Maintenance	3	8	5	120
3	Raw Material Quality	3	7	9	189
4	Case packer reliability	9	6	5	270
5					0
6					0
7					0
8					0
9					0
10					0

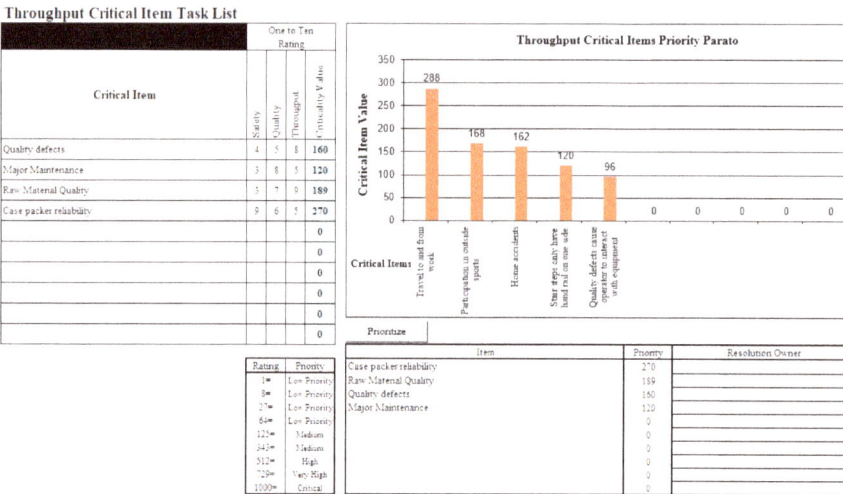

Throughput Critical Items Priority Parato

Rating	Priority
1=	Low Priority
8=	Low Priority
27=	Low Priority
64=	Low Priority
125=	Medium
343=	Medium
512=	High
729=	Very High
1000=	Critical

Prioritize

Item	Priority	Resolution Owner
Case packer reliability	270	
Raw Material Quality	189	
Quality defects	160	
Major Maintenance	120	
	0	
	0	
	0	
	0	
	0	

Supply Chain Critical Items List

The supply chain participants are the raw material suppliers, the transportation providers, the production site, the customers. The rating titles may need to change or there may be a need for additional rating criteria.

The ability to list a specific area and have the supply chain participants evaluate the performance in the various areas provides a collaborative way of addressing issues. The issue discussion is probably more important than the rating.

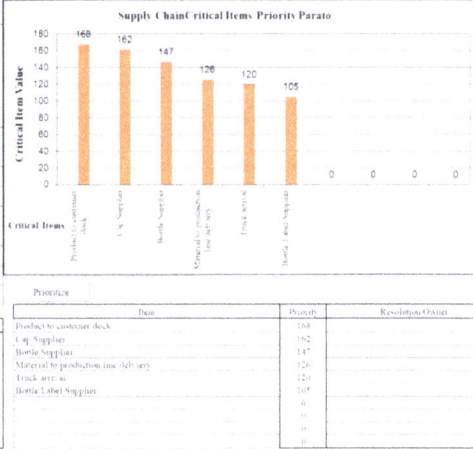

Output Tracking

Output tracking is a powerful way to visualize the performance of an area that is producing a product or providing a service to the next in line.

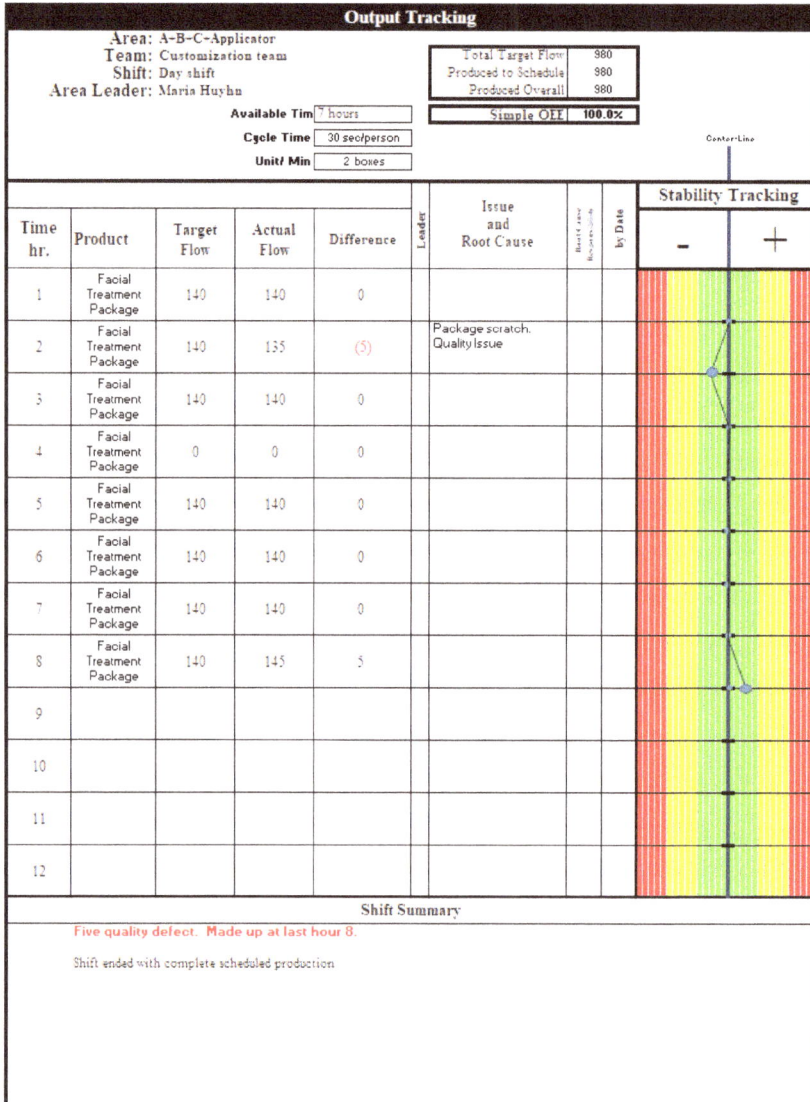

Output Tracking

Area:	A-B-C-Applicator	
Team:	Customization team	
Shift:	Day shift	
Area Leader:	Maria Huyhn	

Available Tim	7 hours
Cycle Time	30 sec/person
Unit/ Min	2 boxes

Total Target Flow	980
Produced to Schedule	980
Produced Overall	980
Simple OEE	100.0%

Center-Line

Time hr.	Product	Target Flow	Actual Flow	Difference	Leader	Issue and Root Cause	Root Case Responsible	by Date	Stability Tracking −	Stability Tracking +
1	Facial Treatment Package	140	140	0						
2	Facial Treatment Package	140	135	(5)		Package scratch. Quality Issue				
3	Facial Treatment Package	140	140	0						
4	Facial Treatment Package	0	0	0						
5	Facial Treatment Package	140	140	0						
6	Facial Treatment Package	140	140	0						
7	Facial Treatment Package	140	140	0						
8	Facial Treatment Package	140	145	5						
9										
10										
11										
12										

Shift Summary

Five quality defect. Made up at last hour 8.

Shift ended with complete scheduled production

Output tracking used at every organizational boundary creates an organizational culture that basis its interactions on specific issues clarified by agreed to measures.

Daily Management Maintenance Tasks List
The goals for the maintenance area are,

☐ To achieve a 100%, line operation request response.

☐ To plan and schedule 90% of maintenance tasks thirty days in advance.

☐ To have 95% of maintenance tasks

☐ To have a maintenance strategy for all equipment

☐ To have a visual annual maintenance schedule.

The maintenance department has multiple responsibilities. There are ten mentioned in this book. This list is not all inclusive.

1. Production Line Support

The maintenance organization team members participate in daily support meeting. They participate to understand the line and department need so they provide the needed support.

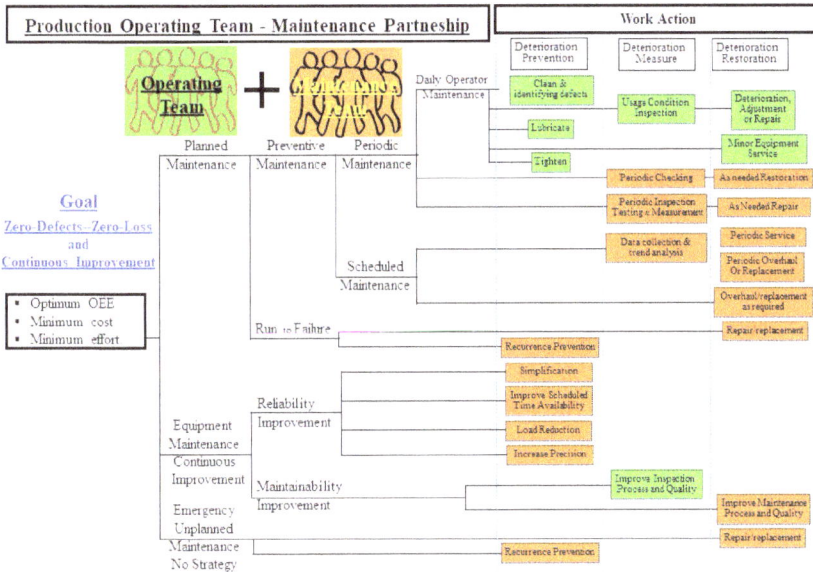

The operating teams establish a close working relationship and clearly identify the work actions each will do. Continuous equipment maintenance improvement to reduce lubrication and inspection time will be discussed and improvements planned. Visual control standards are a key part of new improvements.

3. Break Down Counter Measures

The Maintenance department tracks breakdowns and categorizes them into Major, Moderate, and Minor breakdowns. This data is used as input to loss analysis and setting baseline data for goals to be set from.

Emphasis is placed on breakdown recurrence prevention. Failures are analyzed to root cause and operating standards, maintenance standards, and equipment improvements are put in place to reduce recurrence. Training is created to train technicians in the new standard procedures and equipment improvements are documented for future initiative work

Standards and improvements are reapplied to similar equipment to prevent future failures.

As breakdowns occur, inspections are made of similar equipment to find developing failure situations so that potential breakdowns are immediately addressed.

Aligning rotating equipment, calibrating instruments, and maintaining control loop health are key activities.

Key components are inspected as a result of prevention activities.

As equipment components are maintained at basic and use conditions, poorly designed parts and their application will become apparent. Activities are deployed to make equipment modifications that will improve the life and extend of those components. Phenomena Mechanism Analysis are used to analyze failures due to design weaknesses and correct them

Establishing Maintenance Standards and Procedures

The maintenance standards that should be documented are:
- The standardized work processes
  - Equipment ranking criteria and process
  - Breakdown definition and classification
  - Process failure definition
  - Minor stop definition
  - Equipment logs
- A site wide numbering system for parts/materials, equipment & locations.
- The planning, scheduling, and budgeting maintenance process.
- Countermeasures to Breakdown Elimination daily management system
- Equipment Inspection visual controls
- Lubrication standards
- Planning and scheduling daily management system
- Alignment procedures for rotating equipment
- Instrument calibration and control loop health maintenance procedures

- Rebuild procedures
- Common standardized procedures are instrument calibration methods

The operating team's daily maintenance and operation activities greatly reduce unplanned maintenance and premature component failure. The maintenance resources focus on quality execution of corrective and periodic maintenance. The elimination of unplanned maintenance frees up time for resources to concentrate on developing cost-effective periodic maintenance systems supported by a computerized maintenance information system.

4. **Facilities and tools management**
   - Special tools in place
   - Adequate facilities for maintenance activities
   - Availability of maintenance tools
   - Tools and facilities are maintained at 5S standards.
   - Tools and facilities are improved with a focus of reducing Mean time to repair (MTTR).

5. **Equipment Priority Designation**
   - Identify which equipment on which to focus to improve in the areas of safety, quality, production, cost, delivery and materials.
   - The equipment is ranked yearly
   - Plans are modified to address any changes in business needs.
   - Breakdown elimination activities and operator daily maintain activities are focused on the priority equipment
   - Tracking systems compare the rate of improvement between priority equipment and non-priority equipment.

   Equipment priority designation is used to help establish which equipment and components will receive improvement focus.

6. **Maintenance Planning and Scheduling**
   Line Maintenance Schedule

   This example is presented as a way to show a two-year schedule of the required scheduled maintenance to maintain the line.

This is used by the line team as they operate the production line and each level of the organization. The production planner integrates this information into the production schedule for each production line.

- Priorities for maintenance are set for next maintenance period.
- Related improvement projects are put into the plan.

7. **Lubrication Management system**
   - Easy to maintain, optimized, simplified
   - Transfusion clean lubrication to the required components.
   - Conduct a lubrication survey
   - Lubricant consolidation to the needed lubricants.
   - Color standards and storage standards are created and are visually prominent.
   - Production line operating teams are trained on the purpose, inspection methods, and application methods of lubrication. Maintenance resources provide tentative lubrication standards for the line operating teams and provide coaching, and training as needed.

8. **Maintenance Information System**
   Provide accurate and timely master data that enables maintenance planners to be more efficient and effective
   The maintenance information system answers the following questions,
   - What is your organization for master data creation?
   - What are your change management processes?
   - What % of parts is at the correct location for use by maintenance planners?
   - How many days does it take to register a part?
   - What are your focus areas?

9. **Maintenance and Equipment Cost system**

The maintenance and equipment cost system addresses the following,

- How much is spent on maintenance.
- The size of the maintenance budget.
- Identifies any repetitive maintenance tasks that:
  a. Are particularly expensive.
  b. Vary widely in cost each time they are executed.
- Identifies any equipment that costs more to maintain than similar equipment somewhere else.
- If maintenance spending is predictable.
- If you are on track to support the business need.
- Budget management is a focus in order to automate the analysis and reporting functions needed to control costs. The information used is:
  o Budget summaries,
  o work and materials usage schedules,
  o job priority lists,
  o equipment life forecasts, and
  o tracking maintenance costs by maintenance methods
    - Emergency,
    - Breakdown,
    - Time based maintenance,
    - Condition based maintenance.

10. **Parts and Supplies Control System**

- Parts and supply storage areas are straightened up
- Unnecessary parts are discarded.
- 5S methodology is used to organize the area and assign responsibilities for maintenance of the areas.
- A focus exists for quick retrieval of parts or supplies.
- Spare parts are categorized,
- storage methods are decided,
- Reorder methods are standardized.
- The focus is to reduce the spare part inventory to only the level that is needed to attain equipment availability goals and then reducing time required to find parts through visual control. A key success criterion is to find a needed part in less than 30 seconds.

Stress Free^{TM} *Maintenance Solutions* has more details on all of these systems.

Individual Skill Spider Diagram

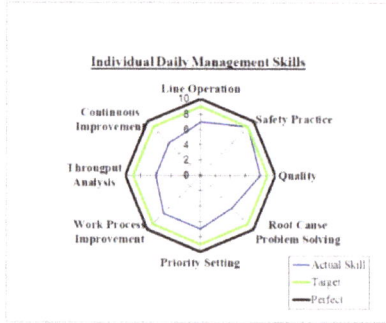

Line Team Skill Spider Diagram

A composited skill spider diagram applied to an operating team identifies the team's skill areas that need to be bolstered.

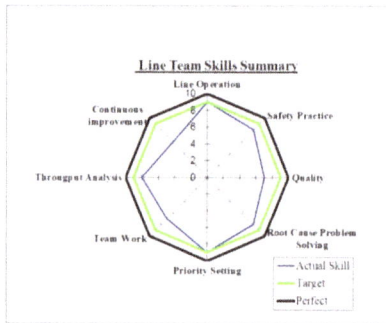

Department Skills Summary

The combined skill diagrams of all the lines provide a visual indication of where the department should focus on increasing the department's skills.

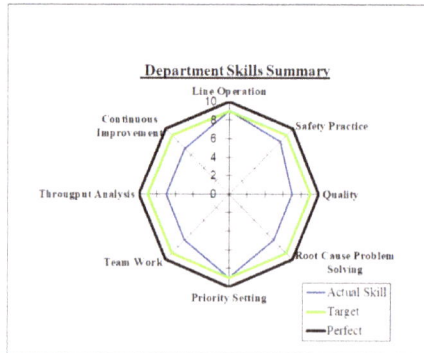

How to use for the total organization

The combining of skills up through the organization may be useful to almost any level. The choice of how high in the organization to go is dependent on the commonality of required skills. For instance, the required skills for support organizations may be significantly different than for the production area.

Organization Zero Loss Assessment

The assessment of losses across the organization can be quickly assessed by using a zero-loss assessment. This assessment when done with the key leaders of the organization requires no data other than what is in the head of each leader.

It is an eighty-five per cent effective process that may take as little as an hour to answer seventy-five questions focused on thirteen parts of the organization and supply chain

Stress Free_{TM}
Maintenance Solutions

Stability Systems

Maintenance Standards & Procedures

Autonomous Maintenance Support

Shutdown Maintenance

Improvement Systems

Maintenance Analysis

Maintenance Improvement

Maintenance Prevention Design

Sustaining Systems

Equipment Ranking

Planning and Scheduling

Lubrication Management

Budget Control

Tools & Facilities Management

Parts & Supplies Management

Technical Data Management

Maintenance Systems

Money to the Bank $

Ron
MUELLER P. E.

Stress Free^{TM} Maintenance Solutions
for
Manufacturing and Production Systems

By: Ron Mueller

Around the World Publishing LLC
4914 Cooper Road Suite 144
Cincinnati, Ohio 45242-9998

ISBN:
ISBN:

Distribution by: Ingram
Cover Picture by: Andrey Popov, Dreamstime.com
Cover Design by: Ron Mueller

Technical Editor:
Gordon Miller P. E.

DEDICATION
To all the dedicated people that strive to optimally maintain the
equipment that transforms raw materials into a finished product.

Table of Content

<u>Overview</u>

Stress Free^{TM} Maintenance Solutions is a system of maintaining and improving the production, safety, and quality systems by stabilizing equipment and processes and by enhancing the skills of all the people involved in maintaining the equipment and systems.

Equipment maintenance is any process used to keep a business's equipment in reliable working order. It includes routine upkeep as well as corrective repair work and periodic rebuild.

Maintenance includes mechanical assets, tools, and computer systems.

The measurable objectives are optimum.

- OEE
- Throughput

And minimum.

- Cost
- Effort

Planned Maintenance System

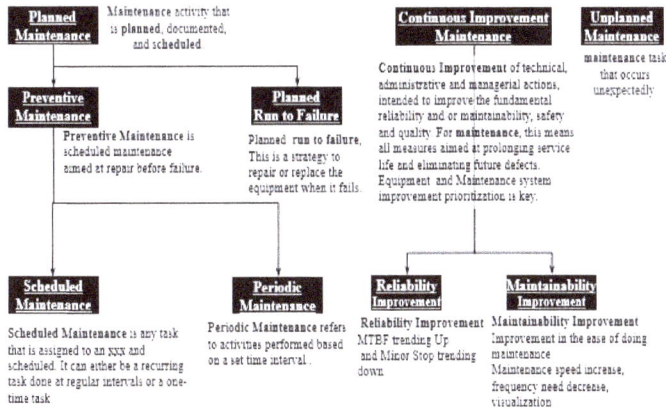

Planned Maintenance — Maintenance activity that is planned, documented, and scheduled

Continuous Improvement Maintenance — Continuous Improvement of technical, administrative and managerial actions, intended to improve the fundamental reliability and or maintainability, safety and quality. For maintenance, this means all measures aimed at prolonging service life and eliminating future defects. Equipment and Maintenance system improvement prioritization is key.

Unplanned Maintenance — maintenance task that occurs unexpectedly

Preventive Maintenance — Preventive Maintenance is scheduled maintenance aimed at repair before failure.

Planned Run to Failure — Planned run to failure. This is a strategy to repair or replace the equipment when it fails.

Scheduled Maintenance — Scheduled Maintenance is any task that is assigned to an xxx and scheduled. It can either be a recurring task done at regular intervals or a one-time task

Periodic Maintenance — Periodic Maintenance refers to activities performed based on a set time interval.

Reliability Improvement — Reliability Improvement MTBF trending Up and Minor Stop trending down

Maintainability Improvement — Maintainability Improvement Improvement in the ease of doing maintenance Maintenance speed increase, frequency need decrease, visualization

A Planned Maintenance System has the following elements.

Planned Maintenance

Preventive Maintenance

The intent is to implement restorative maintenance to prevent failure. This is done using.

Scheduled Maintenance

Scheduled maintenance is any task that is given a deadline and assigned to a maintenance technician. It can be a recurring task done at regular intervals or a one-time task. The primary goals of scheduled maintenance are to reduce unplanned or breakdown maintenance, equipment failure, and maintenance backlog.

Periodic Maintenance

Periodic maintenance is a strategy that requires maintenance tasks to be performed at set time or use frequency intervals while the equipment is still operational. Similar to scheduled maintenance, periodic maintenance activities are planned ahead of time and are performed with or without signs of deterioration. The time or frequency is determined by experience over time. It is intended to help reduce the cost along the supply chain, and to prevent collateral damage to equipment that may occur with an unexpected failure

Planned Run to Failure

Planned run to failure is a maintenance strategy where maintenance is only performed when equipment has failed. Unlike unplanned & reactive maintenance, run-to-failure maintenance is a chosen strategy that is designed to minimize total maintenance costs.

Continuous Improvement Maintenance

1. **Plan:** Identify a maintenance improvement opportunity and plan the improvement.
2. **Do:** Implement the improvement.
3. **Check:** Use data to analyze the results of the improvement and statistically validate whether it made a difference.
4. **Act:** If the improvement was successful, reapply it.

Reliability Improvement

Increasing the line's reliability, increases your production throughput. Increasing production throughput increases the company profit. That increase in company profit is often even bigger than just the throughput gain, because reliable lines operate at lower costs.

Maintainability Improvement

Maintainability involves learning from experience in order to improve the ability to maintain systems or improve the reliability of systems based on maintenance practices.

The measure of maintainability is the **ease** with which maintenance activities can be performed.

This "ease" is achieved through; training, improved documentation, use of similar equipment across the production system, the practice or rapid changeover maintenance and increased planned maintenance.

Unplanned Maintenance

Unplanned maintenance is any maintenance task that occurs unexpectedly. This happens when there is no formal strategy or plan to address repair, replacement, or inspection before it's needed.

The use of Stability Check sheets by both the operating and maintenance teams will minimize the occurrence of unplanned maintenance.

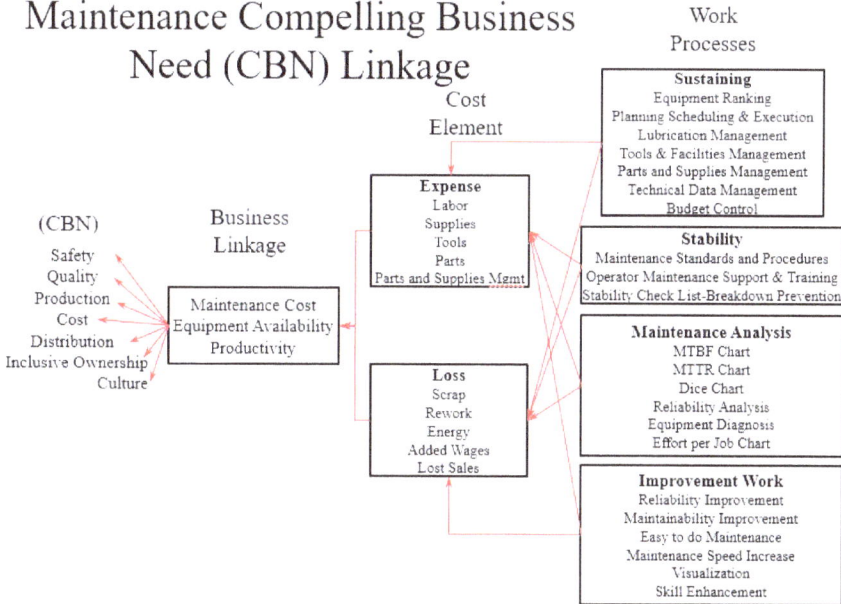

Maintenance Compelling Business Need (CBN) Linkage

The linkage to the business need is an element that the organization needs to emphasize to all personnel. The persons working on the equipment and ensuring the raw materials are converted to the desired product are the primary reason for a successful business.

The work performed must support the business.

Every line person has a maintenance role.

Maintenance Roles

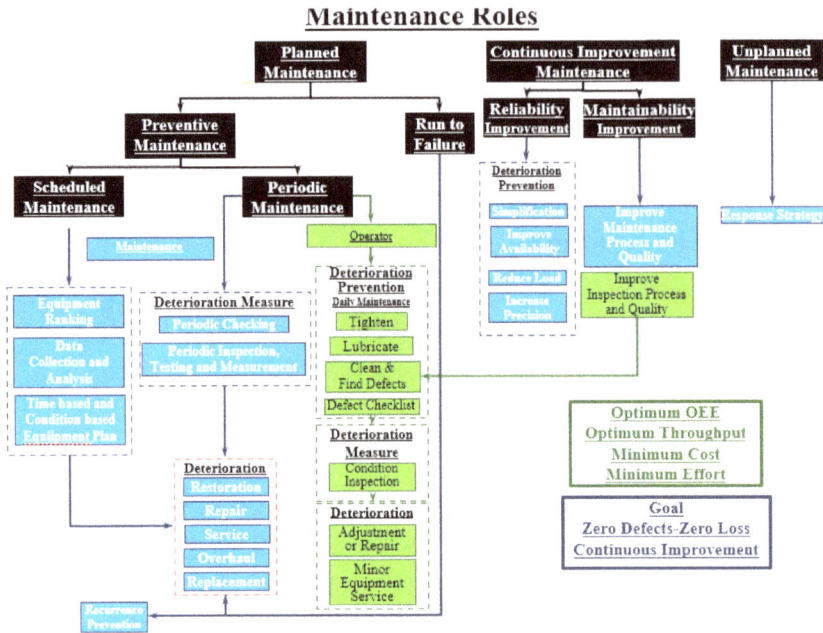

Everyone that interacts with the equipment needs to be involved in keeping it working as intended. The operator needs to understand the basic functions of the equipment.

Loose fasteners represent almost eighty percent of equipment minor stops. Minor stops represents a bigger loss than major breakdowns. Minor stops are often missed, or they require a slowdown of the equipment that often is not recorded as a loss. The first thing I have taught both operators and mechanics is the proper use of a torque wrench. This followed by the proper assembly of the bolt, lock washer and nut. These two learnings greatly reduce the minor stops.

Think of the equipment lubrication like it is blood in your veins. If it is clean, your heart will work for a long time. If the oil is clean the equipment will run for a long time.

The operator of the equipment should be responsible for maintaining basic lubrication. They should know how often to grease, what level to maintain oil levels.

The maintenance tech should be responsible for the more complicated grease and oil application. Complex Lubrication would be what might be associated with the size or the arrangement of the equipment. Lubrication requiring equipment disassembly would fall into this category.

Keep the line healthy and the work becomes easier.

Chapter 1: Maintenance Daily Management

Maintenance Daily Management

Maintenance daily management is by definition the management of the work done by maintenance team to meet the goal keeping the production equipment at its peak condition

Maintenance Daily Management Goal

The goal is to achieve zero product defects, zero material waste and zero lost equipment time.

It requires organizational coordination and adherence to standards.

Each operating team member has a secondary of doing their part to maintain the equipment.

The maintenance personnel are responsible to train the operators in the use of stability inspection check lists and in use of the clean, inspect and lubricate guides

Maintenance Daily Management

	"Drive Stability"															
	Maintenance Leader: Garrett Fortune											8-24-21				
	Safety			Quality			Planned Maintenance		Unplanned	Stability					Cost	
	DOLA	Total Accidents	BOS	Foreign material	Product Weight	Defective Label	Scheduled Minutes	Achieved Minutes	Minutes	MTTR	MTBF	OEE PR	Prior Month Machine Downtime	Current Month Total Machine Downtime	Maintenance Cost	
Maintenance	Thursday October 1, 2021	2	1										Hours	Hours	$	
Product A	Maintenance												Hours	Hours	$	
Line 1																
Line 2																
Line 3																
Line 4																
Line 5																
Product B																
Line 1																
Line 2																
Line 3																
Line 4																
Line 5																
Product C																
Line 1																
Line 2																
Line 3																
Line 4																
Line 5																

Plant Maintenance Priority Problems

Rank	100	80	60
Location	Stuffer 1	Product B	Line 1
Type	Environment	Waste	Equipment
Brief Description			

Improvement focus:

The daily work

Work orders

A maintenance work order provides details about maintenance, repair, or operations work, such as replacing a part, returning equipment to operating condition, or performing an inspection.

The purpose of a work order is to initiate a task, clarify what is to be done, specify completion dates, and give special instructions as needed.

There are different types of work orders. Some of these are.

- General Work Order.
  A general work order is any maintenance task that isn't considered a preventive maintenance, inspection, emergency, or corrective maintenance task.
- Preventive Maintenance work order
- Inspection work order
- Emergency work order
- Corrective Maintenance work order

Breakdown failure reports

A breakdown occurs when the equipment stops functioning. Breakdown is the result of failure and the effect that failure has. For example, if the temperature of your electric motor remains too high, it can melt the internals or it can cause the shaft to snap after the lubrication ceases to function, creating a breakdown.

Describe the failure in specific terms that clearly describes what you see not what may have happened. Get data that might help explain the effect over time and might show a trend. Review previous reports to see if the breakdown is repeating. Check for similar failures in other similar equipment.

Breakdown analysis

Mechanical attributes, spare parts, preventative maintenance procedures and employee skills are all analyzed and reworked to ensure the failure never returns.

| Breakdown Analysis | Date: |
| | By: |

| Picture or Sketch |
| |

5 W-2H	
What ?	
When ?	
Where ?	
Which ?	
Who ?	
How ?	
How Much ?	
Summary	

Why? Facts		
	Question	Answer
Why 1		
Why 2		
Why 3		
Why 4		
Why 5		
Summary		

Action	Comment	Date
Immediate		
Longer Term		
Learning		Date
Maintenance Record		
Operator Standard		
Maintenance Standard		
OPL		

Common causes of equipment breakdowns, stops
- Frequent stops
- Improper operation
- Failure to perform or properly perform preventive maintenance
- Too much preventive maintenance
- Poor reliability culture

Breakdown Reasons

```
                         ┌─────────────┐
                         │  Equipment  │
                         │Deterioration│
                         └─────────────┘
              Yes                          No
         ┌──────────────┐            ┌──────────────┐
         │Deterioration is│          │   Failure    │
         │   Uniform    │            │  Occurred    │
         └──────────────┘            └──────────────┘
         Yes        No
   ┌────────────┐ ┌────────────┐     ┌──────────────┐
   │Clean, Inspect││Clean, Inspect│   │Within Operating│
   │and Lubrication││and Lubrication│  │  Conditions  │
   └────────────┘ └────────────┘     └──────────────┘
                           Yes
  Yes     No    No    ┌──────────────┐  Yes      No
                      │A Maintenance │
                      │Standard Exists│
                      └──────────────┘
                          Yes
┌──────────┐┌──────────┐┌──────────┐┌──────────┐┌──────────┐
│ Natural  ││  Forced  ││ Lack of  ││Weak Point/││Operational│
│Deterioration││Deterioration││Standard Use││ Design  ││  Issue   │
└──────────┘└──────────┘└──────────┘└──────────┘└──────────┘
```

MTTR-MTBF reports
MTTR

The MTTR formula is calculated by dividing the total unplanned maintenance time by the total number of failures that the equipment experienced over a specific period.

The MTTR report summarizes the average downtime to repair.

MTTR is defined with the following formula:

MTTR = repair downtime / number of repairs completed.

MTBF

MTBF calculates the average period between two breakdowns. It is a measure of reliability. (how long the equipment typically works until it has a problem.)

It helps to make data-driven decisions on maintenance scheduling, safety, inventory management, and equipment design without relying on subjective observations.

Equipment records update

Equipment records are the primary data that is associated with the equipment. Each piece of equipment has a maintenance and performance record. The records establish the basic information such as:
- Identification number
- Description
- Account coding
- Dates of maintenance
- Location
- Status

It takes a great deal of time and effort to maintain each asset annually. Compounded by the total number of equipment and combined years of operation, documentation of maintenance tasks can easily get out of hand.

Having clear records of completed tasks can enable maintenance planners to plan out maintenance activities more easily and more efficiently delegate resources.

Keeping maintenance records updated is proof that assets are being taken care of.

Equipment maintenance logs provide data that can be analyzed. Different equipment can be compared by analyzing differences in maintenance costs incurred.

With available technologies, the benefits of having a well-documented equipment maintenance log are more easily achieved than ever.

Scheduling

Nearly all equipment needs some kind of regular maintenance and an equipment maintenance schedule. This type of maintenance is called planned maintenance (PM). Planned maintenance helps reduce the possibility of unexpected failure or repetitive equipment breakdowns.

An example maintenance plan is shown.

The goal is to maintain the line at its peak operating condition. For this to occur maintenance work needs to be closely coordinated with the operation. It is important to schedule major maintenance work, just as it is important to schedule product production.

The maintenance goal is to manage maintenance time in such a way as to optimize the production time.

The production line operator skills are improved to the point that they do the normal line lubrication and minor repairs. This is a key part of growing the production line skills. This operator hands on approach to line maintenance dramatically improves production line performance.

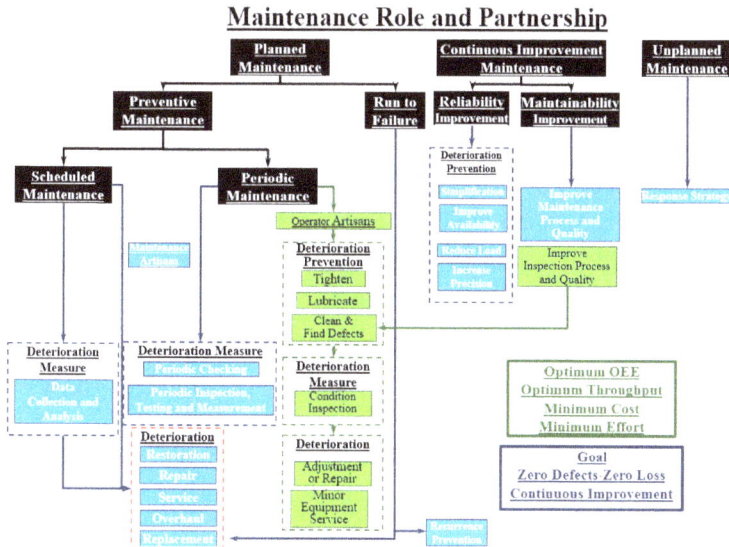

Maintenance Role and Partnership

Backlog report

A backlog report highlights the work that needs to be completed. It is useful information to determine the effectiveness of the maintenance plan, and/or the capacity of the organization to implement the work

Maintenance Cost management

The cost associated with keeping equipment at its top performance by regularly checking it and repairing it is referred to as maintenance cost.

Minimizing cost is the goal of maintenance cost management. The best way to reduce maintenance costs is to prevent equipment malfunctions. Another key is to train the equipment operators and maintenance staff.

One of the most fundamental requirements of business operations is the ability to budget and control cost. Maintenance is a cost is often one of the larger costs of doing business for a production facility.

Spare parts management

The objective of spare parts management is to ensure the lowest overall cost of spare parts without compromising availability. A high level of availability requires spare parts to be available or for the delivery time to be as short as possible.

Key elements of spare parts management
1. Strategically identify all parts and to identify where they are located, and the retrieval time.
2. Utilize and Manage the Bill of Materials (BOM)
3. Simplify the work order process.
4. Centralize and consolidate parts.
5. Utilize a spare parts inventory control system.
6. Give every part a stock location so they can easily be located.

Parts and equipment Supply management

Parts management is the process that used to ensure that right spare part and resources are at the right place at the right time. It includes the purchase of physical goods, information, services, and any other necessary resources that ensure the production system is maintained at a high level of throughput.

Vendor performance report

A vendor performance report documents the good or bad performance of a vendor. Vendor performance can be managed by.

- Defining a vendor management strategy
- Defining performance criteria and expectations
- Collecting performance data and comparing them to the goals

Chapter 2: Stability Systems

A system is said to be stable if its output is under control. A stable system produces at a consistent output. Three key elements; Maintenance Standards, Zero Loss Stability maintenance and the skill of the human are all critical in maintaining production system stability.

Maintenance standards and procedures (SMPs)

Maintenance of equipment is a repeating activity. This by definition means that a procedure can be written and optimized by those doing the work.

The persons writing the procedures should.

- have some training in writing SMPs
- someone involved with safety and environmental hazards should be involved.
- trained job maintenance personnel or subject matter experts should be involved.

The following information should be contained in a standard maintenance procedure.

- Formal title and document number.
- A statement to read the standard maintenance procedure before beginning work.
- Personal protective equipment (PPE) required to do the job.
- Safety and environmental hazards.
  Safety hazards are listed at the beginning of an SMP. Warnings should be repeated for each hazardous step.
  "Warning" to designate personnel harm and the word "Caution" to designate equipment harm.
- A task risk prediction should be the first step in use of the SMP.
  This is a risk prediction that links the risk to the counteraction resources.

Environmental Permit
Structural Barrier
Buddy/Partner
Fire Watch
Fire Protection
Auxilliary Ventilation
Auxilliary Lighting
Sand
Presrue Release System
Pump Lockout
Valve Lock Out
Pneumatic Lockout
Electrical Lockout
Mechanical Lock Out
Enclosed Space Permit
Safety Belt
Safety Shoes
Gloves
Lifting Belt
Electrical chock
How to training
Eye Protection
Air Filter
Hard Hat
Ear Plug

Risk Prediction Number

Counter
Measure

Support
Resource — Risk

Task

36

RISK PREDICTION For:

Task	Rating	Couster Measure

Feedback

Needed additional information for performing the procedure.

- A complete list of tools and materials.
- Listing of other documents needed.
- Needed photos and diagrams.
- Required measurements, standards, and tolerances.
- Required skill level.
- Required time.
- Required number of people.
- Required frequency.
- Required approval and review signatures.
- Space to provide feedback on the SMP's accuracy and effectiveness. Feedback is critical to the success of SMPs. In order for SMPs to be effective and accurate, a formal feedback mechanism should be supplied to the job performer. The SMP should be updated when feedback reveals mistakes or more effective ways to perform the job.

Writing Standard Maintenance Procedures

The SMP should focus on having just enough information to ensure the desired result.

There is no perfect SMP. The proper amount of detail will provide for trained persons to perform the job the first time.

The guiding elements for writing standard maintenance procedures are:

- The goal is to serve the user. The user must understand the procedure.
- Numbered line items and one item per step
- Keep wording short and precise.
- List steps in proper sequence.
- Use step check-offs.
- Whenever possible have the user enter quantitative values.
- Target sixth grade reading level.
- Use graphics to clarify meanings.
- Keep equipment and parts names consistent.
- Begin each step with a verb, action descriptor.
- For jobs with many steps, break the standard into sections.

Standard Maintenance Procedures are necessary to.

- protect personnel the health and safety.
- ensure that everyone performs a task to the same degree of precision.
- save time when performing a task.
- help ensure that standards and regulations are met.
- minimize the effects of personnel turnover.
- increase equipment reliability.
- serve as a training document.
- help document the equipment management procedure.
- help protect the environment.
- provide a basis for accident investigation.

Use Standard Maintenance Procedures

The goal is the consistent use of SMPs. Ensure they are part of the workorder process. Ensure they are periodically trained. Make SMPs 'easy to' documents. Post the SMP's on the equipment or at the operators station.

Zero Loss - Stability Check List application

- ### Create the Zero Loss Inspection Check Sheet

Zero Defect Checksheet (ZDC) - Drives & Rotating Equipment

Area Name | Date
Line Number
Equipment
ZDC Checker

Zero Defect Checksheet (ZDC) - Structure and Fasteners

Area Name: Filler Operations | Date: The beginning of Time | Check Purpose
Line Number
Equipment: Capper
ZDC Checker: John Henry

Equipment to Check	Component to Check	Check For	Check Purpose
			To Discover
Equipment Base Foundation	Top of Equipment standard	Horizontal	Shifting / Vibration and excess loading of parts
	Base	Physical Condition of Concrete / Grout	Cracks / Pitting / Erosion / Grout Problems
	Steel base	Physical Condition of Steel Base	Cracks in the steel / Erosion
	Floor Bolts	Foundation Bolts	Missing or loose bolts / Missing or improperly used washers / Damage or corrosion
	Bolt and Plate In	Level Adjusting Bolt & Receiving Plate	Missing or loose bolts / Shifting or misalignment / Bending cracks, damaged bolt threads / Bolts or support pads not making contact
	Fastener assembly		
	Leveling plate		
	Adjusting Bolts		
Equipment	Rigidity	Equipment position Equipment vibration	Deviation from design / Developing problems
Fastener Nuts - Bolts Screws - Pins Keys - Retaining Rings	Fastener Assembly	Fastener	Erosion / Corrosion / Misalignment
	Joint	Joint	
	Fastener Assembly Parts	Fastener Assembly / Bolts nuts and	Damage to parts / Tool induced damage
	Washers	Washers	Misused washers / Used when they should not be / Incorrect style / Incorrect assembly order

Creating and utilizing specific detailed check sheets for the equipment provides a way to create stability and zero breakdowns. This approach has been successfully applied around the world and achieve significant results.

Operator maintenance and training

Training the personnel in the operation on the basic maintenance that they should perform is a key responsibility of the maintenance department. Skilled operators run stable operations.

Chapter 3: Sustaining and Support Systems

Sustaining

Sustaining systems are those systems that keep the production system healthy within the required performance boundaries. Each of these systems are described below

Equipment ranking

Equipment Ranking is a method used to assess the equipment's risk to maintaining the required production. The rank given to a piece of equipment is used to determine how often the equipment should be inspected or maintained and gives the maintenance scheduler a guide as to which work orders can be rescheduled to a future date, and which require more immediate attention.

Ranking Process

1. Develop the ranking criteria

   Use Production, Quality, Cost, Safety and Moral (PQCDSM) as well as maintainability and operability factors when ranking. Apply a risk prediction approach to properly rank these factors.

2. List all the equipment to be ranked

3. Have a team technically and business diverse team to the ranking.

| Equipment | Rating Impact | | | | | | | | Risk Prediction Number | | | Rank Value |
	Production	Quality	Cost	Delivery	Safety	Moral	Maintainability	Operability	Occurrence Frequency	Ease of dectection	Impact Severity	
Equipment 1												
Equipment 2												
Equipment 3												
Equipment ...												

Note each participant gets to use 1-5 to rate each element The group must agree on the rating for each element. The sum of the agreed to numbers is put into the column
The Rank Value is the multiplication of each value entered for each equipment rating category

4. List the equipment in rank order and determine the maintain action for each equipment.

Planning and Scheduling

Planning and Scheduling flows naturally from the ranking process. It is a critical part of maintaining the health of the production lines. It must be an integral part of the production planning process. Maintenance time should be a key part of the production plan.

Lubrication Management

Think of lubrication management as a blood transfusion process. The act of getting the oil from the lubrication system storage area to the equipment is that transfusion process. It must be clean, sufficient, and done at the proper frequency. Check the equipment manufacturer's guide for lubrication requirements.

It includes both the equipment operators and the maintenance personnel.

It is the L in CIL (Clean, Inspect and Lubricate).

See Lubrication System to understand the design that allows the efficient management of lubrication.

Parts and supplies management

Think of this as having the required part quickly available. It may be in a location that is on site or economically close at hand. And the process of getting it to the line is predefined.

See Parts and Supplies System to understand the design that allows the efficient management of parts and supplies.

Tools and facilities management

Think of the surgeon holding out his hand as he calls out "scalpel". The right tool is immediately at hand, no waiting or fetching. The surgeon is in the operating room and the environment is controlled and the tools are readily available. Both operating and maintenance personnel should be able to function like a surgeon.

See Tools and Facilities System to understand the design that allows the efficient management of tools and facilities.

Technical data management

Technical data management is the process of obtaining, storing, organizing, and maintaining the data created and collected by the technical community. The technical data management process includes a combination of operational, maintenance and business functions that collectively aim to make sure that the data is accurate, available, and accessible.

This information impacts the maintenance planning process.

Shutdown maintenance

Shutdown Maintenance is maintenance that can only be performed while equipment is not in use. Shutting down machinery is costly, but sometimes due to the nature of the defective part/machine, shutdown maintenance is the only viable maintenance procedure.

This is a very common process for many production equipment.

Maintenance Budget Control

The Maintenance Budget is an operating budget that is set aside in a single fiscal year for maintenance activities on the organization's assets. The maintenance budget typically falls into the elements of the Planned Maintenance System.

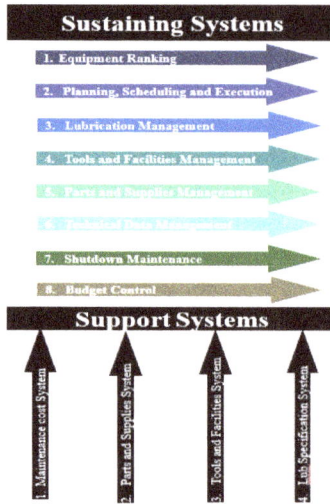

Support

Maintenance Cost System

A maintenance cost system tracks all the maintenance cost elements. This maintenance cost information is utilized in evaluating the equipment and the systems that support maintaining the equipment. It is a fundamental element in determining what the maintenance budget should be.

Parts and Supplies System

The Parts and Supplies System functions to ensure that both repairable and consumable replacement parts are available.

An example of a repairable part is the replacement of a dull cutting blade with a sharp one. The dull blade is then reconditioned to be available to replace the one that will become dull.

An example of a consumable part would be a battery, a light bulb or a motion sensor that gets replaced.

The part and supply system ensures that each type is available in sufficient quantities.

Tools and Facilities System

The Tools and Facilities System functions to ensure that the required tools are sufficient and are available at the point of use. It also ensures that the required facilities are available and are in superior condition.

Lubrication System

The lubrication system ensures that the required lubrication fluid is available.

It ensures that the lubrication is kept in the proper clean condition and is easy to use.

The system optimizes the number of lubricants and the method of dispersing it.

Chapter 4: Maintenance Analysis

Maintenance Analysis is a way to determine how to keep the production system in top shape. It is the method of determining how often the equipment will need attention in order to keep it in good working order.

There are a number of useful analysis tools.

Dice chart application

The dice chart is a visual bar chart of the mechanical, electrical, and pneumatic failures. It provides a visual way to share the problems a production line is experiencing.

Posting such a chart at the production line area communicates to the operations personnel the types of problems that are active on their line.

Dice Chart

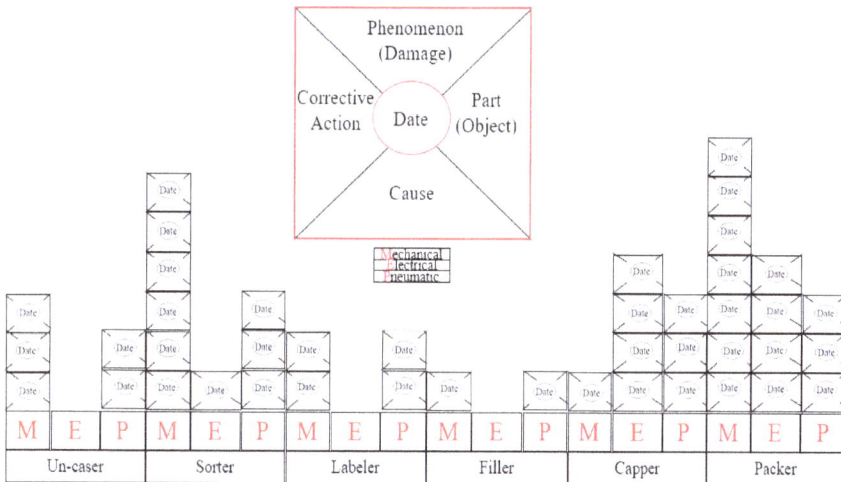

Mean Time Between Failure (MTBF) Chart

The MTBF chart provides a visual way for all personnel to understand the performance of a line and the corrective actions that help to improve the MTBF.

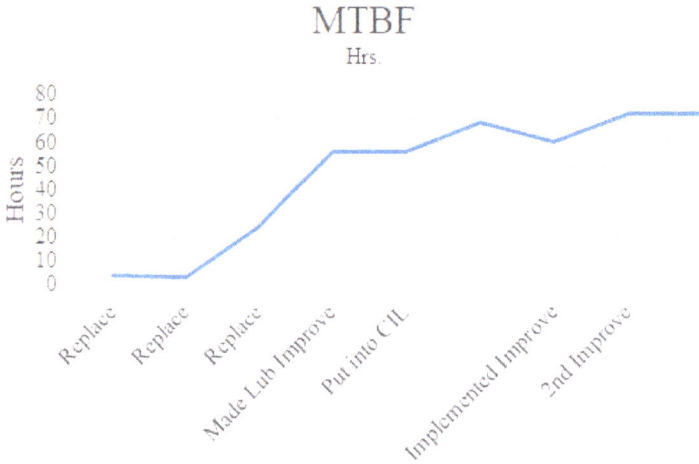

MTBF
Hrs.

(Line chart; Y-axis "Hours" from 0 to 80 in increments of 10. X-axis categories: Replace, Replace, Replace, Made Lub Improve, Put into CIL, Implemented Improve, 2nd Improve. The line starts low near 5, rises through ~20 and ~55, stays around 55–70, dips near 60, then rises to about 72.)

MTTR Chart

The MTTR chart provides a visual way for all personnel to understand the performance of the maintenance actions that help to improve the MTTR. Improvement of MTTR often goes hand-in-hand with improved MTBF.

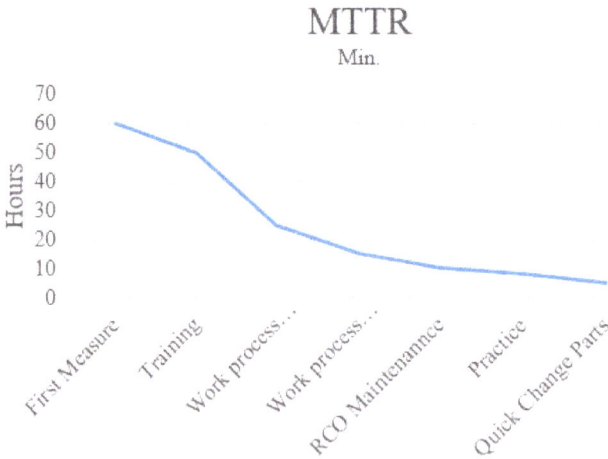

MTTR
Min.

(Line chart; Y-axis "Hours" from 0 to 70 in increments of 10. X-axis categories: First Measure, Training, Work process…, Work process…, RCO Maintenance, Practice, Quick Change Parts. The line starts near 60, decreases through ~50, ~25, ~17, and declines steadily to about 5.)

Reliability Analysis

Reliability is defined as the probability that a production line or process will perform its intended operation for a specified length of time or will operate in a defined environment without failure.

Reliability of a line is calculated as follows.

$$PR = \frac{Net\ Production}{Scheduled\ Time * Target\ Rate}$$

Measurement Intent:

The intent of Process Reliability is to measure the extent to which Scheduled Time invested in Production, Maintenance and improvement activities is converted into Net Production. Some Scheduled time will be utilized to do maintenance and some scheduled time will be lost to unplanned downtime.

Target rate is the intended production target rate. By definition target rate is equal to or less then the ideal rate of the system.

The Reliability Constraint

The constraint is the point in the production system that limits the through put of the system. This point will move as the capability of the constraining point is improved. Ideally the system will be balanced, and a constraint will not be present. However, due to cost, most production systems will have a constraint designed in at the most expensive or costly production transformation.

The improvement focus for a production line should be the constraint and ensuring that other points in the process do not slow down, block or starve the constraint.

Analysis at the constraint

Schedule Utilization $_{Constraint}$ = Scheduled Time $_{Constraint}$ / Calendar Time

Rate Utilization $_{Constraint}$ = Target Rate $_{Constraint}$ / Ideal Rate $_{Constraint}$

PrReliability $_{Constraint}$ = Net Production $_{constraint}$ / Scheduled Time $_{Constraint}$ * Target Rate $_{Constraint}$

Capacity Utilization Constraint = $SU_{constraint}$ * $RU_{constraint}$ * $PR_{constraint}$

Equipment Diagnosis

The use of the Clean, Inspect and Lubricate CIL is a form of equipment diagnosis.

Taking equipment readings of oil level, temperature, vibration is the process of collecting data that allows for early detection of problems.

Determining what type of fault would explain the reading values of various sensors provides the basis for pre-emptive maintenance action.

The operations personnel play a major role in providing this early warning. It benefits them to have a line that is stable and runs continuously. It benefits the maintenance area since it allows for good maintenance planning.

Job Effort analysis

The purpose of job effort analysis is to provide data on how long a job takes. A comparison of how long this takes for an expert to do provides the basis for what others might need training on.

It also provides the basis for evaluating improvements to the work process.

The goal is to make daily work easier to do.

Cost Analysis

A cost analysis is the process of comparing the projected or estimated costs associated with a specific work process or processes.

The goal is to determine how the maintenance budget is being spent. The focus should first be on the big expenditures to see if there is a way to improve the spend situation.

For the maintenance on a production line, the focus should be on the equipment that generates the most cost. This information will aid in the determination of the action to take.

Minimizing over all maintenance cost is always a goal. It should be approached from the actionable level of making maintenance improvements.

Maintenance Measures

Equipment:
- Availability
- Maintainability

Maintenance Efficiency
- MTTR

Maintenance Effectiveness
- Downtime
- Operating Rate
- MTBF

Overall Effectiveness
- Availability
- Performance Rate
- Quality Rate

Chapter 5: Maintenance Improvement and Simplification

Maintenance improvement and simplification is a part of the maintenance daily management process.

Example of a Maintenance Daily Management board

The five Maintenance improvement issues are:

1. Lack of data quality in the PM notifications
2. Inability to capture required data in work orders
3. Incomplete information regarding Activity, Cause, and Damage.
4. Missing data in work orders for problem Analysis
5. Time consuming and high costs of maintenance training

Understanding the loss logic associated with various cause of line stops provides the basis for the action that needs to occur to minimize the loss.

Stops and Loss Logic

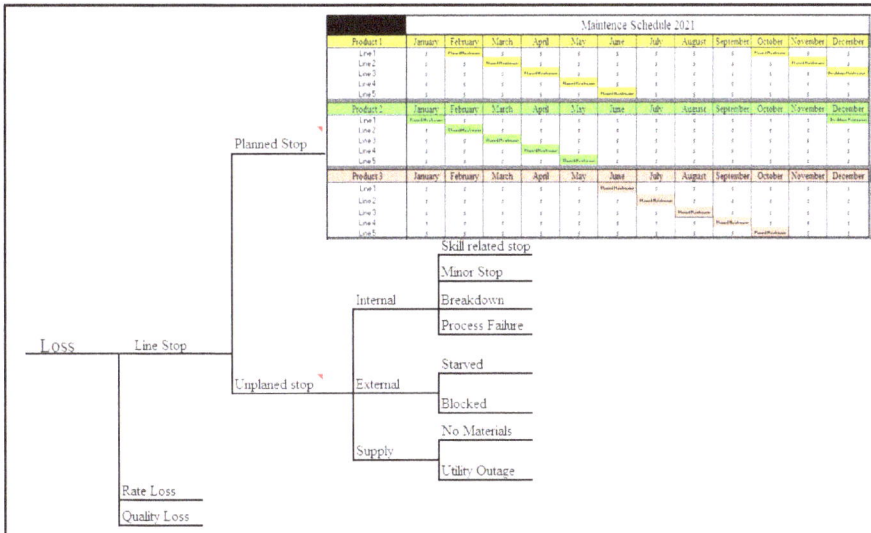

Maintenance improvement will require a close understanding of the work, the equipment, the interaction of the human with the equipment.

However, the focus on making small improvements every day is a critical element that daily management empowers.

Ron Mueller P.E.

- **Integrated Work Systems (IWS) materials author**
- **Coach to dozens of Manufacturing Directors across the world.**
- **Certified TPM Coach.**
- **Tested and proven to enable true breakthrough improvement of Supply Chains.**

A proven leader of smart systems implementation across supply, manufacturing, and distribution to drive out cost, inefficiencies and to establish synchronized Supply Chains. He utilized the best thinking of Japan's TPM leaders and crafted the necessary related pillars and systems that work in Consumer Products Manufacturing. The results delivered include reduction of Raw and Finished Product Inventories by 40%. Delivered over $100 million is loss reduction through focused systems Workshops across dozens of sites. Developed P&G IWS program materials for external sale. Winner of P&G's Diamond Award for Contribution to Product Supply.

Core Competencies include:

- ✓ **Coaching Manufacturing Leadership,**
- ✓ **Implementation of Integrated Work Systems,**
- ✓ **Statistical Replenishment design and implementation,**
- ✓ **Supply Chain Synchronization: author of 3 books in the Stress Free^{TM} series that aid Business and Supply Chain leaders to develop and improve their organization's performance.**

Gordon Miller P.E.

- **Manufacturing Performance Program**
- **Development and Delivery Expert.**
- **Application of Intelligent Manufacturing technology against biggest business challenges with proven business results.**

A record as a collaborative and leading-edge thinker, developing programs to deliver cost, productivity and growth enabling manufacturing technology systems deployed via smart standards and empowered teams. As an early developer of PR/OEE measures and improvement programs, has experience with unlocking organization capability for improvement with smart strategies. Led program that developed initial P&G Manufacturing Execution System, leveraged globally across multiple GBUs. Influenced Beauty and Household Care manufacturing systems changes that enabled and leveraged global standardization for rapid footprint growth. Experience that enabled 50% reduction in OEE losses. Experience as a leader of corporate STEM talent strategy can assess and devise approaches to ensure Talent needs for the challenging future are met.

Core Competencies include:

- ✓ **Global Productivity Program Design and Management,**
- ✓ **Advanced Manufacturing Technology Innovation and Strategy Development,**
- ✓ **Development of Highly Effective Global Teams,**
- ✓ **Vendor development and management, Organization Capability Development,**
- ✓ **Talent Strategy**

This takes you to the Optimum Performance Consulting Web Site

Field proven workshops
are described and available.

www.ingramcontent.com/pod-product-compliance
Lightning Source LLC
Chambersburg PA
CBHW081803200326
41597CB00023B/4134